Standards-Based Lesson Plans for the Busy Elementary School Librarian

Standards-Based Lesson Plans for the Busy Elementary School Librarian

Joyce Keeling

LIBRARIES UNLIMITED™

An Imprint of ABC-CLIO, LLC

Santa Barbara, California • Denver, Colorado

Copyright © 2017 by Joyce Keeling

Library of Congress Cataloging-in-Publication Data

Names: Keeling, Joyce, author.
Title: Standards-based lesson plans for the busy elementary school librarian / Joyce Keeling.
Description: Santa Barbara, California : Libraries Unlimited, an imprint of ABC-CLIO, LLC, [2017] |
    Includes bibliographical references and index.
Identifiers: LCCN 2016053488 (print) | LCCN 2017010208 (ebook) | ISBN 9781440851322
    (paperback : acid-free paper) | ISBN 9781440851339 (ebook)
Subjects: LCSH: Elementary school libraries—Activity programs—United States. | Information literacy—Study and
    teaching (Elementary)—United States. | Information literacy—Standards—United States. | Language arts
    (Elementary)—United States. | Language arts (Elementary)—Standards—United States. | School librarian
    participation in curriculum planning—United States. | Education, Elementary—Curricula—United States.
Classification: LCC Z675.S3 K43 2017 (print) | LCC Z675.S3 (ebook) | DDC 025.5/6782220973—dc23
LC record available at https://lccn.loc.gov/2016053488

ISBN: 978–1–4408–5132–2
EISBN: 978–1–4408–5133–9

21 20 19 18 17   1 2 3 4 5

This book is also available as an eBook.

Libraries Unlimited
An Imprint of ABC-CLIO, LLC

ABC-CLIO, LLC
130 Cremona Drive, P.O. Box 1911
Santa Barbara, California 93116-1911
www.abc-clio.com

This book is printed on acid-free paper ∞

Manufactured in the United States of America

This is dedicated to my sons, Chad Keeling and Rob Keeling and their families (Jan, Carisa, Adam, Katie, Allie, Ava, and Blake). It is also dedicated to the Clarion-Goldfield-Dows School students and to all elementary students all over the world.

Contents

Chapter 5—Fourth-Grade Lesson Plans **177**

Chapter 6—Fifth-Grade Lesson Plans **221**

Introduction

Standards in the School Library Curriculum and Other Information Related to This Book

School libraries like all school classrooms have a standards-based curriculum, as educational standards place a knowledge-expected framework for learning. Just as in the main classroom, the library classroom involves a teaching team, as a school librarian and all teachers work together for information literate students of today and for student future literary needs in an ever-changing world. Current standards are set to meet the needs for the twenty-first-century student. For clarification in this book, the term school librarian refers to a teacher librarian, library media specialist, and elementary school librarian teacher. This book has connected some of the current major literacy and English language arts standards to active learning with easy to access and use lesson plans and resources for the busy elementary school librarian.

A school librarian may use all of the standards or select some of the standards given with each lesson in this book. A school library's standards are usually based on American Association of School Librarians (AASL) standards and then are most likely set within school districts' standards from state guidelines and suggested national standards as well. With every lesson in this book, the English language arts and literacy learning standards are set from AASL literacy standards, the McREL Compendium of Standards and Benchmarks, and the Common Core State Standards (CCSS). English language arts and literacy standards create an effective library learning curriculum program. Since this book is built on standards, it is noteworthy to know about standards, the AASL, McREL, and CCSS standard choices for this book, and how those standards are different but yet similar, and it is noteworthy to look at other crucial elements of this book, as all seen as essential for quality elementary school library programs.

California studies show that effective school library programs based on English language arts and as taught by certified school librarians provide a positive link to student achievement (Ong 2010). South Carolina studies prove that effective school library programs contribute to student success, especially when those programs that teach literary, informational text skills, and research are taught by certified school librarians (Gavigan and Curry 2016). When state standards and consequently school-wide standards are developed and instigated in school libraries and aligned with other classrooms by school librarian teachers, student achievement increased (New York Comprehensive Center 2011). Iowa school reading scores with well-developed library programs (Scholastic 2008). School library programs are more successfully taught with educational standards.

Educational standards are deemed important in education, as standards point out what students are expected to learn and what areas of learning should be tested (Great Schools 2014). Standards provide specific guidelines for commercial products so that one can purchase more reliable products (IEEE-SA 2011), and since standards are set in the commercial world, standards are set in education for reliability learning guidelines as well. Most importantly, educational standards form the learning basis, but teachers provide the learning (Kendall 2011).

Standards not only provide a learning purpose or goal but also provide ways to increase student achievement, which then clarifies and increases learning expectations, especially when standards are clearly stated (McREL 2015). Since educational school standards are regarded as essential (Great Schools 2014), school library teachers and all other teachers address those mandated or suggested standards in the school classroom. Educational standards are given or suggested in U.S. laws, including the previous No Child Left Behind Act as first set in 2002 and through other such laws (Great Schools 2014). The No Child Left Behind Act set out to establish learning standards for all children, with states setting their own learning standards in reading, math, and science (Great Schools 2014). The No Child Left Behind Act also mandated testing and worked at accountability (Korte 2015).

The No Child Left Behind Act was set under the 1965 Elementary and Secondary Act, thus showing many years of standards-based approach to learning in the United States (Shepard, Hannaway, and Baker 2009). The No Child Left Behind Act was replaced by the Every Student Succeeds Act in 2015 (Garland 2016). The Every Student Succeeds Act was set so that there could be higher academic standards for each state's educational programs, so helping all students to achieve, while giving more student accountability, and allowing fewer but better assessments according to the White House (Earnest, White House Office of the Press 2015). The Every Student Succeeds Act encouraged states to adopt the Common Core Standards, but did not require that adoption of the standards (Korte, 2015). With the Every Student Succeeds Act, there was a goal for clearer and more stringent educational standards so that students could better excel (Shepard, Hannaway, and Baker 2009).

Along with the United States and other countries examining educational national standards, associations and other entities also look at both national and international educational standards. For example, both the National Council of Teachers of English and the International Reading Association joined to form language arts standards (National Council of Teachers of English 2012). Those national and international English and reading standards and others are seen in still other educational standards like in the McREL Compendium Standards and Benchmarks (McREL 2015). The CCSS are linked with international standards too (Garland 2016). National and international association education standards create connected learning across the globe.

When discussing national standards, President Obama stated, "We must ensure that we are doing a better job helping all our students master critical thinking, adaptability, collaboration, problem solving and creativity skills that goes beyond the basics" (Earnest, White House Office of the Press 2015). Going beyond the basics are where well-written and researched educational standards come into play in the school library and in all other school classrooms. If not adapting the national-suggested educational standards of the CCSS, some states have capitalized on their own quality standards (Finn, Julian, and Petrilli 2006). Furthermore, schools and subsequently school libraries adopted their states educational standards. Library standards include English language and literacy standards among others and most assuredly include AASL or the American Association of School Librarians literacy standards.

The AASL standards or American Association of School Librarians literacy standards identify standards approaching student problem solving needs and more (AASL 2007). The AASL literacy standards are literacy standards for the twenty-first-century student learners and student learning for life (L4L). With the AASL Learners and L4L, students identify facts, pull relevant information, document, and apply knowledge for critical thinking (Stephens and Franklin 2009). Students also acquire and enrich independent information literacy and literature appreciation with the AASL standards.

Ultimately, the four AASL standards for the twenty-first-century learner basically involve inquiring, thinking critically, gaining knowledge, drawing and making informed decisions and conclusions, sharing knowledge, and working toward personal growth (Stephens and Franklin 2009).

The L4L or Learners and L4L standards of the American Association for School Librarians standards for the twenty-first-century learner are one of the sets of standards that are most assuredly used in school libraries. The AASL standards are linked to state and national language arts and literacy standards, where students think critically. Texas school libraries include the use of ALA standards like inquiry, critical thinking, creating, and using new knowledge of relevant and current print and nonprint sources as combined with an ethical approach for student growth (Texas Library Association 2010). When standards are used in carefully planned school library lessons including print and technology sources, those library lessons resulted in higher reading and writing achievements in the 2013 Pennsylvania study according to Lance and Kachel (2013). As with all school libraries, access to good current print and technology is not enough, as students need direction in using those sources from school librarians who teach students how to inquire, gain knowledge, make informed decisions and apply new knowledge, share knowledge ethically, and follow personal student learning and more in information literacy, as suggested in the Lance and Kachel (2013) studies.

Information literacy, although not isolated in library skills, will continue to be forefront for student instruction in the library classroom, especially with the overwhelming and constantly changing array of technological and print resources in the twenty-first century and centuries to come. When first approaching the multitude of resources, students need a background of knowing what and how to find quality information in an efficient manner, which is met not just with one-on-one school librarian assistance but is seen in the school library standards-based curriculum. Since students live in an information-rich age, information literacy in the school library is even more important (Scholastic 2008).

As individual student's needs and resources change, students could develop an overwhelming feeling for information literacy support, which is met better with a school librarian teacher's assistance and classroom teacher's assistance. Additionally, student's informational literacy learning is built upon current and progressive skills with those skills flowing into student futures. Information literacy standards and English language arts standards or a standards literacy base are needed for current and future student learning in the school library.

Information literacy standards and similar skills as seen in English language arts and literacy standards equip learners for their twenty-first century in the school library and classroom. A school librarian is instrumental in shaping student readiness for the twenty-first-century learning (AASL 2009). School library programs are built on standards, and those standards provide the goals for student learning. Information literacy standards enable students to become equipped for academic and future work needs for a lifetime. Being able to find, critique, and use self-filtered useable information in today's information age is being information literate (Eisenberg 2008).

According to the American Association of Librarians (2009), the school library and its program with information literacy and more should be set around the constructivist theory. With information literacy in the school library, a constructivist theory is where knowledge is found rather than just used (Tanner and Tanner 2008). With AASL standards and other standards in school libraries, the constructivist theory shows that students not only find accurate information in an active learning environment but also develop that information and so creating new knowledge. Because of the changing global world of learning, students need to be able to critique, evaluate, and assimilate new knowledge.

Global information literacy enables students to be prepared for global communication, travel, and the global workforce. Changing communication and technology creates a continual need for solid literacy learning (Quebec School Librarians Network 2014). Information literacy skills in the twenty-first century are seen with gathering and processing print and technology sources. Global work skills include being more flexible and creative (Christensen and Schneider 2010), with creativity, flexibility, and many such skills taught in the library and other classrooms. Global work skills are defined as knowing how to access effective information, create, and then communicate effectively with others across the globe with modern technology. Global information literacy falls under technology and information literacy skills as taught from the school library.

School library global information and technology literacy skills involve critical thinking skills that are connected and taught in progressive increments in elementary lessons and through consequent student learning experiences. Literacy skills involve not just print but technology resources with problem solving skills, which involves being able to use, understand, and ethically use all resources in an ever-changing landscape of an abundance of sources. Problem solving and thinking critically when meeting many resource needs means having information literacy competences (American Library Association 2004). According to the Lance, Rodney, and Hamilton-Pennell (2000) study, there is an achievement difference in reading and information literacy according to the time given to students to learn information literacy, as compared to those who were not given instructional time, and to those students actually having access to print and technology. Consequently, both print and technology information literacy lessons are seen in school library lessons with English language arts and literacy in this book.

Information technology does not isolate learning to just the Internet but to multiple library sources (Kuhlthau 2009). Technology is not the ultimatum on knowledge research but plays a major role in school library learning and information literacy today, as students know how to find safe, credible sources and be able to summarize that information in a changing techno world that connects them globally. The 2000 Pennsylvania study by Lance, Rodney, and Hamilton-Pennell states that reading scores are directly linked to information technology, information literacy, and other such factors. A 2010 study shows students achieve higher scores when there are school library programs, access to more resources, and when students have more time in the school library (Francis, Lance, and Lietzau 2010).

Educational standards and the teaching of those standards in the school library program create independent learners and critical thinkers when approaching new information and learning skills for life (L4L) (Stephens and Franklin 2010). Reading growth and reading enjoyment are then seen in school libraries, along with a knowledgeable acquisition of facts (AASL 2007). The school library curriculum strengthens reading, understanding, and appreciation through library instruction, which includes meeting diverse needs (American Association of School Librarians and Association for Educational Communications and Technology 1998). AASL standards, CCSS, and the McREL Compendium of Standards and Benchmarks standards also connect various components and elements of reading, reading appreciation, as well as teaching information literacy with print and technology. Reading appreciation development is seen with AASL standards, CCSS, and with the McREL Compendium of Standards and Benchmarks, as students read or hear, and then study many different types of fiction and nonfiction (fairy tales, folklore, fiction, and more), and in many other areas in school library programs.

School library programs are often founded on the AASL standards and then school library programs may often combine those standards with state-required or other recommended educational standards. AASL standards suggest ways to help students achieve, as does the Common Core and the McREL Compendium of Standards and Benchmarks. The AASL or American Association of School Librarians standards can often be reflected in the CCSS, in the McREL Compendium of Standards and Benchmarks, and in other information-rich literacy standards.

Since the CCSS are suggested with the Every Student Succeeds Act of 2015, it is given with lessons in this book. CCSS (2015) were written to help students across the country have success in their futures from clearly written guidelines (Common Core 2015). The benefits of CCSS show a consistent standard building block for student preparation for college and work and a rigorous and clear set of standards, although there are objections to the CCSS. Those CCSS objections include federal government involvement and that standards alone do not always provide quality education (Chen 2015).

Common Core English language arts literacy standards vary by states (Arp and Woodard 2003). As of this writing, one or more states have only adapted the Language Arts section of the Common Core, some states made slight changes to the Language Arts section and many states adapted all of the Common Core (Kendall, Ryan, Alpert, Richardson, and Schwols 2012). Furthermore, for those states that have not adapted Common Core, other well-written English language educational and literacy standards are into effect (Carmichael, Wilson, Magee, and Martino 2010). According to Garland (2016) and Kendall (2011), withstanding some differences among states, the CCSS are an improvement for many state standards, especially showing strength in English language arts and showing an alignment of learning among grade levels.

There are many equal strengths of the English language section of CCSS when compared to the McREL Standards and Benchmarks and as compared to AASL standards. If CCSS are adapted by the school librarian's state, the Common Core is most likely used with AASL standards in the library curriculum, as the AASL standards and CCSS standards connect with such things as complex nonfiction and in many other literacy areas too. A more in-depth comparison of those standards are given here. The English language arts part of the CCSS approaches information literacy with rigor. The McREL Compendium of Standards and Benchmarks standards suggest balancing informational texts with literary texts, as does Common Core standards (Uecker, Kelly, and Napierala 2015).

While looking at teaching the balance of informational sources with fictional texts in a library, a school librarian teacher can help other teachers in their classroom, as well as teachers helping the school librarian in his or her library classroom (Uecker, Kelly, and Napierala 2015). With the English language arts and literacy part of CCSS and other such standards, students will reflect, pose an inquiry, gather, evaluate, and use that gathered information for sharing (Kuhlthau 2013), as reflected in the school library curriculum. With nonfiction sources, both the McREL Compendium of Standards and Benchmarks English language standards and the Common Core standards suggest teaching the correct use, understanding, and summarizing of print and nonprint sources, which is a major part of information literacy with library lessons, and thus seen in this book's nonfiction suggested sources. Furthermore, the school librarian can assure quality nonfiction sources and show how students can access and use multiple nonfiction sources, when not just teaching a class, but when school librarians consult one-on-one for student assistance.

When continuing the comparison and a partial description of this book's standards, the AASL standards and the CCSS show a need for students to find credible, multiple print, and technology resources and involve reading skills for informational and literacy abilities for career and college readiness (Kuhlthau 2013). The McREL Compendium of Standards and Benchmarks, Common Core standards, and AASL standards involve research skills and ethics. Eisenberg (2008) suggests structured and understood information research. Processes for effective information users include knowing technology and information retrieval processes based on real needs for successful student learning and researching for now and for student futures in the school library.

The school library curriculum learning involves student inquiry, research, and analyses in CCSS (Kuhlthau 2013), and as also seen in ways, in both the McREL Compendium of Standards and Benchmarks and AASL standards. This chapter and consequently this book refer to part of the English language arts and literacy part of the CCSS and the McREL Compendium of Standards and Benchmarks, and AASL standards. In this book, the mix of all three standards of CCSS, McREL, and AASL are chosen for elementary school library skills, but those standards could be used individually.

The CCSS literacy focus on inquiry, balancing literary, and informational sources and building on learning from those sources, increasing the complexity of the sources and then providing outcomes based on those sources (AASL 2013, November). This section of the chapter will continue to compare some areas of the English Language and literacy standards of CCSS to the McREL Compendium of Standards and Benchmarks and in some cases as compared to AASL standards. For instance, both the McREL Compendium of Standards and Benchmarks and the English language arts and literacy parts of the CCSS create not just a need to use nonfiction as well as fiction print and technological sources but to look at different cultures, genres, and formats. Student learnings from this book's lessons provide the jumpstart for students to be ready for their current and present information literacy-rich lives, all of which can be seen in this book's stated standards, especially with the proverbial AASL standards.

When using AASL standards and with either or both the McREL Compendium of Standards and Benchmarks and CCSS in the school library curriculum, standards will affect student learning for their academic, career, and personal lives, as students grow in literary knowledge and literary appreciation. Various educational standards like McREL, CCCS, and AASL interlink as could other quality literacy or English language arts standards, and thus provide a common strength literacy goal of learning and education. No matter which educational standards are carefully studied and adapted, increased student achievement is the purpose for educational standards (Korte 2015). With the McREL Compendium of Standards and Benchmarks, Common Core standards, and/or AASL standards or other such quality literacy and English arts standards, there is a focus and striving drive for student current and future needs.

The McREL Compendium of Standards and Benchmarks plays an important part of the school library curriculum and in other classrooms. The McREL Compendium of Standards and Benchmarks for K–12 learners have often been seen as national-type standards guidelines, since it underlines rigorous student learning standards, which also engages learning aligned with other standards (McREL 2015). When setting up the McREL standards, "McREL analyzed 137 significant subject-area documents produced by state education agencies and national subject-area organizations," stated Kendall (2000). The McREL Compendium of Standards and Benchmarks became over a hundred national standards in many content areas that were aligned with the curriculum (Schmoker and Marzano 1999).

The McREL Compendium of Standards and Benchmarks has the underlining goal to ensure successful student career and academic lives (McREL 2015), which can be seen with Common Core and AASL standards too. The McREL Compendium of Standards and Benchmarks have been used with many schools, especially when schools have already adopted the McREL Content Knowledge and so used the completion of that McREL Content Knowledge with the McREL Compendium of Standards and Benchmarks (Schmoker and Marzano 1999). Some of the many specific literacy characteristics of the McREL Compendium of Standards and Benchmarks for a school library are the benchmarks of learning book parts, meaning clues for K–2, the uses of variety of sources to research, and more.

The McREL Compendium of Standards and Benchmarks approach nonfiction print and nonprint resources and reading, along with reading elements, as does CCSS. Schools can modify those McREL standards, and likewise when comparing McREL standards to Common Core, CCSS allow for some slight modifications too. The McREL Compendium of Standards and Benchmarks give benchmarks for technology. What is more, McREL supports Common Core standards too (McREL 2015). This book approaches AASL standards, and both the educational standards of the McREL Compendium of Standards and Benchmarks and the CCSS as not all states and entities use Common Core or the McREL Compendium of Standards and Benchmarks.

Regardless of which educational standards are the standards studied, chosen and implemented by states and then adapted by school teachers and school librarian teachers, the bottom line is that standards are used in the school library curriculum. Literacy standards in library lessons ensure that students are receiving an information literacy education, which enables students to be college and career ready. President Obama believes in the best of education for student futures and for their global world (Earnest, White House Press Secretary 2015).

Since preparation for student's future college or higher education is a school library educational goal, it is important to also take a brief look at the ACRL or the Association of College and Research Libraries standards (American Library Association 2004), which shows that there is an information literacy need for students to know when information is needed and where students can find, summarize, and use credible information in print and technology means. ACRL also asserts the need to establish lifelong learners, thus showing connection to the global world (American Library Association 2004). The global world of information literacy also means knowing how to critically access and use quality information in ever-changing print and technological sources, as well as learning about other cultures through nonfiction and fiction sources in the school library, which is mentioned or suggested in Common Core, AASL standards, and the McREL Compendium of Standards and Benchmarks.

Conversely, this book does not attempt to isolate or focus on just one standard type but to integrate AASL foundational school library standards with some of the current Common Core English language arts and literacy standards, and the McREL Compendium of Standards and Benchmarks in English language and literacy, that are adapted by many states and subsequently adapted in the school library curriculum, with a focus on getting students ready for their future. The AASL standards surely provide the foundation for English language and literacy standards in the school library. Time and space does not allocate using every state or other entities' library or literacy educational standards in this book but does allow for AASL, some of the CCSS, and the McREL Compendium of Standards and Benchmarks that are applicable with each lesson. As Schmoker and Marzano (1999) state, it is more important to look at the quality of standards, as compared to examining the quantity.

Standards direct teaching and provide a measurement for improvement (Schmoker and Marzano 1999). Standards-based student learning provides a focus on student learning and guidance for both improvement and [then] success (Shepard, Hannaway, and Baker 2009). A foot forward in educational reform is standards (Chen 2015). If set clearly, language arts and literacy standards set purposes and goals for student learning in the school library. Standards are given in curriculum content areas of main classrooms, and so they are seen in the school library classroom too.

Standards state what students will be able to accomplish in all content or subject areas (Ornstein and Hunkins 2009), and so are seen in all elementary curriculums. When looking at standards, ultimately teachers are the major component of student success (Kendall 2011). Educational standards provide the pathway for the successful outcomes of student learning and accountability. As President George H. W. Bush advised, education must show accountability (Ornstein and Hunkins 2009). Literacy appreciation and accountability in the school library classroom are seen with standards-based lessons and are not only taught but also monitored for success. Standards alone will not create student success, but the use of those standards will raise achievement (Loertscher and Lewis 2013).

Educational standards provide targets for learning. Even though standards can be questioned, educational standards do set effective learning goals, especially if research time is given to those standards (Shepard, Hannaway, and Baker 2009). However, it can be difficult to always show links of effective language arts and literacy standards when testing to the goals of closing reading gaps with all students, as students have different educational goals, languages, and abilities, and also some standards and assessments can be interpreted differently (Shepard, Hannaway, and Baker 2009). Most importantly, it is the effect of using standards with student learning or with test results of clearly set taught standards that provide a base for strong learning.

In the United States, the Every Child Succeeds Act has reenergized the need to approach and use researched educational standards in all classrooms. Educators, such as the school librarian, approach clearly set educational standards in the library classroom, so that learners are better equipped for their futures. School library standards are surely set in a strong foundation of the American Association of School Librarians standards and move onward with state-driven educational standards as well. Those standards involve information literacy and English language arts standards, as seen in both print and technological quality resources. Since the advent of the Common Core or CCSS, this school librarian felt that the Common Core along with the commonly known and used the McREL Compendium of Standards and Benchmarks should both be approached in this lesson plan book for the busy elementary school librarian.

The school librarian is not only a manager of library resources and the information specialist and a teacher but also the information literacy curriculum leader, which starts in the school library classroom (ASLA 2014). The school librarian embraces standards in a leadership method. The school librarian provides a learning curriculum program centering on visual and technology literacy and information, with an inquiry approach (AASL 2009). The school librarian teacher collaborates with other educators to help achieve standard-based information literacy success.

The school librarian along with other educators are role models of teaching, as the school librarian teacher and other teachers work for current and future student successes through a carefully orchestrated classroom of learning balanced on current sources, the needs of students, active learning, and as finally set on quality English language arts and literacy standards. The school library classroom is targeted with focused instruction with literacy and English language arts, especially when aligned standards are used and implemented in all classrooms. All in all, standards alone cannot change education, but with the empowered focus of standards on student learning from school librarian teachers, other teachers, and school leaders, those standards-based lessons will bring increased positive academic change (AASL, 2013, November).

After the lengthy discourse on standards, it is time to look more closely at this book's lessons and other related variables in relationship to this book's given standards. School librarians will find standards applicable to their library curriculum in this book, including the use of the American Librarian Association literacy standards. Clearly taught standards-based lessons will provide the key for student global learning for the twenty-first-century skills. Along with standards and teaching to those standards with library lessons, there are lesson resources and other related elements given with every lesson in this book.

The many resources given in this book were narrowed down to provide quality and current sources for each lesson. The lessons will provide quick access to those popular, quality resources, which will be easily found in school libraries. Lessons in this third book are totally new lessons as compared to the other two books on lessons for the busy elementary school librarian. Each lesson in this book is about twenty minutes in teaching and learning length and has been tested.

This book's lessons show individual learning and collaborative student learning. Individual and collaborative inquiries are seen in learning and teaching principles of school library programs (American Association of School Librarians and Association for Educational Communications and Technology 1998). Cooperative or collaborative learning with students placed in careful groups will not only help students collaborate on learning but also help the busy school librarian teacher as that teacher and other teachers monitor the learning groups (Hoover 2006). The school librarian is part of a school's learning team, which is essential for student learning (State Library of Iowa: Iowa Department of Education 2007). Moreover, some of what English language teachers teach, school librarian teachers also teach (National Council of Teachers of English 2008).

Consequently, lessons in this book show team teaching, which adds value to the standards-based lessons, as students achieve through the help of not one but one or more teachers. Furthermore, main classroom teaching find better student literacy rates when teaching is collaborated with certified school librarians (Lance, Rodney, and Schwarz 2009). When school librarians work with other teachers to support learning with librarian given resources, students do better on standardized tests (Scholastic 2008).

Since a multitude of ever-changing print and technology literacy is at stake, team teaching plays a more urgent important role. Team teaching can have disadvantages, due to a lack of time to plan, but it can provide extra learning for students (Day and Hurrell 2012). Teacher collaboration with the school librarian is instrumental in shaping student readiness for the twenty-first-century learning in the fast moving information age as student are encouraged to be independent and lifelong users (AASL 2009).

According to the Day and Hurrell (2012) study, team teaching holds benefits, rather it be team teaching the entire lesson, sharing parts of the lesson, or just working with part of the class. A library program is often not just taught by school librarians but with the collaboration of other teachers to ensure more success (Texas Library Association 2010). There are benefits to having a social studies teacher help teach social studies subjects, an art teacher helping with art subjects or crafts, and then others with expertise in their teaching fields. With many subject expert teachers, student objectives are better met.

Student objectives are given for each lesson in this book. There is an urgency due to page space and the desire to keep the lessons set in a more speedy and efficient harness of interactive library learning, which evolved in concise and efficient lessons for the busy school librarian. Also there is urgency when trying to be concise with directions, due to time limitations for the busy school librarian. In an effort to keep lessons concise, this school librarian teacher only selected standards that held a perfect fit for each lesson. Finally, as lessons are given in the book, there are suggested assessments that could occur in school library classrooms. As for the school librarian self-assessment, professional self-assessments are seen when the professional school librarian takes note of lesson outcomes and reflects on taught lessons.

Suggested student assessments for the lessons in this book are student self-assessments and teacher observation. In the endeavor for a school librarian teacher's preference of assessment means and in the interest of time, assessments will only be mentioned here and so assessments will not be given with each of the book's lessons. Student assessments can take many forms, and judgments fall to teachers (CCSS 2012).

Formative assessments in the form of journaling and peer reviews work well for library lessons, as do summative and other assessments (AASL 2009). It is essential for the school librarian teacher and teaching team to view and comment on student self-assessments and other such assessments. AASL (2007) suggest student self-assessment strategies or summative assessments in the library classroom, as that leads to reflection, and reflection leads to growth.

Due to time limitations when teaching library classes, student self-assessments are recommended but other assessments may be desired. The school library program is channeled through assessment results and the school librarian teacher is instrumental in shaping student readiness for the twenty-first-century learning (AASL 2009). Instruction creates assessment needs. Student self-assessments and other such assessments with teacher observations for the busy school librarian teacher and their teaching team will quickly assure students and teachers that information literacy and the twenty-first-century goals were met and success occurred or that instruction needs to be repeated.

The American Association of School Librarians and Association for Educational Communications and Technology (1998) have developed a mission of the school library program, which includes successful teaching of goals with "active, authentic learning for information literacy." Active learning is needed for the twenty-first-century global skills, as information must be responsibly acquired, understood, and shared (AASL 2009). This book provides lessons for active and thus successful learning. When this book's lessons evoke higher student problem solving, group or paired work is suggested to ensure success for all learners. This book's standards-based lessons show literacy appreciation and knowledge for informational learning for the twenty-first-century student learning.

All lessons will pave the way for career and college readiness throughout the grade-level alignment of quality standards and the application of those standards. Furthermore, expectations and then achievement lead to successful information and reading literacy (Scholastic 2008). This book's lessons were first created under the foundation of standards, then further created with quality resources including many aspects of multiculturalism and technology, team teaching, and finally centered upon active learning. Students learn more when actively engaged, and so they are more successful (Ornstein and Hunkins 2009). The elementary school librarian will find student success with this book, as this school librarian teacher also found success with this book's active lessons that her students enjoyed.

This third book on lessons for the busy elementary school librarian teacher provides the school librarian teacher or those teaching elementary library skills or informational literacy skills a refreshing new set of lessons based on newer and popular resources, as well as suggesting a few traditional favorite sources. All suggested lesson sources are recommended and are easily found in school libraries. Creditable recommended Internet sites are also given. A library is an active learning environment where students find current books and resources and obtain assistance for information literacy needs and for reading appreciation and where school librarian teachers teach. As Kendall (2011) suggested, it is crucial that students are engaged in learning. The school librarian is busy, and this book will quickly help the curriculum area of the busy school librarian teacher's program. Due to extensive researching for this book, the resources are tested and trusted resources, the lessons are tested, and then there are standard choices for each interactive lesson.

This book focuses on standards, and those standards are current and can be quickly applied to this book's lessons. Since the CCSS, the McREL Compendium of Standards and Benchmarks, and the AASL standards can be intermingled in many ways, this book will provide a good link for any or all of those standards that the school librarian teacher uses with his or her elementary library curriculum. Albeit, other researched and credible standards may also be used in conjunction with the book's lesson. Credible standards with other possible quality language arts and literacy standards in the school library will find a compelling standards match for lessons in this book.

With the standards given in this book or with other quality researched standards, the CCSS, the McREL Compendium of Standards and Benchmarks, and the AASL standards either used alone or together will provide a solid foundation for focused learning and purposeful guided instruction in the school library. English language arts, literacy appreciation, and knowledge for informational learning standards will meet success when used in school library classes and with collaboration with other teachers. The busy school library is the hub for print and technology information literacy instruction for student futures and requires quality standard-based school library instruction for successful student careers and college pathways. Today's elementary school library students will be actively prepared for their future literacy learning needs in a global society and will see increased reading appreciation and increased literacy skills from the standards-based lessons in this book that the elementary school librarian clearly instructs in his or her busy libraries.

A Personal Note to Elementary School Librarian Co-Teachers

My elementary school library students thoroughly enjoyed these lessons, and some students even wanted to do what other grades were doing. The learning excitement was contagious. Along with enjoying the lessons, maximum student learning was indeed seen. Your students will enjoy these lessons too! Keep up your dedicated work of teaching literacy skills, which raises reading scores, directing libraries, advocating quality research at all times, increasing reading appreciation, and much more appreciated work in your busy school libraries.

References

AASL (American Association of School Librarians). *Standards for the 21st Century Learner.* Chicago, IL: American Association of School Librarians, 2007.

AASL (American Association of School Librarians). *Empowering Learners: Guidelines for School Library Media Programs.* Chicago, IL: American Association of School Librarians, 2009.

American Association of School Librarians and Association for Educational Communications and Technology. *Information Power: Building Partnerships for Learning.* Chicago, IL: American Library Association, 1998.

American Library Association. *Information Literacy Competency Standards for Higher Education,* 2004. Accessed January 2016. http://www.ala.org/acrl.standards/informationliteacy competency

Arp, Lori and Beth S. Woodard, Eds. "Information Literacy in School Libraries: It Takes a Community." *Reference and User Services Quarterly* (2003):42(3), 215.

ASLA (Australian School Library Association). *What Is a School Librarian Teacher?,* 2014. Accessed November 2015. http://www.asla.org.au/advocacy/what-is-a-teacher-librarian.aspx

Carmichael, Sheila Byrd, Stephen W. Wilson, Kathleen Porter Magee, and Gabrielle Martino. *The State of State Standards – and the Common Core – in 2010.* Washington, DC: Thomas B. Fordham Institute, 2010.

Chen, Grace. *National Education Standards: Both Sides of the Debate. Public School Review,* 2015. Updated 2015. http://www.publicschoolreview.com

Christensen, Kathleen and Barbara Schneider. *Workplace Flexibility: Realigning 20th-Century Jobs for a 21st-Century Workforce.* Ithaca, NY: Cornell University, 2010.

Common Core. *Common Core State Standards,* 2015. Updated 2015. http://www.core standards.org

Day, Lorraine and Derek Hurrell. "A Teaching Team: More than the Sum of Its Parts." In Creating an Inclusive Learning Environment: Engagement, Equity, and Retention. *Proceedings of the 21st Annual Teaching Learning Forum.* Fremantle, West Australia: University of Notre Dame Australia, 2012. http://otl.curtin.edu.au/tlf/tlf2012/refereed/day.html

Earnest, Josh, White House Press Secretary. *Every Student Succeeds Act,* 2015. Accessed January 2016. http://www.whitehouse.gov

Eisenberg, Michael B. "Information Literacy: Essential Skills for the Information Age." *Journal of Library and Information Technology* (2008):28, 39–47.

Finn, Chester, Liam Julian, and Michael Petrilli. *The State of State Standards.* Washington, DC: Thomas Fordham Foundation, 2006.

Francis, Briana Hovendick, Curry Lance, and Zeth Leitzauh. *School Librarian Teachers Continue to Help Students Achieve Standards: The Third Colorado Study.* Denver, CO: Colorado Department of Education, 2010.

Garland, Sarah. "How Does Common Core Compare?" The Hechinger Report. *The Huff Post,* 2013. Accessed 2016. http://www.huffingtonpost.com/2013/10/15/common-core-compare_n_4102973.html

Gavigan, Karen and Keith Curry. "SC Study Shows Link between School Librarians and Higher Test Scores." *School Library Journal* (2016). Accessed January 2017. http://www.slj.com/2016/03/industry-news/sc-study-shows-link-between-school-librarians-and-higher-test-scores/

Great Schools. *Why Are Standards Important?,* 2014. Accessed December 2015. http://www.greatschools.org/gk/articles/why-are-standards-important/

Hoover, Clara. "Research-Based Instructional Strategies." *School Library Media Activities Monthly* (2006):22, 26.

IEEE-SA. *What Are Standards? Why Are They Important?,* October 11, 2011. Accessed January 2016. http://standardsinsight.com/ieee_company_detail/what-are-standards-why--are-they-important

Kendall, John. "Topics: A Roadmap to Standards." *NASSP Bulletin* (2000):84, 37.

Kendall, John. *Understanding Common Core State Standards.* Alexandria, VA: ASCD and Denver, CO: McREL, 2011.

Kendall, John, Susan Ryan, Alan Alpert, Amy Richardson, and Amitra Schwols. *State Adoption of the Common Core State Standards: The 15 Percent Rule.* Denver, CO: Mid-continent Research for Education and Learning, 2012.

Korte, Gregory. "The Every Student Succeeds Act vs No Child Left Behind: What's Changed?" *USA Today,* December 11, 2015. Accessed January 2016. htttp:/www.usatoday.com/story/news/politics/2015/12/10/every-student-succeeds-act-vs-no-child-left-behind-whats-changed?

Kuhlthau, Carol Collier. "Guided Inquiry: School Libraries in the 21st Century." *School Libraries World Wide.* Jefferson City, MO: International Association of School Librarianship, 2009, 17–28.

Kuhlthau, Carol Collier. "Inquiry Inspires Original Research." *School Library Media Monthly* (November 2013):30(2).

Lance, Keith Curry and Debra Kachel. "Achieving Academic Standards through the School Library Program." *School Librarian Teacher* (2013):40(5), 8–13.

Lance, Keith Curry, Marcia J. Rodney, and Bill Schwarz. *The Idaho School Library Impact Study-2009: How Idaho Librarians, Teachers, and Administrators Collaborate for Student Success. Idaho Commission for Libraries.* Boise, ID: Idaho Commission for Libraries, 2010.

Lance, Keith Curry, Marcia Rodney, and Christine Hamilton-Pennell. *Measuring up to Standards: The Impact of School Library Programs and Information Literacy in Pennsylvania Schools.* Greenburg, PA: Pennsylvania Citizens for Better Libraries, 2000.

Loertscher, David V. and Kathryn Roots Lewis. *Implementing the Common Core State Standards: The Role of the School Librarian Teacher.* Chicago, IL: American Association of Teacher Librarians and Achieve, 2013.

McREL. "Standards and Curriculum." *McREL International*, 2015. Accessed January 2016. http://www.mcrel.org/standards-curriculum/

National Council of Teachers of English. *NCTE/IRA Standards for English Language Arts*, 2012. Accessed December 2015. http://www.ncte.org/standards/ncte-ira

National Council of Teachers of English. *Resolution on Supporting School and Community Libraries.* Updated 2008. http://www.ncte.org/positions/statements/supportinglibraries

New York Comprehensive Center. *Informational Brief: Impact of School Libraries on Student Achievement.* New York: New York Comprehensive Center, 2011.

Ong, Faye, Ed. *Model School Library Standards for California Public Schools, Kindergarten Through Grade Twelve.* Sacramento, CA: California Department of Education, 2010.

Ornstein, Allan and Frankcis P. Hunkins. *Curriculum Foundations, Principles, and Issue.* New York: Pearson, 2009.

Quebec School Librarians Network. *Standards of Practice for School Library Learning Commons in Canada*, 2014. Updated 2014. http://qslin.org/cla-standards-for-canadian-school-libraries/

Schmoker, Mike and Robert Marzano. "Realizing the Promise of Standards-Based Education." *Educational Leadership* (1999):56, 17.

Scholastic. *School Libraries Work!* New York: Scholastic, 2008.

Shepard, Lorrie, Jane Hannaway, and Eva Baker, Eds. *Standards, Assessments, and Accountability. Education Policy White Paper.* Washington, DC: National Academy Education, 2009.

State Library of Iowa: Iowa Department of Education. *Iowa School Library Program Guidelines: Libraries, Literacy and Learning for the 21st Century.* Des Moines, IA: Iowa Department of Education, 2007.

Stephens, Clarie Gatrell, and Pat Franklin. "Managing AASL's New Standards for the 21st Century Learner." *School Library Monthly* (September 2009):34–36.

Tanner, Daniel and Laurel Tanner. *Curriculum Development: Theory and Practice.* Upper Saddle River, NJ: Pearson Education, 2008.

Texas Library Association. *It's Not Just Books and Stories!* Updated 2010. http://www.txla.org/sites/tla/files/forparents/School%20library%20standards%202010.pp

Uecker, Ruth, Shelly Kelly, and Marni Napierala. "Implementing the Common Core State Standards: What is the School Librarian Teacher's Role?" *Knowledge Quest.* Chicago, IL: American Librarian Association, 2015.

Standards

AASL Standards for the 21st Century Learner

American Association of School Librarians (AASL) Standards for the 21s Century Learner

    The following AASL or American Association of School Librarians standards are linked with Common Core and McREL standards, which all reflect information literacy and promised student growth. Part or all of the following AASL standards will be connected to every lesson in this book for the busy elementary school librarian.

AASL (American Association of School Librarians) Standards for the 21st Century Learner

- Inquire, think critically, and gain knowledge. (AASL 1)
- Draw conclusions, make informed decisions, apply knowledge to new situations, and create new knowledge. (AASL 2).
- Share knowledge and participate ethically and productively as members of our democratic society. (AASL 3)
- Pursue personal and aesthetic growth (AASL 4)

Excerpted from *Standards for the 21st-Century Learner* by the American Association of School Librarians, a division of the American Library Association, copyright © 2007 American Library Association. Available for download at http:// www.ala.org/aasl/standards. Used with permission.

Common Course Language Arts Literacy Standards CCSS

Kindergarten

Kindergarten Common Core (Literacy)-Reading Literature

CCSS.ELA-Literacy.RL.K.1
- With prompting and support, ask and answer questions about key details in a text.

CCSS.ELA-Literacy.RL.K.2
- With prompting and support, retell familiar stories, including key details.

CCSS.ELA-Literacy.RL.K.3
- With prompting and support, identify characters, settings, and major events in a story, using key details.

CCSS.ELA-Literacy.RL.K.5
- Recognize common types of texts (e.g., storybooks, poems).

CCSS.ELA-Literacy.RL.K.6
- With prompting and support, name the author and illustrator of a story and define the role of each in telling the story.

CCSS. ELA-Literacy.RL.K.7
- With prompting and support, describe the relationship between illustrations and the story in which they appear (e.g., what moment in a story an illustration depicts).

Kindergarten Common Core (Literacy), Reading Informational Texts.

CCSS.ELA-Literacy.RI.K.2
- With prompting and support, identify the main topic and retell key details of a text.

CCSS.ELA-Literacy.RI.K.5
- Identify the front cover, back cover, and title page of a book.

First-Grade

First Grade Common Core (Literacy)-Reading Literature

CCSS.ELA-Literacy.RL.1.1
- Ask and answer questions about key details in a text.

CCSS.ELA-Literacy.RL.1.3
- Describe characters, settings, and major events in a story, using key details.

CCSS.ELA-Literacy.RL.1.4
- Identify words and phrases in stories or poems that suggest feelings or appeal to the senses.

CCSS.ELA-Literacy.RL.1.5
- Explain major differences between books that tell stories and books that give information, drawing on a wide reading of a range of text types.

CCSS.ELA-Literacy.RL.1.7
- Use illustrations and details in a story to describe its characters, setting, or events.

First-Grade Common Core (Literacy), Reading Informational Texts.

CCSS.ELA-Literacy.RL.1.1
- Ask and answer questions about key details in a text.

CCSS.ELA-Literacy.RL.1.7.
- Use illustrations and details in a text to describe its key ideas.

Second Grade

Second-Grade Common Core (Literacy)-Reading Literature

CCSS.ELA-Literacy.RL.2.1
- Ask and answer such questions as who, what, where, when, why, and how to demonstrate understanding of key details in a text.

CCSS.ELA-Literacy.RL.2.2
- Recount stories, including fables and folktales from diverse cultures, and determine their central message, lesson, or moral.

CCSS.ELA-Literacy.RL.2.4
- Describe how words and phrases (e.g., regular beats, alliteration, rhymes, repeated lines) supply rhythm and meaning in a story, poem, or song.

CCSS. ELA-Literacy.RL.2.5
- Describe the overall structure of a story, including describing how the beginning introduces and story and the ending concludes the action.

CCSS.ELA-Literacy.RL.2.9
- Compare and contrast two or more versions of the same story (e.g., Cinderella stories) by different authors or from different cultures.

Second-Grade Common Core (Literacy), Reading Informational Texts.

CCSS.ELA-Literacy. RI.2.1
- Ask and answer such questions as who, what, where, when, why, and how to demonstrate understanding of the key details in a text

CCSS.ELA-Literacy.RI.2.6
- Identify the main purpose of a text, including what the author wants to answer, explain, or describe.

Third-Grade

Third-Grade Common Core (Literacy)-Reading Literature

CCSS. ELA-Literacy.RL.3.1
- Ask and answer questions to demonstrate understanding of a text, referring explicitly to the text as the basis for the answers.

CSS.ELA-Literacy.RL.3.2
- Recount stories, including fables, folktales, and myths from diverse cultures; determine the central message, lesson, or moral and explain how it is conveyed through key details in the text.

CCSS. ELA-Literacy. RL.3.3
- Describe characters in a story (e.g., their traits, motivations, or feelings) and explain how their actions contribute to the sequence of events.

CCSS.ELA-Literacy. RL.3.5
- Refer to parts of stories, dramas, and poems, when writing or speaking about a text, using terms such a chapter, scene, and stanza, describe how each successive part builds on earlier sections.

Third Grade Common Core (Literacy), Reading Informational Texts

CCSS.ElA-Literacy. RI.3.1
- Ask and answer questions to demonstrate understanding of a text, referring explicitly to the text for answers.

CCSS.ELA-Literacy. RI. 3.7
- Use information gained from illustrations (e.g., maps, photographs) and the words in a text to demonstrate understanding of the text (e.g., where, when, why, and how key events occur).

Governors Association Center for Best Practices and Council of Chief State School Officers (2010). Common Core State Standards (Literacy). Washington, D.C: National Governors Association Center for Best Practices and Council of Chief State School Officers. Retrieved from http://www .corestandards.org/

Fourth-Grade

Fourth-Grade Common Core (Literacy)-Reading Literature

CCSS. ELA-Literacy.RL.4.1
- Refer to details and examples in a text when explaining what the text says explicitly and when drawing inferences from the text.

CCSS.ELA.RL.4.2
- Determine a theme of a story, drama, or poem from details in the text; summarize the text.

CCSS. ELA. RL.4.9
- Describe in depth a character, setting, or event in a story or drama, drawing on specific details in the text (e.g. a character's thoughts, words, or actions).

CCSS.ELA-Literacy. RL.4.9
- Compare and contrast the treatment of similar themes and topics (e.g., opposition of good and evil) and patterns of events (e.g., the quest) in stories, myths, and traditional literature from different cultures.

*Fourth Grade Common Core (Literacy), Reading Informational Texts

CCSS.ElA-Literacy. RI.4.1
- Refer to details and examples in a text, when explaining what the text says explicitly and when drawing inferences from the text.

CCSS.ELA-Literacy. RI. 4.7
- Interpret information presented visually, orally, or quantitatively (e.g., in charts, graphs, diagrams, timelines, animations, or interactive elements on Web pages) and explain how the information contributes to an understanding of the text in which it appears.

Fifth-Grade

Fifth-Grade Common Core (Literacy)-Reading Literature

CCSS. ELA-Literacy.RL.5.2

- Determine a theme of a story, drama, or poem from details in the text, including how characters in a story or drama respond to challenges or how the speaker in a poem reflects upon a topic; summarize the text.

CCSS.ELA.RL.5.3

- Compare and contrast two or more characters, setting, or events in a story or drama, drawing on specific details in a text (e.g., how characters interact).

CCSS.ELA-Literacy. RL.5.7

- Analyze how visual and multimedia elements contribute to the meaning, tone, or beauty of a text (e.g., graphic novel, multimedia presentation of fiction, folktale, myth, poem).

CCSS.ELA-Literacy. RL.5.9

- Compare and contrast stories in the same genre (e.g., mysteries and adventure stories) on their approaches to similar themes and topics.

Fifth Grade Common Core (Literacy), Reading Informational Texts

CCSS.ElA-Literacy. RI.5.3

- Explain the relationships or interactions between two or more individuals, events, ideas, or concepts in a historical, scientific, or technical text based on specific information in the text.

CCSS.ELA-Literacy. RI. 5.7

- Draw on information from multiple print or digital sources, demonstrating the ability to locate an answer to a question quickly or to solve a problem efficiently.

CCSS.ELA-Literacy.R.I.5.9

- Integrate information from several texts on the same topic in order to write or speak about the subject knowledgeably.

Governors Association Center for Best Practices and Council of Chief State School Officers (2010). Common Core State Standards (Literacy). Washington, D.C: National Governors Association Center for Best Practices and Council of Chief State School Officers. Retrieved from http://www.corestandards.org/

McREL Compendium of Standards and Benchmarks From Content Knowledge Language Arts

Kindergarten-Second Grades

Writing Standards and Benchmarks (Grades K-2)

Standard 4

Gathers and uses information for research purposes.

- Uses a variety of sources to gather information (e.g., informational books, pictures, charts indexes, video, television programs, guest speakers, internet, own observation).

Language Arts Reading Standards and Benchmarks (Grades K-2)

Standard 5

Uses the general skills and strategies of the reading process.
- Uses meaning clues (e.g., pictures, captions, illustrations, title, cover, headings, story structure, story topic) to aid comprehension and make predictions about content (e.g., action, events character's behavior).

Standard 6

Uses skills and strategies to read a variety of literary texts.
- Reads [Hear] a variety of familiar literary passages and texts (e.g., fairy tales, folktales, fiction, nonfiction, legends, fables, myths, poems, nursery rhymes, picture books, predictable books).
- Knows setting, main characters, main events, sequence, narrator, and problems in stories.

Standard 7

Uses skills and strategies to read a variety of informational texts.
- Summarizes information found in texts (e.g., retells in own words).
- Relates new information to prior knowledge and experience.

Third-Fifth Grades

Writing Standards and Benchmarks (Grades 3-5)

Standard 4

Gathers and uses information for research purposes.
- Uses a variety of strategies to plan research (e.g., identifies possible topic by brainstorming, listing questions, using idea webs, organizes prior knowledge about a topic; develops a course of action, determines how to locate necessary information).
- Uses encyclopedias to gather information for research topics.
- Uses electronic media to gather information (e.g., databases, Internet, CD-ROM, television shows, videos, pull-down menus, word searches).

Language Arts Reading Standards and Benchmarks (Grades 3-5)

Standard 5

Uses the general skills and strategies of the reading process.
- Uses word reference materials (e.g., glossary, dictionary, thesaurus) to determine the meaning, pronunciation, and derivations of unknown words.

Standard 6

Uses skills and strategies to read a variety of literary texts.
- Reads a variety of literary passages and texts (e.g., fairy tales, folktales, fiction, nonfiction, myths, poems, fables, fantasies, historical fiction, biographies, autobiographies, chapter books).
- Knows the defining characteristics (e.g., rhyme and rhythm in poetry; settings and dialogue in drama, make believe in folktales and fantasies, life stories in biography; illustrations in children's stories) and structural elements (e.g., chapter, scene, stanza, verse, meter) of a variety of genres
- Understands the basic concept of plot (e.g., main problem, conflict, resolution, cause-and-effect).
- Knows themes that recur across literary works.

- Understands similarities and differences within and among literary works from various genre and cultures (e.g., in terms of settings, character types, events, point of view; role of natural phenomena).

Standard 7

Uses skills and strategies to read a variety of informational texts.
- Uses the various parts of a book (e.g., index, table of contents, glossary, appendix, preface) to locate information.
- Summarizes and paraphrases information in texts (e.g., includes the main idea and significant supporting details of a reading selection).
- Understands similarities and differences within and among literary works from various genre and cultures (e.g., in terms of settings, character types, events, point of view, role of natural phenomena).

McREL Language Arts Standards from Content Knowledge (Online Edition) http://www2 .mcrel.org/compendium/SubjectTopics.asp?SubjectID=7. Reprinted by permission of McREL.

Chapter 1

Kindergarten

Kindergarten library lesson plans will help the busy school librarian strive to meet the demanding needs of a school library including that of teaching literacy skills and reading appreciation. The following interactive standards-backed elementary lessons will meet the needs of today's students. In this book, the school library curriculum is based on literacy, as addressed in the American Association of School Librarian (AASL) standards, and with the McREL Compendium of Standards and Benchmarks and Common Core State Standards.

The quality-researched standards of AASL, Common Core State Standards (CCSS), and McREL are applied with each school library lesson for purposeful school library instruction. The parts of the standards chosen for this book were those that were the most essential for library instruction and could be met in the time allotment of twenty minutes. The standards may be used together as already given, individually, or lessons may be set to other quality literacy and English language arts standards.

Student learning objectives are given for each lesson. Lessons include students working individually or with others for more efficient student learning. Team teaching is seen, as more can be accomplished when working together. Quality-researched resources are suggested. The streamlined standards-based lessons for the busy school librarian will provide interactive and successful student learning. The AASL standards are stated in the first chapter as they are universally seen with all lessons in some way. The following McREL and CCSS standards are used specifically with this grade level.

Kindergarten Library Standards with Language Arts Benchmarks from McREL Language Arts Writing Standards and Benchmarks and Common Core Language Arts Literacy Standards (CCSS)

Kindergarten students:

*Kindergarten Common Core (Literacy), Reading Literature

1. With prompting and support, ask and answer questions about key details in a text. (CCSS.ELA-Literacy.RL.K.1)
2. With prompting and support, retell familiar stories, including key details. (CCSS.ELA-Literacy.RL.K.2)
3. With prompting and support, identify characters, settings, and major events in a story, using key details. (CCSS.ELA-Literacy.RL.K.3)
4. Recognize common types of texts (e.g., storybooks, poems). (CCSS.ELA-Literacy.RL.K.5)
5. With prompting and support, name the author and illustrator of a story and define the role of each in telling the story. (CCSS.ELA-Literacy.RL.K.6)
6. With prompting and support, describe the relationship between illustrations and the story in which they appear (e.g., what moment in a story an illustration depicts). (CCSS.ELA-Literacy.RL.K.7)

Kindergarten Common Core (Literacy), Reading Informational Texts

7. With prompting and support, identify the main topic and retell key details of a text. (CCSS.ELA-Literacy.RI.K.2)
8. Identify the front cover, back cover, and title page of a book. (CCSS.ELA-Literacy.RI.K.5)

Governors Association Center for Best Practices and Council of Chief State School Officers *Common Core State Standards (Literacy)*. Washington, DC: National Governors Association Center for Best Practices and Council of Chief State School Officers, 2010. Retrieved from http://www.corestandards.org/

McREL Compendium of Standards and Benchmarks Language Arts Writing Standards and Benchmarks (Grades K–2)

*Gathers and uses information for research purposes. Standard 4

1. Uses a variety of sources to gather information (e.g., informational books, pictures, charts, indexes, video, television programs, guest speakers, internet, own observation). (McREL)

McREL Compendium of Standards and Benchmarks Language Arts Reading Standards and Benchmarks (Grades K–2)

*Uses the general skills and strategies of the reading process. Standard 5

2. Uses meaning clues (e.g., pictures, captions, illustrations, title, cover, headings, story structure, story topic) to aid comprehension and make predictions about content (e.g., action, events, character's behavior). (McREL)
   *Uses skills and strategies to read a variety of literary texts.
3. Reads [Hear] a variety of familiar literary passages and texts (e.g., fairy tales, folktales, fiction, nonfiction, legends, fables, myths, poems, nursery rhymes, picture books, predictable books). (McREL)
4. Know setting, main characters, main events, sequence, narrator, and problems in stories. (McREL)

*Use skills and strategies to read a variety of informational texts.

5. Summarize information found in texts (e.g., retell in own words). (McREL)
6. Relate new information to prior knowledge and experience. (McREL)

McREL. *Language Arts Standards*, 2015. Retrieved from http://www2.mcrel.org/compendium/standard

Library Mouse

The Story of Library Mouse

Once there was a mouse, named Library Mouse. He was playing on the school playground. He saw a school child's backpack. He went inside it. The backpack was picked up by a child. The backpack with Library Mouse was taken into the school library. The mouse crawled out of the backpack and looked. He saw many books. He liked books to read and <u>chew</u>. Because the mouse was so excited, he ran on the books and tried to chew on one. The library teacher caught him and showed him to the children. The children told the mouse that he cannot chew books. The mouse said, "okay." The mouse waved goodbye. He would see the children again. The end.

Help Library Mouse. Draw some ways to take care of library books for the mouse. Color the bottom Library Mouse, before he runs.

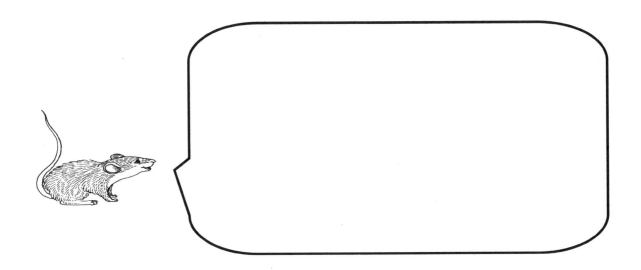

Library Mouse

Standards

Student(s)

- Inquire, think critically, and gain knowledge. (AASL 1)
- Draw conclusions, make informed decisions, apply knowledge to new situations, and create new knowledge. (AASL 2)
- Share knowledge and participate ethically and productively as members of our democratic society. (AASL 3)
- Pursue personal and aesthetic growth. (AASL 4)
- With prompting and support, identify characters, settings, and major events in a story, using key details. (CCSS 3)
- Recognize common types of texts (e.g., storybooks, poems). (CCSS 4)
- [Reads] Hears a variety of familiar literary passages and texts (e.g., fairy tales, folktales, fiction, nonfiction, legends, fables, myths, poems, nursery rhymes, picture books, predictable books). (McREL 3)
- Knows setting, main characters, main events, sequence, narrator, and problems in stories. (McREL 4)

Objectives

Students

- Recognize characters and the main event.
- Illustrate ways to take care of library books.

Directions

1. The reading teacher reads and shows a mouse in a library or school fiction story. Discusses characters and major event, as could be related to the school or school library.
2. The school librarian reads the worksheet story and discusses the character and major event.
3. Guided by the school librarian, students discuss how to care for library books.
4. Guided by teachers, students illustrate how to take care of books for the mouse and for themselves. Students color the illustrations.

Teaching Team

Reading and school librarian teachers.

Suggested Sources

Kirk, Daniel. *Library Mouse.* New York: ABRAMS, 2012.
Kirk, Daniel. *Library Mouse: A World to Explore.* New York: ABRAMS, 2010.
Numeroff, Laura Joffe. *A Mouse Cookie First Library.* New York: Laura Geringer Books, 2007.
Numeroff, Laura Joffe. *If You Take a Mouse to School.* New York: HarperCollins, 2002.

Fire Trucks to the Rescue

1. Circle what the fire truck did: Put out a fire or rested

2. Circle the color of the fire truck: Blue   Yellow   Red

3. Connect the dots to find a fire truck going to the rescue.

Color the fire trucks.

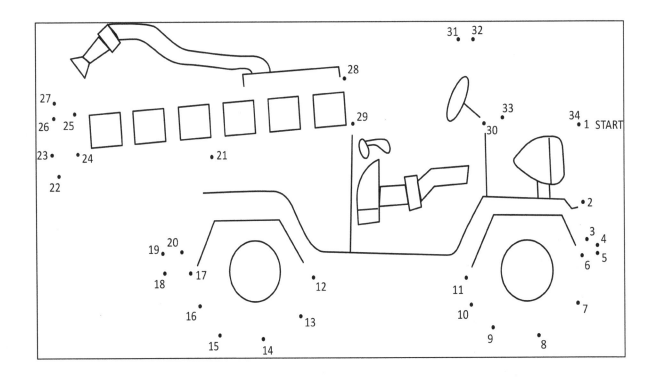

From *Standards-Based Lesson Plans for the Busy Elementary School Librarian* by Joyce Keeling.
Santa Barbara, CA: Libraries Unlimited. Copyright © 2017.

Fire Trucks to the Rescue

Standards

Student(s)

- Inquire, think critically, and gain knowledge. (AASL 1)
- Draw conclusions, make informed decisions, apply knowledge to new situations, and create new knowledge. (AASL 2)
- Share knowledge and participate ethically and productively as members of our democratic society. (AASL 3)
- With prompting and support, name the author and illustrator of a text and define the role of each in telling the story. (CCSS 5)
- With prompting and support, identify the main topic and retell key details of a text. (CCSS 7)
- Uses a variety of sources to gather information (e.g., informational books, pictures, charts, indexes, videos, television programs, guest speakers, Internet, own observation). (McREL 1)
- Uses meaning clue (e.g., pictures, captions, illustrations, title, cover, headings, story structure, story topic) to aid comprehension and make predictions about content (e.g., action, events, character's behavior). (McREL 2)
- Relates new information to prior knowledge and experience. (McREL 6)

Objectives

Students

- Recall facts about fire trucks from prior and new knowledge.
- Define author.

Directions

1. After first discussing the author, the school librarian reads and shows a fiction fire truck book. The book's key details, the fire truck color, and what happened in the story are discussed.
2. After first discussing the author, the reading teacher reads, shows, and discusses a brief nonfiction fire truck book. Students compare the information to what they knew.
3. The teachers guide students as students answer worksheet questions.
4. Students complete a dot-to-dot and color a fire truck.

Teaching Team

Reading and school librarian teachers.

Suggested Sources

Fiction

> Austin, Mike. *Fire Engine No. 9*. New York: Random House, 2015.
> Middleton, Susan. *Fire! Fuego! Brave Bomberos*. New York: Bloomsbury, 2012.

Nonfiction

> Graubart, Norman. *Fire Trucks*. New York: Power Kids Press, 2015.
> Riggs, Kate. *Fire Trucks*. Mankato, MN: Creative Education, 2016.

ABC Order

Easy books (E) are fiction. Fiction books are in ABC order. They are in ABC order by the last name of the author.

Find a book   Find it on a shelf

(1) Circle an A, B, or C. Find the   on the A, B, or C   .

(2) Look at the   .   Draw what you liked from it.

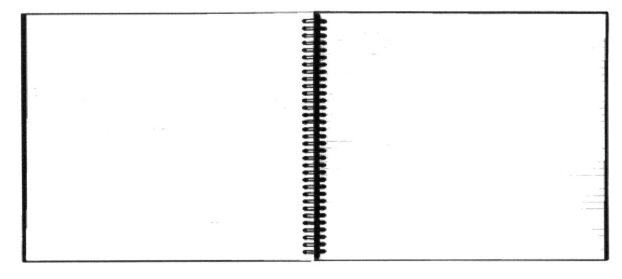

ABC Order

Standards

Student(s)

- Inquire, think critically, and gain knowledge. (AASL 1)
- Draw conclusions, make informed decisions, apply knowledge to new situations, and create new knowledge. (AASL 2)
- Share knowledge and participate ethically and productively as members of our democratic society. (AASL 3)
- Pursue personal and aesthetic growth. (AASL 4)
- With prompting and support, ask and answer questions about key details in a text. (CCSS 1)
- Uses meaning clues (e.g., pictures, captions, illustrations, title, cover, headings, story structure, story topic) to aid comprehension and make predictions about content (e.g., action, events, character's behavior). (McREL 2)
- [Reads] Hear a variety of familiar literary passages and texts (e.g., fairy tales, folktales, fiction, nonfiction, legends, fables, myths, poems, nursery rhymes, picture books, predictable books). (McREL 3)

Objectives

Students

- Discover the ABC order of books.
- Find a book on the A, B, or C shelf.
- Illustrate the key idea.

Directions

1. The reading teacher reads and shows an entertaining ABC book. The key detail is discussed.
2. The school librarian shows and discusses how books are put in ABC order by the first letter of the author's last name, in the easy fiction book library section. Those A, B, and C sections are the focus of the lesson and are marked with a sticky note identifying each section as an A, B, or C shelf.
3. As guided by teachers and the worksheet, students select a book and then find the book on the A, B, or C shelf.
4. On the worksheets, students illustrate the key detail from the book that they found.

Teaching Team

Reading and school librarian teachers.

Suggested Sources

Andreae, Giles. *ABC Animal Jamboree*. Wilton, CT: Tiger Tales, 2012.
Katz, Susan. *ABC School's For Me!* New York: Scholastic Press, 2015.
Rock 'N Learn Alphabet [DVD]. Conroe, TX: Rock 'N Learn Studio, 2012.
Scieszka, Jon. *Race from A to Z*. New York: Simon & Shuster Books for Young Readers, 2016.
Soble, June. (2006). *Shiver Me Letters: A Pirate ABC*. Boston, MA: Sandpiper/Houghton Mifflin Harcourt, 2006.

Fall Fun

What are some fun things that you can do in the Fall? Draw fun Fall things on the leaf.

Fall Fun

Standards

Student(s)

- Inquire, think critically, and gain knowledge. (AASL 1)
- Draw conclusions, make informed decisions, apply knowledge to new situations, and create new knowledge. (AASL 2)
- Pursue personal and aesthetic growth. (AASL 4)
- With prompting and support, ask and answer questions about key details in a text. (CCSS 1)
- Explain major differences between books that tell stories and books that give information, drawing on a wide reading of a range of text types. (First Grade, CCSS 4)
- Uses a variety of sources to gather information (e.g., informational books, pictures, charts, indexes, videos, television programs, guest speakers, Internet, own observation). (McREL 1)
- Use meaning clues (e.g., pictures, captions, illustrations, title, cover, headings, story structure, story topic) to aid comprehension and make predictions about content (e.g., action, events, character's behavior). (McREL 2)

Objectives

Students

- Recall the differences between fiction and nonfiction.
- Illustrate ways to have fun with research.

Directions

1. The school librarian discusses differences between fiction and nonfiction. One or two Fall nonfiction books are read, shown, and discussed as books that give information.
2. The reading teacher reads, shows, and discusses a Fall fiction book.
3. The class summarizes what they learned about Fall fun from the fiction and nonfiction books. Students then illustrate ways to have fun in the Fall.

Teaching Team

Reading and school librarian teachers.

Suggested Sources

Fiction

Mayer, Mercer. *The Fall Festival*. New York: HarperCollins, 2009.
Raczka, Bob. *Fall Mixed Up*. Minneapolis, MN: Carolrhoda, 2011.

Nonfiction

Lindeen, Mary. *Let's Play Football*. Chicago, IL: Norwood House Press, 2016.
Nagelhout, Ryan. *I Lover Soccer*. Milwaukee, WI: Gareth Stevens Publishing, 2015.
Shores, Erika. *Pumpkins—Celebrate Fall*. Mankato, MN: Capstone, 2016.
Smith, Sian. *Fall*. Portsmouth, NH: Heinemann, 2009.
Yee, Herbert Wong. *My Autumn Book*. New York: Henry Holt and Co, 2015.

On a Hunt

You are going on a lion or bear hunt. What will you see? In the boxes, draw what you see. Color and cut out the binoculars and boxes. Add the boxes to connect it all. Fold on the dotted lines when connecting the boxes to the binocular top and bottom.

On a Hunt

Standards

Student(s)

- Inquire, think critically, and gain knowledge. (AASL 1)
- Draw conclusions, make informed decisions, apply knowledge to new situations, and create new knowledge. (AASL 2)
- Share knowledge and participate ethically and productively as members of our democratic society. (AASL 3)
- With prompting and support, ask and answer questions about key details in a text. (CCSS 1)
- With prompting and support, identify characters, settings, and major events in a story, using key details. (CCSS 3)
- Uses meaning clues (e.g., picture captions, illustrations, title, cover, headings, story structure, story topics) to aid comprehension and make predictions about content (e.g., action, events, character's behavior). (McREL 2)
- Summarizes information found in texts (e.g., retell in own words). (McREL 5)

Objectives

Students

- Summarize setting, characters, and major events, and other key details.
- Illustrate two major events.
- Create binoculars to act out the story hunt.

Directions

1. The school librarian reads and shows an entertaining book about going on a lion or bear hunt.
2. The reading teacher guides student discussion and summary of the setting, characters, major events, and other key details of the story.
3. Under guidance from the art, reading, and school librarian teachers, students illustrate major events from the story on the two worksheet squares.
4. The art teacher guides student construction of the binoculars. Students color and cut out the binoculars. After cutting out the worksheet squares, students fold on the dotted lines. The two folded squares are placed between the two binoculars, in order to connect the top and bottom binoculars into one binocular. The squares are positioned and taped at the far right and then far left inside the binocular set, while leaving an open viewing space in the middle of the binoculars.
5. Students act out the lion or bear hunt story using their binoculars.

Teaching Team

Art, reading, and school librarian teachers.

Suggested Sources

Cuyler, Margery. *We're Going on a Lion Hunt*. New York: Two Lions, 2008.
Rosen, Michael. *We're Going on a Bear Hunt*. New York: Walker Books, 2015.

Pig Goes on a Ride

Pig goes on a big hot air balloon ride. First, draw pig's adventure on the balloon. After coloring pig, put pig in the balloon with a new friend for a new adventure.

Pig Goes on a Ride

Standards

Student(s)

- Draw conclusions, make informed decisions, apply knowledge to new situations, and create new knowledge. (AASL 2)
- Share knowledge and participate ethically and productively as members of our democratic society. (AASL 3)
- With prompting and support, identify characters, settings, and major events in a story, using key details. (CCSS 3)
- With prompting and support, describe the relationship between illustrations and the story in which they appear (e.g., what moment in a story an illustration depicts). (CCSS 6)
- Uses meaning clues (e.g., pictures, captions, illustrations, title, cover, headings, story structure, story topic) to aid comprehension and make predictions about content (e.g., action, events, character's behavior). (McREL 2)
- Knows setting, main characters, main events, sequence, narrator, and problems in stories. (McREL 4)

Objectives

Students

- Compare title pages of two books by the same author.
- Recognize the characters, setting, and main events.
- Illustrate one story adventure or one major event.

Directions

1. The school librarian reads and shows two fiction books by the same author, in which a pig is a major character. The author, illustrator, and title on the title page are briefly discussed.
2. Through illustrations, the reading teacher leads a discussion on the comparison of character, setting, and main events or main plot of both books.
3. With both teachers' assistance, students illustrate one adventure or major book event on the worksheet balloon. Students color pig and put pig into the balloon with the new friend, so they can go on the adventure.

Teaching Team

Reading and school librarian teachers.

Suggested Sources

Astley, Neville. *Peppa Pig: The Balloon Ride* [DVD]. Toronto, ON: Entertainment One Film, 2012.
Astley, Neville. *Peppa Pig: Best Friends*. New York: Scholastic, 2015.
Astley, Neville. *Peppa Pig: Peppa's First Sleepover*. New York: Scholastic, 2015.
Willems, Mo. *I Will Take a Nap!* New York: Hyperion Books for Children, 2015.
Willems, Mo. *My New Friend Is So Fun!* New York: Hyperion Books for Children, 2014.
Willems, Mo. *Should I Share My Ice Cream?* New York: Hyperion, 2011.

Many Turkeys

Read an easy book about turkeys. Color the turkeys the same colors. Attach the pages to make a flip book, so the turkeys move.

My Turkey Flip Book

Many Turkeys

Standards

Student(s)

- Inquire, think critically, and gain knowledge. (AASL 1)
- Draw conclusions, make informed decisions, apply knowledge to new situations, and create new knowledge. (AASL 2)
- With prompting and support, identify characters, settings, and major events in a story, using key details. (CCSS 3)
- With prompting and support, describe the relationship between illustrations and the story in which they appear (e.g., what moment in a story an illustration depicts). (CCSS 6)
- Identify the front cover, back cover, and title page of a book. (CCSS 8)
- Uses meaning clues (e.g., pictures, captions, illustrations, title, cover, headings, story structure, story topic) to aid comprehension and make predictions about content (e.g., action, events, character's behavior). (McREL 2)
- [Reads] Hear a variety of familiar literary passages and texts (e.g., fairy tales, folktales, fiction, nonfiction, legends, fables, myths, poems, nursery rhymes, picture books, predictable books). (McREL 3)
- Knows setting, main characters, main events, sequence, narrator, and problems in stories. (McREL 4)

Objectives

Students

- Recognize title page and book cover.
- Define setting, character, and plot.
- Create a flip book to retell the story.

Directions

1. Students first discuss the title page and the cover of the humorous turkey fiction book. Then the school librarian reads the book and shows the illustrations.
2. Under the reading teacher's guidance, the class discusses character, setting, and plot from the turkey book illustrations.
3. Students color the turkeys the same colors for their turkey flip book, cut out the turkeys, and staple the turkeys into a booklet, and then illustrate story parts on the back of the pages.

Teaching Team

Reading and school librarian teachers.

Suggested Sources

Cantin, Emily Wheeler. *Tom Turkey the Truthful Storyteller*. Mustang, OK: Tate Publishing, 2011.
Johnston, Tony. *10 Fat Turkeys*. New York: Scholastic, 2004.
Slonim, David. *10 Turkeys in the Road*. Tarrytown, NY: Marshall Cavendish Children, 2011.
White, Linda Arms. *Too Many Turkeys*. New York: Holiday House, 2011.

Baker's Dozen

Listen to the Baker's Dozen story. Color the main character and the cookie jar. On one cookie, draw one event. On the other cookie, draw another event. Cut out the cookies and put them into the cookie jar.

Baker's Dozen

Standards

Student(s)

- Inquire, think critically, and gain knowledge. (AASL 1)
- Draw conclusions, make informed decisions, apply knowledge to new situations, and create new knowledge. (AASL 2)
- Share knowledge and participate ethically and productively as members of our democratic society. (AASL 3)
- With prompting and support, identify characters, settings, and major events in a story using key details. (CCSS 3)
- Identify the front cover, back cover, and title page of a book. (CCSS 8)
- [Reads] Hear a variety of familiar literary passages and texts (e.g., fairy tales, folktales, fiction, nonfiction, legends, fables, myths, poems, nursery rhymes, picture books, predictable books). (McREL 3)
- Knows setting, main characters, main events, sequence, narrator, and problems in stories. (McREL 4)

Objectives

Students

- Understand the elements of a fairy tale.
- Summarize title page and book cover.
- Define theme, characters, and main events.
- Illustrate two main events.

Directions

1. The school librarian reads and shows *The Baker's Dozen* story and also discusses the book cover and title page.
2. The reading teacher guides discussion of the main events, characters in the story, why the book was a fairy tale, and discusses the theme.
3. The teachers guide students as they illustrate two main events on the cookies.
4. Students color the baker and cookie jar, cut the dotted line on the cookie jars, and cut out the cookies so that cookies can be put back into the cookie jar.

Teaching Team

Reading and school librarian teachers.

Suggested Sources

Forest, Heather. *The Baker's Dozen.* Little Rock, ARK: August House, 2013.
Shepard, Aaron. *The Baker's Dozen: A Saint Nicholas Tale.* Friday Harbor, WA: Skyhook Press, 2010.

Christmas Dog

Draw what happened to the dog in the middle of the story:

Christmas Dog

Standards

Student(s)

- Inquire, think critically, and gain knowledge. (AASL 1)
- Draw conclusions, make informed decisions, apply knowledge to new situations, and create new knowledge. (AASL 2)
- Share knowledge and participate ethically and productively as members of our democratic society. (AASL 3)
- With prompting and support, ask and answer questions about key details in a text. (CCSS 1)
- With prompting and support, identify characters, settings, and major events in a story, using key details. (CCSS 3)
- Recognize common types of texts (e.g., storybooks, poems). (CCSS 4)
- [Reads] Hear a variety of familiar literary passages and texts (e.g., fairy tales, folktales, fiction, nonfiction, legends, fables, myths, poems, nursery rhymes, picture books, predictable books). (McREL 3)
- Knows setting, main characters, main events, sequence, narrator, and problems in stories. (McREL 4)

Objectives

Students

- Summarize character, setting, and plot of both books.
- Illustrate the plot of one book.

Directions

1. The school librarian and reading teacher each read and show a Christmas dog book.
2. Under the teachers' guidance, the class summarizes the books by discussing the character, setting, and plot.
3. With teachers' assistance, students illustrate the plot from one book.
4. Students color the worksheet illustrations and cut out the two boxes. The top box fastens with a metal fastener to the bottom dog box for a gift card.

Teaching Team

Reading and school librarian teachers.

Suggested Sources

Bateman, Teresa. *The Christmas Pups*. Mankato, MN: Weigl, 2013.
Brown, Margaret Wise. *Jingle Paws*. New York: Parragon Publishers, 2014.
Drummond, Ree. *Charlie and the Christmas Kitty*. New York: HarperCollins, 2015.
Grogan, John. *A Very Marley Christmas*. New York: HarperCollins, 2014.
Wells, Rosemary. *McDuff's Christmas*. New York: Hyperion Book, 2005.

Tractors and Trucks to the Rescue

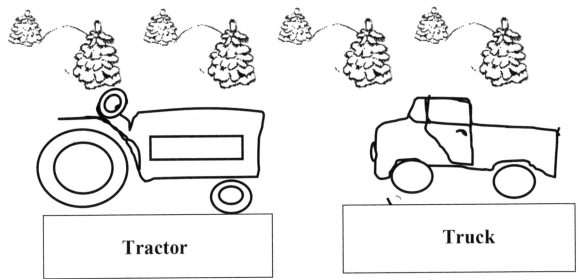

Tractor	Truck

Read a story about a tractor and truck rescue on a snowy day. Compare tractor and truck by drawing the plot in the following sections. Tractor and truck drive on the snowy road.

What happened? **Tractor**   What happened? **Truck**

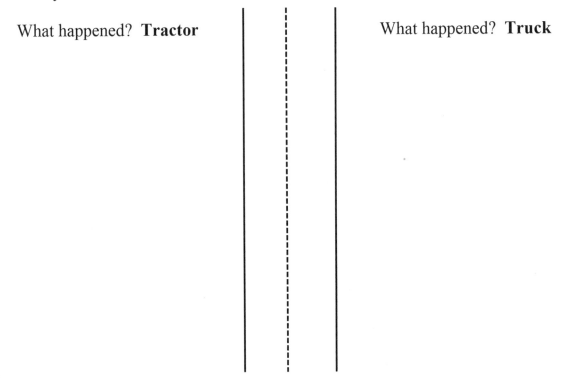

Tractors and Trucks to the Rescue

Standards

Student(s)

- Inquire, think critically, and gain knowledge. (AASL 1)
- Draw conclusions, make informed decisions, apply knowledge to new situations, and create new knowledge. (AASL 2)
- With prompting and support, identify characters, settings, and major events in a story, using key details. (CCSS 3)
- With prompting and support, describe the relationship between illustrations and the story in which they appear (e.g., what moment in a story an illustration depicts). (CCSS 6)
- Uses meaning clues (e.g., pictures, captions, illustrations, title, cover, headings, story structure, story topic) to aid comprehension and make predictions about content (e.g., action, events, character's behavior). (McREL 2)
- [Reads]] Hear a variety of familiar literary passages and texts (e.g., fairy tales, folktales, fiction, non-fiction, legends, fables, myths, poems, nursery rhymes, picture books, predictable books). (McREL 3)

Objectives

Students

- Recognize the rhyming book format.
- Compare and discuss characters, settings, and main plots.
- Illustrate a major event for each main character.

Directions

1. The teachers each read a rhyming book that shows a tractor and truck coming to the rescue at Christmas or another rescue time. Students make predictions throughout the books. Teachers also point out the rhyming format of the books.
2. Under the reading teacher and school librarian's guidance, the class discusses and compares the character, setting, and main plot of the two books.
3. With teachers' assistance, students illustrate an event for tractor and then for truck.
4. Students color the tractor and truck scene. Worksheets should be copied on card stock. Cut out the tractor and truck with the attached name boxes. Bend the box at the box top, so that the vehicles drive down the dotted line road.

Teaching Team

Reading and school librarian teachers.

Suggested Sources

Long, Loren. *An Otis Christmas*. New York: Penguin, 2013.
Long, Loren. *Otis and the Scarecrow*. New York: Penguin, 2015.
Schertle, Alice. *Little Blue Truck's Christmas*. Boston, MA: HMH, 2014.
Schertle, Alice. *Little Blue Truck Leads the Way*. Boston, MA: Harcourt, 2009.
Steers, Billy. *Tractor Mac Builds a Barn*. New York: Farrar Straus Giroux, 2015.
Steers, Billy. *Tractor Mac Saves Christmas*. New York: Farrar Straus Giroux, 2015.

Dog and His Bone

 *The Dog and His Bone*

The dog had a bone. He walked over a bridge with his bone. He saw his reflection in the water. He thought that there was a dog with a bigger bone in the water. He barked to get the bone. When he barked, his own bone fell into the water. Now, he did not have a bone.

Moral: Be happy with what you have.

Color and cut out story pictures. Glue the pictures on the bones in the story order.

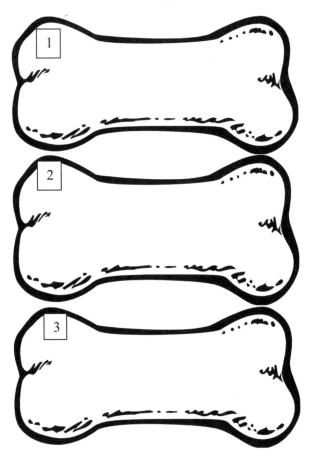

Dog and His Bone

Standards

Student(s)

- Inquire, think critically, and gain knowledge. (AASL 1)
- Draw conclusions, make informed decisions, apply knowledge to new situations, and create new knowledge. (AASL 2)
- Share knowledge and participate ethically and productively as members of our democratic society. (AASL 3)
- With prompting and support, ask and answer questions about key details in a text. (CCSS 1)
- With prompting and support, retell familiar stories, including key details. (CCSS 2)
- With prompting and support, identify characters, settings, and major events in a story, using key details. (CCSS 3)
- [Read] Hear a variety of familiar literary passages and texts (e.g., fairy tales, folktales, fiction, nonfiction, legends, fables, myths, poems, nursery rhymes, picture books, predictable books). (McREL 3)
- Know setting, main characters, main events, sequence, narrator, and problems in stories. (McREL 4)

Objectives

Students

- Realize the definition of a fable and moral.
- Discuss the problem, moral, and story events.
- Organize the story in order of what happened and create a booklet for story retelling.

Directions

1. The reading teacher discusses and defines fable and moral.
2. The school librarian reads the "Dog and His Bone" fable, which also has the title of "Dog and His Shadow" or "The Dog and His Reflection."
3. The class discusses the order of events as well as the problem and then moral of the fable.
4. With both teachers' guidance, students color and cut out the pictures and put them in order by gluing the pictures on the large numbered dog bones. Dog bones are cut out and stapled together for a booklet for a story retelling.

Teaching Team

Reading and school librarian teachers.

Suggested Sources

Daily, Don. "Dog and His Bone." *The Classic Treasury of Aesop's Fables*. Philadelphia, PA: Running Press Kids, 2007.

McGovern, Ann. "The Dog and His Shadow." *Aesop's Fables*. New York: Scholastic, 2013.

Pinkney, Jerry. "Dog and His Shadow." *Aesop's Fables*. New York: North-South Books, 2000.

Ross, Linda. *Dog and His Reflection*. Louisville, KY: Newmark, 2015.

Three Little Kittens

Three Little Kittens,

They lost mittens.

Then…

Mittens were found,

Kittens made a happy
sound.

Meow, Meow, Meow.

Three Little Kittens

Standards

Student(s)

- Inquire, think critically, and gain knowledge. (AASL 1)
- Draw conclusions, make informed decisions, apply knowledge to new situations, and create new knowledge. (AASL 2)
- With prompting and support, retell familiar stories, including key details. (CCSS 2)
- With prompting and support, identify characters, settings, and major events in a story, using key details. (CCSS 3)
- Recognize common types of text (e.g., storybooks, poems). (CCSS 4)
- [Reads] Hear a variety of familiar literary passages and texts (e.g., fairy tales, folktales, fiction, non-fiction, legends, fables, myths, poems, nursery rhymes, picture books, predictable books). (McREL 3)
- Knows setting, main characters, main events, sequence, narrator, and problems in stories. (McREL 4)

Objectives

Students

- Summarize characters, rhymes, and major events.
- Create hand puppets to act out the repeated rhymes.

Directions

1. Students need duplicate worksheet copies, copied on card stock. The reading and school librarian teachers introduce the rhyming format of *Three Little Kittens* rhyming book.
2. The school librarian reads the *Three Little Kittens* story twice, and the class recites rhyming sections.
3. As encouraged by teachers, students discuss major events, characters, and rhymes.
4. The reading teacher leads the class in learning the worksheet kitten rhyme.
5. Students color the kittens and one mitten.
6. Students cut out the extra mitten from the duplicate sheet and tape the two mittens together while leaving the bottom open, so that students wear the paper mitten with four fingers. Students act out the rhyme or book with their mitten.

Teaching Team

Reading and school librarian teachers.

Suggested Sources

Anderson, Steven. *Three Little Kittens (Sing-Along Animal Songs)* [CD]. Mankato, MN: Cantata Learning, 2016.

Engelbreit, Mary. *Mary Engelbreit's Mother Goose: One Hundred Best-Loved Verses*. New York: HarperCollins, 2005.

Galdone, Paul. *Three Little Kittens: A Folk Tale Classic*. New York: Houghton Mifflin Harcourt, 2011.

Pinkney, Jerry. *Three Little Kittens*. New York: Dial Books for Young Readers, 2010.

Valentine Cats—the Cat's Meow

It is Valentine's Day,

And cats are at play.

Valentine Cats—the Cat's Meow

Standards

Student(s)

- Inquire, think critically, and gain knowledge. (AASL 1)
- Draw conclusions, make informed decisions, apply knowledge to new situations, and create new knowledge. (AASL 2)
- Share knowledge and participate ethically and productively as members of our democratic society. (AASL 3)
- Pursue personal and aesthetic growth. (AASL 4)
- With prompting and support, describe characters, settings, and major events in a story, using key details. (CCSS 3)
- Recognize common types of tests (e.g., storybooks, poems). (CCSS 4)
- Uses meaning clues (e.g., pictures, captions, illustrations, title, cover, headings, story structure, story topic) to aid comprehension and make predictions about content (e.g., action, events, character's behavior). (McREL 2)
- [Reads] Hear a variety of familiar literary passages and texts (e.g., fairy tales, folktales, fiction, nonfiction, legends, fables, myths, poems, nursery rhymes, picture books, predictable books). (McREL 3)
- Knows setting, main characters, main events, sequence, narrator, and problems in stories. (McREL 4)

Objectives

Students

- Discover and summarize the rhyming format.
- Recognize the rhymes, main character, and the major events.
- Illustrate the main event.

Directions

1. The reading and school librarian teachers introduce the rhyming format of the valentine rhyming cat book. The school librarian then reads and shows the rhyming cat book.
2. Under teachers' guidance, the class discusses the character, events of the story, and the rhymes.
3. Students illustrate an event from the story on the top heart with cats.
4. Students color and cut out the two hearts and fasten the bottom heart to the illustrated top heart with a metal fastener, so the top heart swings open to reveal the student illustrated event.

Teaching Team

Reading and school librarian teachers.

Suggested Sources

Dean, James. *Pete the Cat: Valentine's Day Is Cool*. New York: Harper, 2013.
Farley, Robin. *Mia: The Sweetest Valentine*. New York: HarperFestival, 2012.
Scotten, Rob. *Splat the Cat Funny Valentine*. New York: HarperFestival, 2012.

Bear's Letter

Dear Bear,

I liked your book,

Thanks for the look.

I liked this best:

From,

To: Bear_____

Bear's Letter

Standards

Student(s)

- Draw conclusions, make informed decisions, apply knowledge to new situations, and create new knowledge. (AASL 2)
- Share knowledge and participate ethically and productively as members of our democratic society. (AASL 3)
- With prompting and support, identify characters, settings, and major events in a story, using key details. (CCSS 3)
- Recognize common types of texts (e.g., storybooks, poems). (CCSS 4)
- With prompting and support, name the author and illustrator of a story and define the role of each in telling the story. (CCSS 5)
- [Read] Hear a variety of familiar literary passages and texts (e.g., fairy tales, folktales, fiction, nonfiction, legends, fables, myths, poems, nursery rhymes, picture books, predictable books). (McREL 3)
- Knows setting, main characters, main events, sequence, narrator, and problems in stories. (McREL 4)

Objectives

Students

- Recognize the author and compare books by the same author.
- Define character, setting, and main event.
- Illustrate the main event for a letter.

Directions

1. The school librarian reads and shows two fiction books about bears by the same author. Author and illustrator are discussed.
2. The reading teacher leads a comparison discussion on characters, settings, and main event of the books. The class discusses the events that they liked.
3. With both teachers' assistance, students finish the worksheet letter to bear by illustrating the event they enjoyed the most from one book. Students color the bear and his cave.
4. Students cut out the letter. While cutting the envelope out, they cut out and keep all envelope parts connected. The bottom envelope folds to the back of the first envelope part. The sides of the front envelope fold to hold the folded letter. The letter is delivered (attached) to bear's cave.

Teaching Team

Reading and school librarian teachers.

Suggested Sources

Wilson, Karma. *Bear Snores On.* New York: Little Simon, 2005.
Wilson, Karma. *Bear Feels Scared.* New York: Little Simon, 2008.
Wright, Maureen. *Sleep, Big Bear, Sleep.* New York: Two Lions, 2009.
Wright, Maureen. *Sneeze, Big Bear, Sneeze!* New York: Two Lions, 2011.

Bunny's Spring

Bunny hears, smells, and sees spring. Add some more things for Bunny to see, hear, and smell. Then make your own bunny ears.

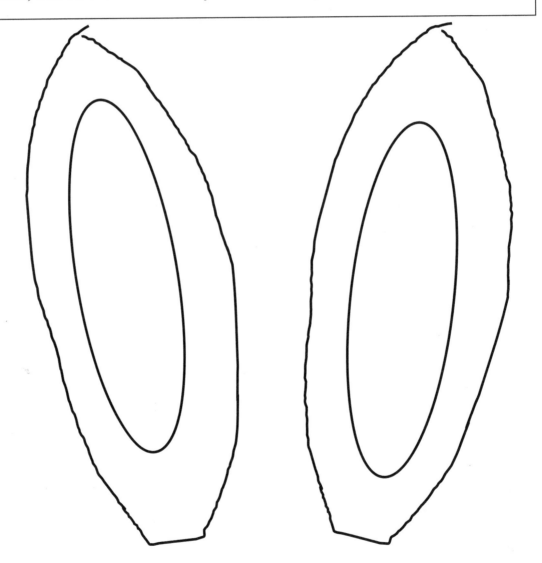

Bunny's Spring

Standards

Student(s)

- Inquire, think critically, and gain knowledge. (AASL 1)
- Draw conclusions, make informed decisions, apply knowledge to new situations, and create new knowledge. (AASL 2)
- With prompting and support, identify characters, settings, and major events in a story, using key details. (CCSS 3)
- Explain major differences between books that tell stories and books that give information, drawing on a wide reading of a range of text types. (First Grade, CCSS 4)
- With prompting and support, identify the main topic and retell key details of a text. (CCSS 7)
- Uses meaning clues (e.g., pictures, captions, illustrations, title, cover, headings, story structure, story topic) to aid comprehension and make predictions about content (e.g., action, events, character's behavior). (McREL 2)
- Relates new information to prior knowledge and experience. (McREL 6)

Objectives

Students

- Explain character and setting.
- Illustrate and retell.
- Recognize fiction and nonfiction differences.

Directions

1. The worksheet is copied on card stock, with the word strip copied twice more for a headband.
2. The science teacher briefly reads and shows a nonfiction rabbit book. Students discuss spring.
3. The school librarian shows and reads a fiction book about rabbits in spring. Students recognize fiction and nonfiction contrasts. They also discuss character and what things that rabbit saw in spring.
4. As guided by teachers, students relate their prior knowledge of spring with their new knowledge. At the top of the worksheet, students add two more spring things that were discovered.
5. Students use the word sheet strip and additional strips for the bunny ears headband. Students color and cut out the bunny ears, which are attached at the base of the headband.

Teaching Team

Science and school librarian teachers.

Suggested Sources

Fiction

Henkes, Kevin. *When Spring Comes*. New York: Greenwillow, 2016.
Loughrey, Anita. *Rabbit's Spring Adventure*. Edina, MA: QEB Publishing, 2012.
McCue, Liza. *Quiet Bunny's Many Colors*. New York: Sterling, 2010.

Nonfiction

Murray, Julie. *Rabbits*. Mankato, MN: ABDO Kids, 2015.
Zoble, Derek. *Rabbits*. Minneapolis, MN: Bellwether Media, 2011.

Fish, Fish

In the fish bubble, draw what the fish would say at the end of the story. Now, get the fish bowl ready. Color the water blue and the ferns green. Color fish.

Fish, Fish

Standards

Student(s)

- Inquire, think critically, and gain knowledge. (AASL 1)
- Draw conclusions, make informed decisions, apply knowledge to new situations, and create new knowledge. (AASL 2)
- With prompting and support, identify characters, settings, and major events in a story, using key details. (CCSS 3)
- Explain major differences between books that tell stories and books that give information, drawing on a wide reading of a range of text types. (First Grade, CCSS 4)
- With prompting and support, identify the main topic and retell key details of a text. (CCSS 7)
- Uses a variety of sources to gather information (e.g., informational books, pictures, charts, indexes, video, television programs, guest speakers, internet, own observation). (McREL 1)
- Summarizes information found in texts (e.g., retell in own words). (McREL 5)

Objectives

Students

- Compare a fiction book to a nonfiction book.
- Recognize character, key ideas, and what happened in the beginning.
- Illustrate the ending.

Directions

1. The science teacher shows and discusses illustrations of a nonfiction clownfish book.
2. The school librarian reads and shows a fiction clownfish book and then compares the nonfiction to the fiction clownfish book.
3. The class discusses character and the beginning and ending of the fiction story. In the fish speaking bubble, students draw what fish would say at the end of the story.
4. With both teachers' assistance, students color the fish, fish bowl water, and green fern and draw a line to put fish back in the bowl.

Teaching Team

Science and school librarian teachers.

Suggested Sources

Fiction

Diesen, Deborah. *The Pout-Pout Fish Goes to School*. New York: Farrar Straus Giroux, 2014.
Pfister, Marcus. *Rainbow Fish to the Rescue*. New York: North-South Books, 2014.

Nonfiction

Gibbs, Maddie. *Clownfish*. New York: Power Kids Press, 2014.
Meister, Carl. *Clownfish*. Minneapolis, MN: Jump, 2014.
Stille, Darlene. *I Am a Fish: The Life of a Clown Fish*. Mankato, MN: Picture Window Books, 2005.

Lost Lamb

Lamb was lost. Where did it go?

Lamb was gone,

What a song.

Where did he go?

I do not know!

Lost Lamb

Standards

Student(s)

- Draw conclusions, make informed decisions, apply knowledge to new situations, and create new knowledge. (AASL 2)
- Share knowledge and participate ethically and productively as members of our democratic society. (AASL 3)
- With prompting and support, retell familiar stories, including key details. (CCSS 2)
- Recognize common types of texts (e.g., storybooks, poems). (CCSS 4)
- [Reads] Hear a variety of familiar literary passages and texts (e.g., fairy tales, folktales, fiction, nonfiction, legends, fables, myths, poems, nursery rhymes, picture books, predictable books). (McREL 3)
- Knows setting, main characters, main events, sequence, narrator, and problems in stories. (McREL 4)

Objectives

Students

- Recognize and retell rhymes.
- Summarize characters and major events.
- Create a new story event.

Directions

1. The reading and school librarian teachers read humorous and traditional Little Bo Peep and Mary Had a Little Lamb rhymes. Students retell the rhymes.
2. Guided by teachers, students discuss characters, story events, and rhymes.
3. Teachers help students brainstorm new story ideas for lamb's tale, like the lamb could follow Mary to the park. Students color and cut out their worksheet illustrations in order to create a new lamb story. Students put the worksheet poem on the front of a folded paper and add the lamb and newly created illustrated story on the inside, so that the poem is answered with the story.
4. Students learn the worksheet rhyme.

Teaching Team

Reading and school librarian teachers.

Suggested Sources

Bixley, Donovan. *Little Bo Peep and More Favourite Nursery Rhymes*. Kingston, ON: Upstart Press, 2015.

Duran, Alan. *Little Bo-Peep's Missing Sheep*. Mankato, MN: Crabtree, 2013.

Dweck, Mary and Williams, Wilson. *Mary Had a Sleepy Sheep*. Allentown, PA: Sleepy Sheep Productions, 2014.

Hale, Sarah Josepha Buell. *Mary Had a Little Lamb*. North Mankato, MN: Child's World, 2011.

Wegwerth, A. I. *Little Bo Peep and Her Bad, Bad Sheep: A Mother Goose Hullaballoo*. Mankato, MN: Capstone, 2016.

Opening White House Facts

My White House Book

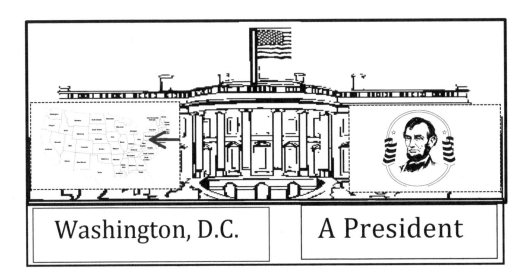

Washington, D.C. | A President

1. Where is the White House? Color the word box, Washington D.C., blue.

2. Who lives at the White House? Color the word box, A President, red.

3. Color the flags red, white, and blue.

4. Cut out the White House boxes.

Opening White House Facts

Standards

Student(s)

- Inquire, think critically, and gain knowledge. (AASL 1)
- Draw conclusions, make informed decisions, apply knowledge to new situations, and create new knowledge. (AASL 2)
- Share knowledge and participate ethically and productively as members of our democratic society. (AASL 3)
- With prompting and support, identify the main topic and retell key details of a text. (CCSS 7)
- Uses a variety of sources to gather information (e.g., informational books, pictures, charts, indexes, videos, television programs, guest speakers, Internet, own observation). (McREL 1)
- Relates new information to prior knowledge and experience. (McREL 6)

Objectives

Students

- Summarize a White House fiction story and two key details of a nonfiction book.
- Discuss and then color the purpose and the location of the White House.

Directions

1. The school librarian reads a White House fiction book and discusses it.
2. The social studies teacher shows and skims a nonfiction White House book to briefly point out two key details, which are the purpose (where the President lives) and location of the White House (DC), and other brief facts. Students relate their prior knowledge to the book.
3. Students color the Washington, DC word box light blue and the president word box light red, so that the words can still be read. Students color the flags red, white, and blue.
4. Students cut out and then attach the two White House squares by stapling at the far left side for a White House booklet, which opens up to facts.

Teaching Team

School librarian and social studies teachers.

Suggested Sources

Fiction

Marciano, John Bemelman. *Madeline at the White House.* New York: Puffin, 2016.
Zappitello, Beth. *First Dog.* Mankato, MN: Sleeping Bear Press, 2009.

Nonfiction

Gaspar, Joe. *The White House.* New York: PowerKids Press, 2014.
GPO [Government Publishing Office]. *White House.* Updated 2015. Retrieved from https://bensguide.gpo.gov/
Murray, Julie. *White House.* Mankato, MN: Abdo Publishing, 2003.
Yanuck, Debbie. *The White House.* Mankato, MN: Capstone Press, 2003.

Shark's Tale

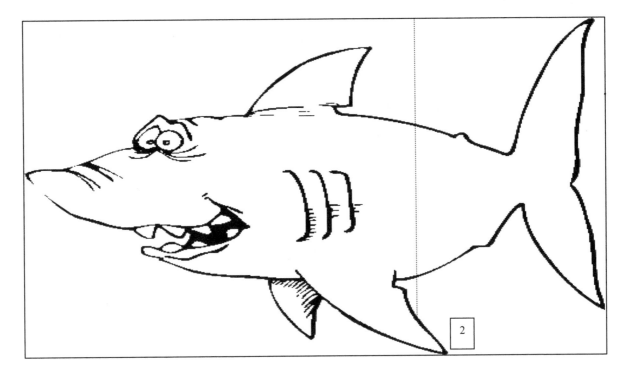

Shark had a tale.

1. Draw the start of the story on 1.

2. Draw the end of the story on 2.

Tape the two tails so that shark can

flip his tail and tell his tale.

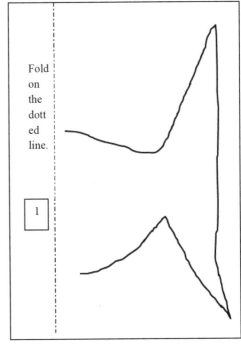

Fold on the dotted line.

Shark's Tale

Standards

Student(s)

- Inquire, think critically, and gain knowledge. (AASL 1)
- Draw conclusions, make informed decisions, apply knowledge to new situations, and create new knowledge. (AASL 2)
- With prompting and support, retell familiar stories, including key details. (CCSS 2)
- With prompting and support, describe the relationship between illustrations and the text in which they appear (e.g., what person, place, thing, or idea in the text an illustration depicts). (CCSS 6)
- Uses meaning clues (e.g., pictures, captions, illustrations, title, cover, headings, story structure, story topic) to aid comprehension and make predictions about content (e.g., action, events, character's behavior). (McREL 2)
- [Reads] Hear a variety of familiar literary passages and texts (e.g., fairy tales, folktales, fiction, nonfiction, legends, fables, myths, poems, nursery rhymes, picture books, predictable books). (McREL 3)

Objectives

Students

- Identify the relationships between story and illustrations.
- Illustrate the beginning and ending of the story.
- Retell a story.

Directions

1. The reading teacher reads and shows a shark fiction book, while discussing the relationship between the illustrations and the story.
2. The school librarian guides discussion on the beginning and end of the story.
3. Students illustrate the beginning of the story on the shark tail in the box and illustrate the end of the story on the shark's actual tail. Students will lightly color the rest of the shark.
4. The box with the shark tail will be cut out and folded on the dotted line. The shark's tail box will be taped on the x part of the shark. It looks like the shark is flipping his tail.
5. The shark tale will be retold by students with their worksheets.

Teaching Team

Reading and school librarian teachers.

Suggested Sources

Gill, Timothy. *Flip & Fin: We Rule the School.* New York: Greenwillow Books, 2014.
Gill, Timothy. *Flip & Fin Sharks to the Rescue.* New York: Greenwillow Books, 2016.
Hale, Bruce. *Clark the Shark.* New York: HaperCollins, 2013.
Hale, Bruce. *Clark the Shark Dares to Share.* New York: HarperCollins, 2013.
Sauer, Tammi. *Nugget & Fang: Friends Forever or Snack Time.* New York: Scholastic, 2015.

All Bugs

Find bug facts. Draw a fact in each bug box. Color the flowers. Color the bugs. Cut out the bug and fact box together. Put the bugs back into the flowers.

All Bugs

Standards

Student(s)

- Inquire, think critically, and gain knowledge. (AASL 1)
- Draw conclusions, make informed decisions, apply knowledge to new situations, and create new knowledge. (AASL 2)
- With prompting and support, describe the relationship between illustrations and the text in which they appear (e.g., what person, place, thing, or idea in the text an illustration depicts). (CCSS 6)
- With prompting and support, identify the main topic and retell key details of a text. (CCSS 7)
- Uses a variety of sources to gather information (e.g., informational books, pictures, charts, indexes, videos, television programs, guest speakers, Internet, own observation). (McREL 1)
- Uses meaning clues (e.g., pictures, captions, illustrations, title, cover, headings, story structure, story topic) to aid comprehension and make predictions about content (e.g., action, events, character's behavior). (McREL 2)

Objectives

Students

- Recognize nonfiction or informational books.
- Discover and illustrate a fact for each bug.

Directions

1. The science teacher introduces the bee and butterfly research by discussing and showing illustrations of both bees and butterflies on flowers or in a similar setting.
2. The school librarian discusses nonfiction and presents simple bee and butterfly nonfiction.
3. Students find and then discuss one bee and butterfly fact from the pictures or simple text. They illustrate one newly found fact in bug fact blank boxes.
4. With guidance of both teachers, students color the flower garden and the bugs and cut out the combination of each bug with their attached fact box. The dotted lines in the garden should be cut before, so that students can put their bugs back into the garden at the dotted lines.

Teaching Team

Science and school librarian teachers.

Suggested Sources

Frisch, Aaron. *Bees.* Mankato, MN: Creative Education, 2015.
Frisch, Aaron. *Butterflies.* Mankato, MN: Creative Education, 2015.
Gray, Rita. *Flowers Are Calling.* Boston, MA: Houghton Mifflin Harcourt, 2015.
Hansen, Grace. *Bees.* Mankato, MN: ABDO Kids, 2015.
Hansen, Grace. *Butterflies.* Mankato, MN: ABDO Kids, 2015.
Thorp, Claire. *All about Flowers.* Chicago, IL: Heinemann, 2015.

Chapter 2

First-Grade Lesson Plans

These first-grade library lesson plans were created to help the busy school librarian, as he or she strives to meet the demanding needs of a school library including that of teaching literacy skills and reading appreciation. The following interactive standards-backed elementary lessons will meet the globally literate needs of today's students. The lessons are set to different standards in the desire to meet the school librarians' state or school library, Common Core State Standards (CCSS) or McREL literacy, or English language arts standards, which include the proverbial American Association of School Librarians (AASL) standards.

The quality-researched AASL standards, CCSS, and the McREL Compendium of Standards and Benchmarks are applied with each school library lesson for purposeful school library instruction and student achieved skills. The parts of the standards chosen for this book were those that were the most essential for library instruction and could be met in the lesson time allotment of twenty minutes. The standards may be used together as given, individually, or lessons may be set to other quality standards.

Based on standards, student learning objectives are given for each lesson. Lessons include students working individually or with others for more efficient student learning. Team teaching is seen, as more can be accomplished when working together. Quality-researched resources are suggested. The streamlined, standards-based lessons for the busy school librarian will provide interactive and successful student learning. The AASL standards are stated in the first chapter as they are universally seen with all lessons in some way. The following McREL and CCSS standards are used specifically with this grade level.

First-Grade Library Standards with Language Arts Benchmarks (McREL Compendium of Standards and Benchmarks) and CCSS

First-grade students:

*First-Grade Common Core (Literacy), Reading Literature

1. Ask and answer questions about key details in a text. (CCSS.ELA-Literacy.RL.1.1)
2. Describe characters, settings, and major events in a story, using key details. (CCSS.ELA-Literacy.RL.1.3)
3. Identify words and phrases in stories or poems that suggest feelings or appeal to the senses. (CCSS.ELA-Literacy.RL.1.4)
4. Explain major differences between books that tell stories and books that give information, drawing on a wide reading of a range of text types. (CCSS.ELA-Literacy.RL.1.5)
5. Use illustrations and details in a story to describe its characters, setting, or events. (CCSS.ELA-Literacy.RL.1.7)

First-Grade Common Core (Literacy), Reading Informational Texts

6. Ask and answer questions about key details in a text. (CCSS.ELA-Literacy.RL.1.1)
7. Use illustrations and details in a text to describe its key ideas. (CCSS.ELA-Literacy.RL.1.7)

Governors Association Center for Best Practices and Council of Chief State School Officers. *Common Core State Standards (Literacy)*. Washington, DC: National Governors Association Center for Best Practices and Council of Chief State School Officers, 2010. Retrieved from http://www.corestandards.org/

McREL Language Arts Writing Standards and Benchmarks (Grades K–2)

*Gathers and uses information for research purposes. Standard 4

1. Uses a variety of sources to gather information (e.g., informational books, pictures, charts, indexes, video, television programs, guest speakers, internet, own observation). (McREL)

McREL Language Arts Reading Standards and Benchmarks (Grades K–2)

*Uses the general skills and strategies of the reading process. Standard 5

2. Uses meaning clues (e.g., pictures, captions, illustrations, title, cover, headings, story structure, story topic) to aid comprehension and make predictions about content (e.g., action, events, character's behavior). (McREL)

*Uses skills and strategies to read a variety of literary tests.

3. Reads [Hear] a variety of familiar literary passages and texts (e.g., fairy tales, folktales, fiction, nonfiction, legends, fables, myths, poems, nursery rhymes, picture books, predictable books). (McREL)
4. Knows setting, main characters, main events, sequence, narrator, and problems in stories. (McREL)

*Uses skills and strategies to read a variety of informational texts.

5. Summarize information found in texts (e.g., retell in own words). (McREL)
6. Relate new information to prior knowledge and experience. (McREL)

McREL. *Language Arts Standards*, 2015. Retrieved from http://www2.mcrel.org/compendium/standard

Monster Manners

The monster may need manners in the library.

Show how the monsters acted in the story.

On the bookmark, draw ways for the monster to have library manners.

Monster Manners

Standards

Student(s)

- Inquire, think critically, and gain knowledge. (AASL 1)
- Draw conclusions, make informed decisions, apply knowledge to new situations, and create new knowledge. (AASL 2)
- Share knowledge and participate ethically and productively as members of our democratic society. (AASL 3)
- Pursue personal and aesthetic growth. (AASL 4)
- Use illustrations and details in a story to describe its characters, setting, or events. (CCSS 5)
- [Reads] Hear a variety of familiar literary passages and texts (e.g., fairy tales, folktales, fiction, nonfiction, legends, fables, myths, poems, nursery rhymes, picture books, predictable books). (McREL 3)
- *Knows* setting, main characters, main events, sequence, narrator, and problems in stories. (McREL 4)

Objectives

Students

- Illustrate main event or plot.
- Describe character.
- Describe library manners and create a bookmark.

Directions

1. The reading teacher and school librarian read and show a book about monsters in the library or monsters and manners. They lead a discussion on character and main plot or main event.
2. The school librarian leads a discussion on library manners.
3. With both teachers' guidance, students illustrate the main plot or main event or how monsters were in the story.
4. Students color, illustrate, and then create bookmarks that show good library manners. Students cut out their bookmarks.

Teaching Team

Reading and school librarian teachers.

Suggested Sources

Bailey, Catherine. *Mind Your Monsters.* New York: Sterling Children's Books, 2015.
Mortensen, Lori. *Monsters Matter in the Library.* Mankato, MN: Capstone Press, 2011.
Spurr, Elizabeth. *Monsters Mind Your Manners!* Park Ridge, IL: Albert Whitman, 2011.

Fox on TV

The fox tricked the stork. He gave the stork soup that the stork could not eat, because the stork's beak was long. The fox thought it was funny. Then the stork tricked the fox. The stork gave the fox something that the fox could not eat either.

Moral (lesson): Be nice to others or they may not be nice to you.

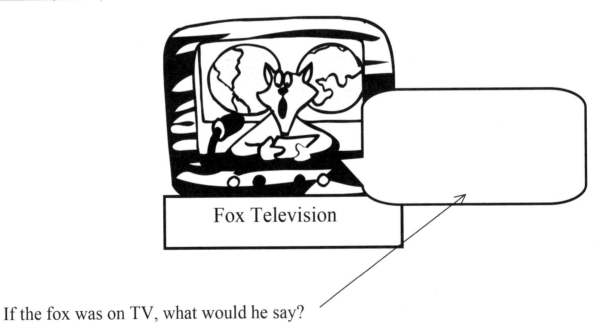

Fox Television

If the fox was on TV, what would he say?

Fox on TV

Standards

Student(s)

- Inquire, think critically, and gain knowledge. (AASL 1)
- Draw conclusions, make informed decisions, apply knowledge to new situations, and create new knowledge. (AASL 2)
- Share knowledge and participate ethically and productively as members of our democratic society. (AASL 3)
- Pursue personal and aesthetic growth. (AASL 4)
- Describe characters, settings, and major events in a story using key details. (CCSS 2)
- [Reads] Hear a variety of familiar literacy passages (e.g., fairy tales, folktales, fiction, nonfiction, legends, fables, myths, poems, nursery rhymes, picture books, predictable books). (McREL 3)
- Knows setting, main characters, main events, sequence, narrator, and problems in stories. (McREL 4)

Objectives

Students

- Analyze the "Fox and the Stork" fable and the moral.
- Recall main event, characters, and setting.
- Discuss the fox character and write or illustrate what the fox would say.

Directions

1. The school librarian describes a fable and a moral, and then reads *The Fox and the Stork* fable.
2. The reading teacher leads a class discussion on characters, main event, setting, and the moral. Students discuss what would have been a better thing for the characters to do.
3. Teachers lead a class discussion on what the fox would say if he had to report his story as a news reporter on television. Students either write a short sentence or illustrate what the fox would say in the word speech bubble.
4. Students color the illustrations and share their worksheet answers.

Teaching Team

Reading and school librarian teachers.

Suggested Sources

Library of Congress. *Fox & the Stork. Aesop for Children*. Updated 2015. Retrieved from http://www.read.gov/aesop/016.html

McDermott, Gerald. *The Fox and the Stork*. Boston, MA: Harcourt, 2003.

McGovern, Ann. *Aesop's Fables*. New York: Scholastic, 2013.

Parker, Vic. *The Fox and the Stork and Other Fables*. Milwaukee, WI: Gareth Publishing, 2015.

Pirotta, Saviour. *Aesop's Fables*. Boston, MA: Kingfisher, 2007.

Fisherman and the Fish

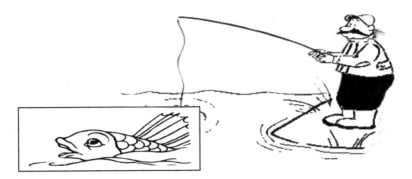

Story: There once was a fisherman who caught a magical fish. The man's wife wanted wishes from the magical fish. The man asked the fish for wishes: (1) The man's wife asked for a nicer house. (2) She asked for a castle. (3) She asked to be king. Because she asked for too much, the wife then had nothing.

1. At the top, add the man's wife to the picture. Also draw their house. Color.
2. Follow the fish trail to see what the wife learned. Write the words you found:

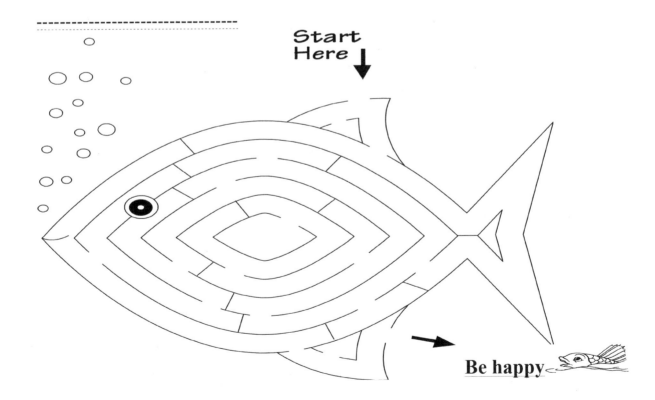

Start Here

Be happy

From *Standards-Based Lesson Plans for the Busy Elementary School Librarian* by Joyce Keeling. Santa Barbara, CA: Libraries Unlimited. Copyright © 2017.

Fisherman and the Fish

Standards

Student(s)

- Inquire, think critically, and gain knowledge. (AASL 1)
- Draw conclusions, make informed decisions, apply knowledge to new situations, and create new knowledge. (AASL 2)
- Share knowledge and participate ethically and productively as members of our democratic society. (AASL 3)
- Explain major differences between books that tell stories and books that give information, drawing on a wide reading of a range of text topics. (CCSS 4)
- Use illustrations and details in a story to describe its characters, setting, or events. (CCSS 5)
- [Reads] Hear a variety of familiar literacy passages (e.g., fairy tales, folktales, fiction, nonfiction, legends, fables, myths, poems, nursery rhymes, picture books, predictable books). (McREL 3)
- Knows setting, main characters, main events, sequence, narrator, and problems in stories. (McREL 4)

Objectives

Students

- Recognize a fairy tale and describe the main events.
- Visualize and illustrate the setting and characters.
- Locate and write the moral.

Directions

1. Reading and school librarian teachers show and read "The Fisherman and His Wife" tale.
2. The teachers lead a class discussion on characters, moral, and what happened first, in the middle, and at the end. Students discuss what made the story a fairy tale, and discuss that the story is not real.
3. Students follow the fish trail maze to find the moral and copy the discovered words (Be Happy). They add the wife and the house to the worksheet illustrated setting and color it.
4. Teachers follow up by reading and discussing a different version.

Teaching Team

Reading and school librarian teachers.

Suggested Sources

Felix, Rebecca. *The Fisherman and His Wife*. North Mankato, MN: Child's World, 2014.
Hoffman, Mary. "The Fisherman and His Wife." *First Book of Fairy Tales*. New York: DK, 2001.
HowStuffWorks. *The Fisherman and His Wife*. Updated 2015. Retrieved from http://www.howstuffworks.com/the-fisherman-and-his-wife-story.htm
Isadora, Rachel. *The Fisherman and His Wife*. New York: G. P. Putnam's Sons, 2008.
Stewart, Whitney. *A Catfish Tale: A Bayou Story of the Fisherman and His Wife*. Mankato, MN: AV2 Weigl, 2015.

Pumpkin Patch

First-Grade Pumpkin Patch

Read two books about pumpkins in a pumpkin patch. Color the big pumpkin. "Pick" two other pumpkins from the pumpkin patch. Draw a character from each pumpkin book on each smaller pumpkin. Cut out the little pumpkins. Glue the small pumpkins and other pictures on the big pumpkin.

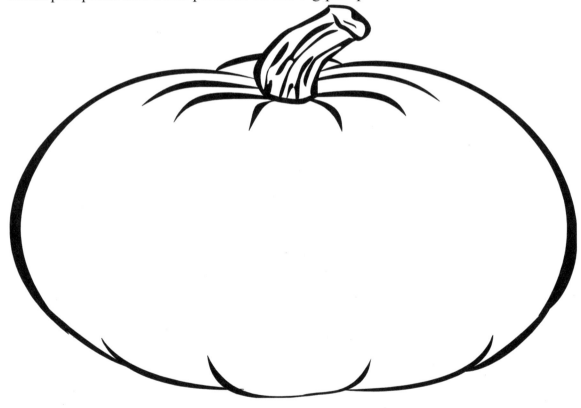

Pumpkin Patch

Standards

Student(s)

- Inquire, think critically, and gain knowledge. (AASL 1)
- Draw conclusions, make informed decisions, apply knowledge to new situations, and create new knowledge. (AASL 2)
- Share knowledge and participate ethically and productively as members of our democratic society. (AASL 3)
- Ask and answer questions about key details in a text. (CCSS 1)
- Use the illustrations and details in a text to describe its characters, setting, or events. (CCSS 5)
- Uses meaning clues (e.g., pictures, captions, illustrations, title, cover, headings, story structure, story topic) to aid comprehension and make predictions about content (e.g., action, events, character's behavior). (McREL 2)
- [Reads] Hear a variety of familiar literacy passages (e.g., fairy tales, folktales, fiction, nonfiction, legends, fables, myths, poems, nursery rhymes, picture books, predictable books). (McREL 3)
- Summarizes information found in texts (e.g., retell in own words). (McREL 5)

Objectives

Students

- Describe the differences in the two books' characters, setting, and events or plot.
- Illustrate character and setting.

Directions

1. The reading and school librarian teachers each read and show a pumpkin patch-type fiction book, while pointing out a pumpkin patch.
2. Teachers discuss and compare the two books' characters, settings, and events or plot.
3. Teachers guide student illustrations of a character of each book on each smaller pumpkin. Students lightly color the smaller and large pumpkins.
4. Students "pick" or rather cut out the two illustrated pumpkins and glue those on the larger pumpkin. Students color or add pictures to the large pumpkin to illustrate the setting of a pumpkin patch.

Teaching Team

Reading and school librarian teachers.

Suggested Sources

Cox, Judy. *Pick a Pumpkin, Mrs. Millie*. New York: Two Lions, 2009.
Holub, Joan. *Pumpkin Patch Fun*. Mankato, MN: AV2 by Weigl, 2015.
Moulton, Mark Kimball. *The Very Best Pumpkin*. New York: Simon & Schuster Books for Young Readers, 2010.
Steers, Billy. *Tractor Mac, Harvest Time*. New York: Farrar Straus Giroux, 2015.
Wallace, Nancy Elizabeth. *Pumpkin Day!* New York: Two Lions, 2006.

Blast Off!

After hearing a space adventure, put yourself in the story as an astronaunt. Draw yourself in the astronaunt mask. Draw your adventure too.

Blast Off!

Standards

Student(s)

- Inquire, think critically, and gain knowledge. (AASL 1)
- Draw conclusions, make informed decisions, apply knowledge to new situations, and create new knowledge. (AASL 2)
- Share knowledge and participate ethically and productively as members of our democratic society. (AASL 3)
- Ask and answer questions about key details in a text. (CCSS 1)
- Use illustrations and details in a story to describe its characters, settings, and events in the story. (CCSS 5)
- Uses meaning clues (e.g., pictures, captions, illustrations, title, cover, headings, story structure, story topic) to aid comprehension and make predictions about content (e.g., action, events, character's behavior). (McREL 2)
- Knows setting, main characters, main events, sequence, narrator, and problems in stories. (McREL 4)

Objectives

Students

- Define characters, setting, and main plot or main event.
- Illustrate themselves as astronauts from the story.

Directions

1. The school librarian reads and shows an astronaut picture book.
2. Using the illustrations, the reading teacher leads discussion on characters, setting, and main event or main plot.
3. Students illustrate themselves as the astronaut of the story. With the teacher's guidance, students illustrate themselves in the astronaut helmet shield. Then students illustrate their astronaut adventure either on the flag or at the base of the astronaut.
4. Students color their sheets.

Teaching Team

Reading and school librarian teachers.

Suggested Sources

Barrett, Judi. *Cloudy with a Chance of Meatballs 3: Planet of the Pies*. New York: Simon & Schuster, 2013.

Brett, Jan. *Hedgie Blasts Off* [Audio]. Holmes, NY: Spoken Arts, 2015.

Kelly, Mark. *Mousetronaut: Based on a (Partially) True Story*. New York: Simon & Schuster Books, 2012.

Kelly, Mark. *Mousetronaut Goes to Mars*. New York: Simon & Schuster for Young Readers, 2013.

Mini, Grey. *Space Dog*. New York: Alfred A. Knopf, 2015.

Bats, Bats, Bats

> Bats, bats, bats!
> Bats are at a beach, a library, and other places.
> They can even be seen at baseball bases.
> They are everywhere, and that's that.

1. What is the title of a bat book:_____

_____

What is the title of another bat book:_____

_____

2. Compare the books by drawing events from each book in the boxes.

Bats, Bats, Bats

Standards

Student(s)

- Inquire, think critically, and gain knowledge. (AASL 1)
- Draw conclusions, make informed decisions, apply knowledge to new situations, and create new knowledge. (AASL 2)
- Share knowledge and participate ethically and productively as members of our democratic society. (AASL 3)
- Identify words and phrases in stories or poems that suggest feelings or appeal to the senses. (CCSS 3)
- Use illustrations and details in a story to describe its characters, setting, or events. (CCSS 5)
- [Reads] Hear a variety of familiar literary passages and texts (e.g., fairy tales, folktales, fiction, nonfiction, legends, fables, myths, poems, nursery rhymes, picture books, predictable books). (McREL 3)
- Knows setting, main characters, main events, sequence, narrator, and problems in stories. (McREL 4)

Objectives

Students

- Compare and discuss events, settings, and characters of fiction books by the same author.
- Recall and write book titles.
- Illustrate an event from each book.
- Devise bat banners to retell a story.

Directions

1. Teachers read and show two bat rhyming books by the same author. Then teachers review the author and write the two book titles on the class board.
2. Teachers guide discussion on the characters, main plot, and settings of the two books.
3. As guided by teachers, students write the book titles and illustrate an event from each book.
4. Students discuss and recite the worksheet poem.
5. The art teacher guides students as they create bat banners on a twelve-inch-long ribbon or paper strip, by adding the colored worksheet pictures, the worksheet poem, and other colored illustrations glued on the strip or ribbon.

Teaching Team

Art, reading, and school librarian teachers.

Suggested Sources

Appelt, Kathi. *Bats Around the Clock*. New York: HarperCollins, 2009.
Appelt, Kathi. *Bats Jamboree*. Paradise, CA: Paw Prints Press, 2010.
Lies, Brian. *Bats at the Library*. Boston, MA: HMH Books for Young Readers, 2008.
Lies, Brian. *Bats at the Ballgame*. Boston, MA: HMH Books for Young Readers, 2010.
Lies, Brian. *Bats at the Beach*. Boston, MA: HMH Books for Young Readers, 2011.

Giving Thanks

Read about giving thanks. Write a thankful poem in the box. In each line, list three thankful things. Rhyme the last words of the two lines. Color the picture.

Giving Thanks

_____

_____

From *Standards-Based Lesson Plans for the Busy Elementary School Librarian* by Joyce Keeling.
Santa Barbara, CA: Libraries Unlimited. Copyright © 2017.

Giving Thanks

Standards

Student(s)

- Inquire, think critically, and gain knowledge. (AASL 1)
- Draw conclusions, make informed decisions, apply knowledge to new situations, and create new knowledge. (AASL 2)
- Ask and answer questions about key details in a text. (CCSS 1)
- Identify words and phrases in stories or poems that suggest feelings or appeal to the senses. (CCSS 3)
- Use illustrations and details in the story to describe its characters, setting, or events. (CCSS 5)
- Uses meaning clues (e.g., picture captions, illustrations, title, cover, headings, story structure, story topics) to aid comprehension and make predictions about content (e.g., action, events, character's behavior). (McREL 2)
- [Reads] Hear a variety of familiar literary passages and texts (e.g., fairy tales, folktales, fiction, nonfiction, legends, fables, myths, poems, nursery rhymes, picture books, predictable books). (McREL 3)
- Relates new information to prior knowledge and experience. (McREL 6)

Objectives

Students

- Summarize ways to be thankful from the book and from prior knowledge.
- Define and color a cornucopia.
- Write a class-composed, two- or three-line rhyming poem.

Directions

1. The worksheets are copied on card stock.
2. The reading teacher discusses being thankful at thanksgiving.
3. The school librarian reads and shows a thanksgiving fiction book that shows a cornucopia and ways to be thankful. Students relate the book to what they know about showing thanks.
4. Under guidance of the reading teacher, the class creates and writes a simple, two-line thankful rhyming poem with two to three words a line.
5. The art teacher describes a cornucopia. The art teacher guides student coloring of the cornucopia. Students cut out the cornucopia with the poem attached. The poem will be bent to allow the cornucopia to be self-standing.

Teaching Team

Art, reading, and school librarian teachers.

Suggested Sources

Kimmelman, Leslie. *Round the Turkey: A Grateful Thanksgiving.* Mankato, MN: AV2 Weigl, 2013.
Manushkin, Fran. *Katie Saves Thanksgiving.* Mankato, MN: Picture Window Books, 2011.
Newton, Vanessa. *Thanksgiving for Emily Ann.* New York: Scholastic, 2014.

Book Detective

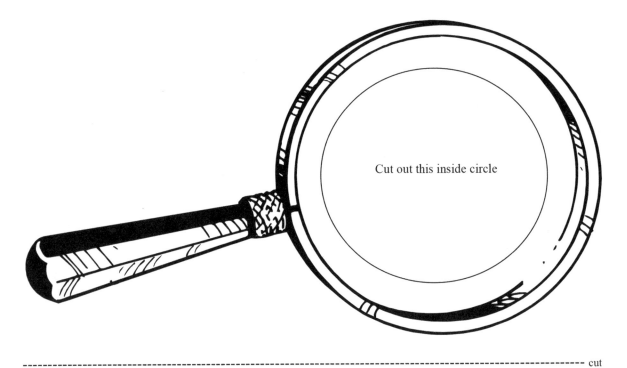

Cut out this inside circle

--- cut

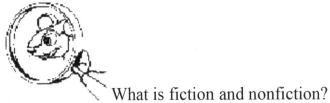 What is fiction and nonfiction?

Fiction is fake for goodness sakes. Nonfiction is real, and that is a deal.

1. Be a detective. Use your magnifying glass to find a nonfiction book or fiction book.

2. Circle the book type: Nonfiction   Fiction

3. Keep being a detective! Find more fiction or nonfiction books.

Book Detective

Standards

Student(s)

- Inquire, think critically, and gain knowledge. (AASL 1)
- Draw conclusions, make informed decisions, apply knowledge to new situations, and create new knowledge. (AASL 2)
- Share knowledge and participate ethically and productively as members of our democratic society. (AASL 3)
- Pursue personal and aesthetic growth. (AASL 4)
- Explain major differences between books that tell stories and books that give information, drawing on a wide reading of a range of text types. (CCSS 4)
- [Reads] Hear a variety of familiar literary passages and texts (e.g., fairy tales, folktales, fiction, nonfiction, legends, fables, myths, poems, nursery rhymes, picture books, predictable books). (McREL 3)

Objectives

Students

- Define a detective in order to become a detective.
- Deduce the differences between nonfiction and fiction books.

Directions

1. The worksheets are copied on card stock.
2. A small display of fiction and nonfiction books is exhibited near their locations.
3. The reading teacher reads a detective fiction book and discusses what a detective does.
4. The school librarian has students repeat the worksheet fiction and nonfiction rhyme and discusses nonfiction and fiction differences. With the teacher's help, some students give examples of where to find fiction and nonfiction in the displays and elsewhere.
5. Students cut out their magnifying glasses with the center circle cut out, so that they can be library detectives who use magnifying glasses to search.
6. When using their magnifying glasses and with the guidance of both teachers, students search for a fiction or nonfiction book and circle a fiction or nonfiction word on their worksheets.
7. With a partner, library detectives find other fiction or nonfiction books and discuss what makes them nonfiction or fiction.

Teaching Team

Reading and school librarian teachers.

Suggested Sources

Deondato, Rick. *Pipsie, Nature Detective*: *The Disappearing Caterpiller.* New York: Two Lions, 2015.

Jennings, Sharon. *Franklin the Detective.* Toronto, ON: Kids Can Press, 2004.

Rock, Brian. *The Deductive Detective.* Mt. Pleasant, SC: Sylvan Dell Publishing, 2013.

Teague, Mark. *Detective LaRue: Letters from the Investigation.* New York: Scholastic, 2004.

Christmas Train

Read a Christmas train story and draw the setting, characters, and main plot on the train box cars.

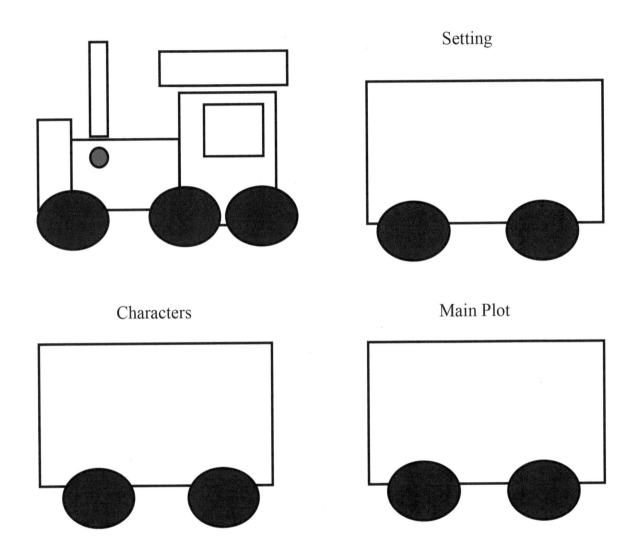

Setting

Characters

Main Plot

Christmas Train

Standards

Student(s)

- Inquire, think critically, and gain knowledge. (AASL 1)
- Draw conclusions, make informed decisions, apply knowledge to new situations, and create new knowledge. (AASL 2)
- Ask and answer questions about key details in a text. (CCSS 1)
- Use illustrations and details in the story to describe its characters, setting, or events. (CCSS 5)
- Uses meaning clues (e.g., picture captions, illustrations, title, cover, headings, story structure, story topics) to aid comprehension and make predictions about content (e.g., action, events, character's behavior). (McREL 2)
- [Reads] Hear a variety of familiar literary passages and texts (e.g., fairy tales, folktales, fiction, nonfiction, legends, fables, myths, poems, nursery rhymes, picture books, predictable books). (McREL 3)

Objectives

Students

- Recall and illustrate setting, characters, and main plot as seen in the story.

Directions

1. The worksheets need to be copied on card stock.
2. The school librarian reads and shows a Christmas train fiction book.
3. The reading teacher discusses the story setting, characters, and main plot.
4. The teachers guide students illustrating of setting, characters, and main plot on the train cars, as seen in the story.
5. The art teacher guides the coloring of the train engine. The card stock copied train cars are cut out and connected.

Teaching Team

Art, reading, and school librarian teachers.

Suggested Sources

Awdry, Rev. W. *Christmas in Wellsworth* (Thomas & Friends). New York: Random House, 2014.
Monson, Thomas. *The Christmas Train: A True Story.* Salt Lake City, UT: Shadow Mountain, 2012.
Van Allsburg, Chris. *Polar Express.* New York: Houghton Miffin, 2015.
Warner Brothers. *Polar Express* [DVD]. Burbank, CA: Warner Brothers, 2006.

Over the River

Put the ride to grandparent's house in order. Put 1, 2, or 3 in each small box.

Woods

Grandparent's house

Over the river

Now, write a two-line poem about the story:

_____

_____

Over the River

Standards

Student(s)

- Inquire, think critically, and gain knowledge. (AASL 1)
- Draw conclusions, make informed decisions, apply knowledge to new situations, and create new knowledge. (AASL 2)
- Identify words and phrases in stories or poems that suggest feelings or appeal to the senses. (CCSS 3)
- Use illustrations and details in the story to describe its characters, setting, or events. (CCSS 5)
- Use meaning clues (e.g., picture captions, illustrations, title, cover, headings, story structure, story topics) to aid comprehension and make predictions about content (e.g., action, events, character's behavior). (McREL 2)
- [Read] Hear a variety of familiar literary passages and texts (e.g., fairy tales, folktales, fiction, nonfiction, legends, fables, myths, poems, nursery rhymes, picture books, predictable books). (McREL 3)

Summarize information found in texts (e.g., retell in own words). (McREL 5)

Objectives

Students

- Discuss rhythm.
- Relate the order of the events as seen in the book.
- Compose a two-line story poem from a summary of the book.

Directions

1. The school librarian points out the poetic rhythm of a song book and then reads and shows the *Over the River and Through the Wood* book.
2. Teachers guide the discussion of setting, characters, and beginning, middle, and end events.
3. The reading teacher guides the class in creation of a simple three-word, two-line poem about the story events. Students copy the class-created poem or write their own poem.
4. Since some versions of this book gave a grandmother or a grandfather as the main character, the worksheet simply says grandparent. Students put the story events in order, as seen in the book, by placing numbers in the small boxes. Worksheets are colored.

Teaching Team

Reading and school librarian teachers.

Suggested Sources

Ashman, Linda. *Over the River & Through the Wood: A Holiday Adventure.* New York: Sterling Publishing, 2015.

Child, Lydia Maria. *Over the River and Through the Wood.* New York: NorthSouth Books, 2014.

Snowy Day

What are two things you can do in the snow?

1.

2.

 Make a snow globe. Shake your snow globe when done making it.

*Color the round shape (snow globe) blue. Color the bottom of it brown or black.

*Cut out the snowman or sled. Cut out the snowflakes. Tape everything in the round circle (snow globe).

Snowy Day

Standards

Student(s)

- Inquire, think critically, and gain knowledge. (AASL 1)
- Draw conclusions, make informed decisions, apply knowledge to new situations, and create new knowledge. (AASL 2)
- Share knowledge and participate ethically and productively as members of our democratic society. (AASL 3)
- Ask and answer questions about key details in a text. (CCSS 6)
- Use illustrations and details in a text to describe its key ideas. (CCSS 7)
- Uses a variety of sources to gather information (e.g., informational books, pictures, charts, indexes, video, television programs, guest speakers, internet, own observation). (McREL 1)
- [Reads] Hear a variety of familiar literary passages and texts (e.g., fairy tales, folktales, fiction, nonfiction, legends, fables, myths, poems, nursery rhymes, picture books, predictable books). (McREL 3)
- Relates new information to prior knowledge and experience. (McREL 6)

Objectives

Students

- List or illustrate fun things to do in the snow.
- Show fun in the snow with a creation of a snow globe.

Directions

1. The reading and school librarian teachers show and read fun snow books. Students discuss ways to have fun in the snow as seen in the books and as compared to prior knowledge.
2. Teachers guide students as students list or illustrate two fun things to do in the snow.
3. The art teacher guides students as students color the snow globe blue, color the globe stand brown or black, cut out the snowflakes, and cut out either the snowman or the boy sledding. The snowman or sled is taped in the top snow globe. The snowflakes are attached with double-sided tape inside the globe, so that the snowflakes appear to have slight motion inside the snow globe.

Teaching Team

Art, reading, and school librarian teachers.

Suggested Sources

Bauer, Marion Dane. *Snow.* New York: Simon Spotlight, 2016.
Bix, Jasper. *Building a Snowman.* Milwaukee, WI: Gareth Stevens, 2016.
Bix, Jasper. *Let's Go Sledding*! Milwaukee, WI: Gareth Stevens, 2016.
Inkpen, Mick. *Kipper's Snowy Day.* London: Hodder & Stoughton, 2015.
Laminack, Lester. *Snowday!* Atlanta, GA: PeachTree, 2010.
McGhee, Alison. *Making a Friend.* New York: Atheneum Books for Young Readers, 2014.

Master Cat (*Puss in Boots*) Fairy Tale

The Fairy Tale of Master Cat (*Puss in Boots*) and the Young Man

Once upon a time, there was a _____ who got a _____ from his dad. The _____ would help the _____, only if the _____ could get some _____. The _____ got _____. So, the _____ helped. He got a _____ for the _____. The _____ and _____ married.

They all lived happily ever after. The end.

Show how Puss in Boots helped:

Master Cat (*Puss in Boots*) Fairy Tale

Standards

Student(s)

- Inquire, think critically, and gain knowledge. (AASL 1)
- Draw conclusions, make informed decisions, apply knowledge to new situations, and create new knowledge. (AASL 2)
- Share knowledge and participate ethically and productively as members of our democratic society. (AASL 3)
- Describe characters, setting, and major events in a story, using key details. (CCSS 2)
- Use illustrations and details in a story to describe its characters, setting, or events. (CCSS 5)
- Reads a variety of familiar literacy passages (e.g., fairy tales, folktales, fiction, nonfiction, legends, fables, myths, poems, nursery rhymes, picture books, predictable books). (McREL 3)
- Knows setting, main characters, main events, sequence, narrator, and problems in stories. (McREL 4)
- Summarizes information found in texts (e.g., retells in own words). (McREL 5)

Objectives

Students

- Recognize and read the fairy tale of Master Cat (*Puss in Boots*).
- Summarize story plot, how the main character helped, and discuss the elements of a fairy tale.
- Illustrate the major event.

Directions

1. The reading and school librarian teachers read and show the Master Cat (*Puss in Boots*) fairy tale.
2. The teachers lead a class discussion on what happened first, in the middle, and what happened at the end, how the cat main character helped, and why the story was a fairy tale.
3. The class will be guided as they read their worksheet Master Cat story together.
4. With teacher's guidance, students write or illustrate the bottom worksheet question and color the worksheet illustrations.
5. Student partners read the story.

Teaching Team

Reading and school librarian teachers.

Suggested Sources

Huling, Jan. *Puss in Cowboy Boots*. New York: Simon & Schuster Books for Young Readers, 2002.

Perrault, Charles. *Puss in Boots*. Minneapolis, MN: Learner, 2014.

Pinkney, Jerry. *Puss in Boots*. New York: Puffin Books, 2015.

Vote for President

What were one to two ideas for a president seen in the book? On the long poster draw the ideas.

Color the flag red and blue and cut it out for a flag pin, so you can help the main character be president.

Vote for President

Standards

Student(s)

- Inquire, think critically, and gain knowledge. (AASL 1)
- Draw conclusions, make informed decisions, apply knowledge to new situations, and create new knowledge. (AASL 2)
- Share knowledge and participate ethically and productively as members of our democratic society. (AASL 3)
- Pursue personal and aesthetic growth. (AASL 4)
- Ask and answer questions about key details in a text. (CCSS 1)
- Use illustrations and details in the story to describe its characters, setting, or events. (CCSS 5)
- Uses meaning clues (e.g., picture captions, illustrations, title, cover, headings, story structure, story topic) to aid comprehension and make predictions about context (e.g., action, events, character's behavior). (McREL 2)
- [Reads] Hear a variety of familiar literary passages and texts (e.g., fairy tales, folktales, fiction, nonfiction, legends, fables, myths, poems, nursery rhymes, picture books, predictable books). (McREL 3)
- Knows setting, main characters, main events, sequence, narrator, and problems in stories. (McREL 4)

Objectives

Students

- Summarize the main character, the story events, and other key text details.
- Illustrate the ideas that the character had for a president.

Directions

1. The school librarian reads and shows a fiction book on being president, while also mentioning author and title.
2. The reading teacher guides student discussion on main character, events, and other key text details. Discussion also involves the main character's ideas for presidency.
3. The teachers guide students as students colorfully illustrate one to two of the main character's ideas for presidency, on the long poster.
4. Students color blue and red around the flag and cut out the flag for a flag pin. They tape the paper flag pin on their shirts to show support of the main character's presidency.

Teaching Team

Reading and school librarian teachers.

Suggested Sources

Cronin, Doreen. *Duck for President*. New York: Simon and Schuster, 2006.
Wells, Rosemary. *Otto Runs for President*. New York: Scholastic, 2008.
Winters, Kay. *My Teacher for President*. New York: Scholastic, 2004.

Wild Cats

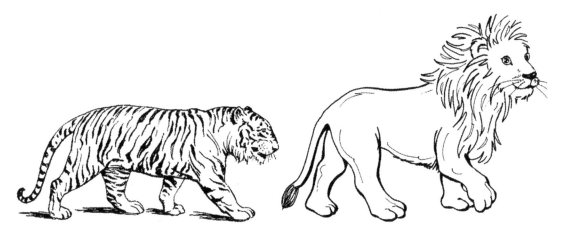

Some big wild cats are lions and tigers. Compare lions and tigers.

(1) Lions

_____

(2) Tigers

_____

Make a lion or tiger eye mask. What color should it be? Should it have stripes or a mane? Add whiskers.

Wild Cats

Standards

Student(s)

- Inquire, think critically, and gain knowledge. (AASL 1)
- Draw conclusions, make informed decisions, apply knowledge to new situations, and create new knowledge. (AASL 2)
- Share knowledge and participate ethically and productively as members of our democratic society. (AASL 3)
- Pursue personal and aesthetic growth. (AASL 4)
- Ask and answer questions about key details in a text. (CCSS 1)
- Explain major differences between books that tell stories and books that give information, drawing on a wide reading of a range of text books. (CCSS 4)
- Use the illustrations and details in a text to describe its key ideas. (CCSS 7)
- Uses a variety of sources to gather information (e.g., informational books, pictures, charts, indexes, video, television programs, guest speakers, internet, own observation). (McREL 1)
- Summarizes information found in texts (e.g., retell in own words). (McREL 5)
- Relates new information to prior knowledge and experience. (McREL 6)

Objectives

Students

- Summarize a fact for a tiger and a lion.
- Design a lion or tiger eye mask that resembles an actual lion or tiger.

Directions

1. From showing simple lion and tiger books, the science teacher leads a discussion on two major differences between a lion and a tiger including the color and fur pattern of each animal.
2. The school librarian emphasizes nonfiction books and shows simple lion and tiger nonfiction books.
3. From viewing the nonfiction book illustrations or from reading brief facts, small groups and then the class summarize a short fact about a lion and then a tiger.
4. Students write a lion and tiger fact, color the lion and tiger, and then design an eye mask to look like a lion or tiger (add stripes or a mane, whiskers, color, and cut out the boxed mask).

Teaching Team

Science and school librarian teachers.

Suggested Sources

Archer, Claire. *Tigers.* Mankato, MN: ABDO, 2015.
Archer, Claire. *Lions.* Mankato, MN: ABDO, 2015.
Franks, Katie. *Lions.* New York: PowerKids, 2015.
Gentle, Victor. *Lions.* Milwaukee, WI: Gareth Stevens, 2002.
Gentle, Victor. *Tigers.* Milwaukee, WI: Gareth Stevens, 2002.
Smith, Lucy Sackett. *Tigers: Prowling Predators.* New York: PowerKids, 2010.

Groundhog Time

When groundhog sees his shadow, what do people say about winter? Here, groundhog says it is time to keep library books safe. On groundhog's sack, illustrate his story. Then glue groundhog's sack on a regular sack.

Groundhog says that it is time to keep your library books safe in a bag.

Groundhog Time

Standards

Student(s)

- Inquire, think critically, and gain knowledge. (AASL 1)
- Draw conclusions, make informed decisions, apply knowledge to new situations, and create new knowledge. (AASL 2)
- Explain major differences between books that tell stories and books that give information, drawing on a wide reading of a range of text types. (CCSS 4)
- Use the illustrations and details in a text to describe its characters, setting, or events. (CCSS 5)
- Uses meaning clues (e.g., picture captions, illustrations, title, cover, headings, story structure, story topics) to aid comprehension and make predictions about content (e.g., action, events, character's behavior). (McREL 2)
- [Reads] Hear a variety of familiar literary passages and texts (e.g., fairy tales, folktales, fiction, nonfiction, legends, fables, myths, poems, nursery rhymes, picture books, predictable books). (McREL3)
- Knows setting, main characters, main events, sequence, narrator, and problems in stories. (McREL 4)

Objectives

Students

- Define Groundhog Day, character, and main event.
- Create a groundhog library book bag from a groundhog story event.

Directions

1. The reading and school librarian teachers read and show a nonfiction and fiction book about Groundhog Day so students become familiar with Groundhog Day.
2. Teachers lead a class discussion on Groundhog Day including character and main event.
3. The art teacher guides student illustrations of the Groundhog fiction story event on the worksheets. The groundhog worksheet glues to a plastic bag for a library book bag.

Teaching Team

Art, reading, and school librarian teachers.

Suggested Sources

Fiction

> Pearlman, Robb. *Groundhog's Day Off*. New York: Bloomsbury, 2015.
> Remenar, Kristen. *Groundhog's Dilemma*. Watertown, MA: Charlesbridge, 2015.
> Vojita, Stemper, Pat. *Mr. Groundhog Wants the Day Off*. McHenry, IL: Raven Tree Press, 2013.

Nonfiction

> Gibbons, Gail. *Groundhog Day*. New York: Holiday House, 2007.
> Lindeen, Mary. *Groundhog Day*. Chicago, IL: Norwood House Press, 2015.

Caring at Valentine's Day

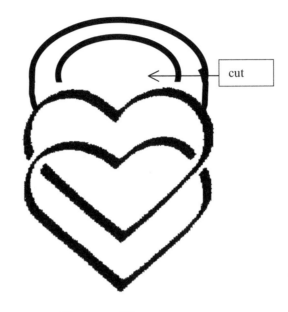

Read two Valentine books.

1. How did one Valentine's book show caring?

2. How did the other Valentine's book show caring?

3. Color the big hearts. Glue the I Care heart on the big ones.

   Cut out the big hearts. Give the heart charm to someone you care.

Caring at Valentine's Day

Standards

Student(s)

- Draw conclusions, make informed decisions, apply knowledge to new situations, and create new knowledge. (AASL 2)
- Share knowledge and participate ethically and productively as members of our democratic society. (AASL 3)
- Describe characters, settings, and major events in a story, using key details. (CCSS 2)
- Identify words and phrases in stories or poems that suggest feelings or appeal to the senses. (CCSS 3)
- Use illustrations and details in a story to describe its characters, setting, or events. (CCSS 5)
- With prompting and support, name the author and illustrator of a story and define the role of each in telling the story. (Kindergarten CCSS 5)
- [Reads] Hear a variety of familiar literary passages and texts (e.g., fairy tales, folktales, fiction, nonfiction, legends, fables, myths, poems, nursery rhymes, picture books, predictable books). (McREL 3)

Objectives

Students

- Illustrate or compare in written form several ways of showing Valentine's Day caring from two books.
- Summarize caring by creating a caring Valentine charm.

Directions

1. The reading and school librarian teachers each read and show a Valentine book about caring. Authors and illustrators are discussed as well.
2. The class discusses and compares the events of the stories. Students list how caring was showed in each book, and teachers write that short caring list on the class board.
3. Students illustrate or write one to two ways of showing Valentine's Day caring from each book.
4. Students color the large Valentine hearts. They cut out the hearts with the top half circle connected, cut out the "I Care" colored heart and glue it on the large hearts, and cut the inside of the top circle for a Valentine jewelry charm to give to someone they care.

Teaching Team

Reading and school librarian teachers.

Suggested Sources

Andrews, Julie. *The Very Fairy Princess: Valentines from the Heart.* New York: Little, Brown and Company, 2015.

Bunting, Eve. *Mr. Goat's Valentine.* Mankato, MN: Sleeping Bear Press, 2016.

Capucilli, Alyssa Satin. *Katy Duck and the Secret Valentine.* New York: Simon Spotlight, 2014.

Friedman, Laurie B. *Ruby Valentine and the Sweet Surprise.* Minneapolis, MN: Carolrhoda Books, 2014.

Jennings, Sharon. *Franklin's Valentines.* Tonawanda, NY: Kids Can Press, 2013.

At the Big Top

In the bottom box, draw what you saw in the circus. Color and cut out the top box. Cut out the bottom box. Attach the big top to the bottom box! Cut on the dotted line and fold, so that the big top can open!

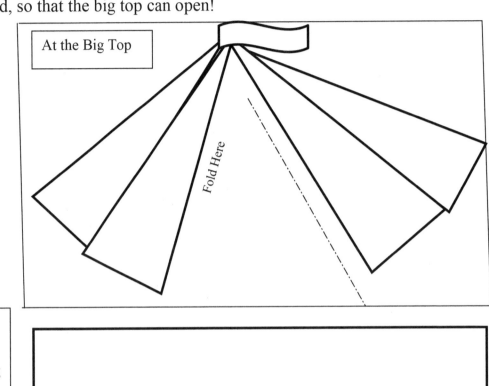

At the Big Top

Fold Here

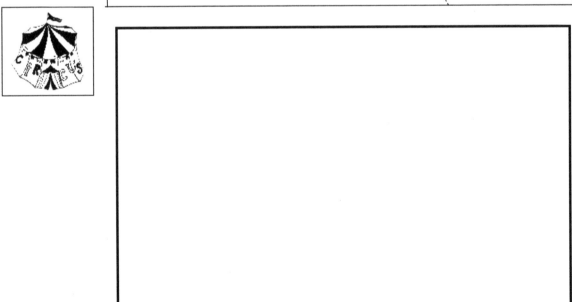

At the Big Top

Standards

Student(s)

- Inquire, think critically, and gain knowledge. (AASL 1)
- Draw conclusions, make informed decisions, apply knowledge to new situations, and create new knowledge. (AASL 2)
- Ask and answer questions about key details in a text. (CCSS 1)
- Use illustrations and details in the story to describe its characters, setting, or events. (CCSS 5)
- With prompting and support, name the author and illustrator of a story and define the role of each in telling the story. (Kindergarten CCSS 5)
- Uses meaning clues (e.g., picture captions, illustrations, title, cover, headings, story structure, story topics) to aid comprehension and make predictions about content (e.g., action, events, character's behavior). (McREL 5)
- [Reads] Hear a variety of familiar literary passages and texts (e.g., fairy tales, folktales, fiction, nonfiction, legends, fables, myths, poems, nursery rhymes, picture books, predictable books). (McREL 3)
- Relates new information to prior knowledge and experience. (McREL 6)

Objectives

Students

- Describe author, title, and illustrator.
- Illustrate a major circus event from the meaning clues.

Directions

1. To show a circus, the school librarian shows some of *Peter Spier's Circus* or similar book.
2. The reading teacher reads and shows a circus fiction book. Author, title, and illustrator are described.
3. Teachers guide student discussion on major circus events of the circus story as seen from meaning clues and as heard. Students relate their prior circus knowledge to the story.
4. The art, reading, and school librarian teachers guide students as students colorfully draw a circus event in the bottom worksheet box.
5. The art teacher guides students in the coloring of the big top and cutting on the dotted line of the big top or top box. Students attach the top box to the bottom box, to be able to open and close their big top on their circus event.

Teaching Team

Art, reading, and school librarian teachers.

Suggested Sources

Bond, Michael. *Paddington at the Circus*. New York: HarperCollins, 2016.
Klise, Kate. *The Circus Goes to Sea*. New York: Algonquin, 2015.
Spier, Peter. *Peter Spier's Circus!* New York: Dragonfly Books, 2002.
Van Dusen, Chris. *Circus Ship*. Somerville, MA: Candlewick Press, 2016.

Chickens Cluck

Find and write two chicken facts from a nonfiction book. Then color the chicken coming out of the egg.

1. _____

_____

_____

2. _____

_____

_____

Chickens Cluck

Standards

Student(s)

- Inquire, think critically, and gain knowledge. (AASL 1)
- Draw conclusions, make informed decisions, apply knowledge to new situations, and create new knowledge. (AASL 2)
- Pursue personal and aesthetic growth. (AASL 4)
- Explain major differences between books that tell stories and books that give information, drawing on a wide range of text types. (CCSS 4)
- Ask and answer questions about key details in a text. (CCSS 6)
- Use a variety of sources to gather information. (e.g., informational books, pictures, charts, indexes, video, television programs, guest speakers, internet, own observation). (McREL 1)
- Summarizes information found in texts (e.g., retell in own words). (McREL 5)
- Relates new information to prior knowledge and experience. (McREL 6)

Objectives

Students

- Distinguish between fiction and nonfiction.
- Select, summarize, and write two chicken facts.

Directions

1. The reading teacher reads and shows a fiction chicken book. Then the teacher shows a nonfiction chicken book, while discussing the differences between fiction and nonfiction.
2. The school librarian provides simple nonfiction chicken books for small group research. Small groups will research through illustrations and the simple text.
3. Small groups share one to two chicken facts with the class, which results in a list of briefly worded chicken facts on the class board.
4. As guided by teachers, students write two chicken facts on their papers.
5. The art teacher guides students as they color the top chick and eggs. The eggs and chicken are cut out together. Once the eggs are folded, the top egg hatches open to the chick.

Teaching Team

Art, reading, and school librarian teachers.

Suggested Sources

Fiction

> Bardhan-Quallen, Sudipta. *Chicks Run Wild*. New York: Simon & Schuster, 2011.
> Stein, David Ezra. *Interrupting Chicken*. Somerville, MA: Candlewick Press, 2010.

Nonfiction

> Hendrix, Emilia. *Chickens and Chicks*. Milwaukee, WI: Gareth Stevens, 2016.
> Murray, Julie. *Chickens*. Mankato, MN: ABDO Kids, 2016.

Gators

Alligator or Crocodile?

1. Alligator has a **U** (U-snout). Draw more about alligator:

2. Crocodile has a **V** (V-snout). Draw more about crocodile:

3. Color the gator in the box. Cut out the gator box and this box. Tape the gator to this box, but leave the bottom open, for a hand puppet.

Gators

Standards

Student(s)

- Inquire, think critically, and gain knowledge. (AASL 1)
- Draw conclusions, make informed decisions, apply knowledge to new situations, and create new knowledge. (AASL 2)
- Explain major differences between books that tell stories and books that give information, drawing on a wide reading of a range of text types. (CCSS 4)
- Use the illustrations and details in a text to describe its key ideas. (CCSS 7)
- Uses a variety of sources to gather information (e.g., informational books, pictures, charts, indexes, video, television programs, guest speakers, internet, own observation). (McREL 1).
- Summarizes information found in texts (e.g., retells in own words). (McREL 5)

Objectives

Students

- Explain the differences between fiction and nonfiction.
- Research and draw facts.
- Create gator hand puppets in order to act out the story.

Directions

1. The school librarian introduces the lesson by reading and discussing a fiction alligator book. The teacher briefly leads discussions on the differences between fiction and nonfiction books.
2. The science teacher shows crocodile and alligator differences by their colors and shows that alligators have U-shaped snouts, but crocodiles have V-shaped snouts.
3. The school librarian guides small groups in finding alligator and crocodile nonfiction resources. Students research the illustrations and simple text of the alligator and crocodiles sources.
4. Individuals in small groups draw a new fact about each gator and share the facts with the class.
5. The art teacher helps students color the boxed gator and create a hand puppet by taping the question box to the gator, while leaving the bottom open for hands. They act out the fiction story.

Teaching Team

Art, science, and school librarian teachers.

Suggested Sources

Fiction

Eastman, P. D. *Aaron Is Cool.* New York: Random House, 2015.

Parsley, Elise. *If You Ever Want to Bring an Alligator to School, Don't!* New York: Little Brown and Company, 2015.

Nonfiction

Herrington, Lia. *Crocodiles and Alligators.* New York: Scholastic, 2016.

Marsh, Laura. *Alligators and Crocodiles.* Washington, DC: National Geographic, 2015.

Smith, Renee. *Crocodiles and Alligator Differences. Science Kids.* Updated 2015. Retrieved from http://www.sciencekids.co.nz/sciencefacts/animals/crocodilealligatordifferences.html

Rabbit's Story

1. Draw (illustrate) the main event of rabbit's story for rabbit:

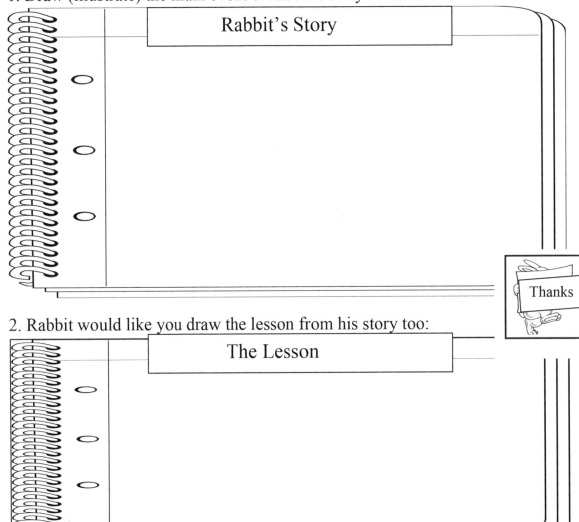

Rabbit's Story

Thanks

2. Rabbit would like you draw the lesson from his story too:

The Lesson

Rabbit's Story

Standards

Student(s)

- Inquire, think critically, and gain knowledge. (AASL 1)
- Draw conclusions, make informed decisions, apply knowledge to new situations, and create new knowledge. (AASL 2)
- Share knowledge and participate ethically and productively as members of our democratic society. (AASL 3)
- Ask and answer such questions about key details in a text. (CCSS 1)
- Use illustrations and details in a story to describe its characters, setting, or events. (CCSS 5)
- [Reads] Hear a variety of familiar literary passages and texts (e.g., fairy tales, folktales, fiction, nonfiction, legends, fables, myths, poems, nursery rhymes, picture books, predictable books). (McREL 3)
- Knows setting, main characters, main events, sequence, narrator, and problems in stories. (McREL 4)

Objectives

Students

- Identify a fable and moral.
- Analyze main event, setting, character, and the moral, and illustrate main event and moral.

Directions

1. The school librarian discusses how books give a lesson or something that can be learned from a story. If it is a fable or similar source, there is a moral or lesson.
2. The reading teacher reads, shows, and discusses a rabbit fable, folktale, or fiction story.
3. Reading and school librarian teachers guide student discussion on main event, setting, character, and moral as seen and heard from the story.
4. Teachers guide students as students illustrate the main event and then the moral for rabbit.
5. Students color the main rabbit and share their illustrated answers with the class.

Teaching Team

Reading and school librarian teachers.

Suggested Sources

Fable/Folklore

Bruchac, James and Joseph Bruchac. *Rabbits Snow Dance: A Traditional Iroquois Story.* New York: Penguin Books for Young Readers, 2012.
Franklin, Phoebe. *Lion and the Rabbit.* Louisville, KY: Newmark, 2015.
George, Shannon. *Rabbit's Gift: A Fable from China.* Boston, MA: Harcourt, 2007.
Kessler, Brad. *Brer Rabbit and Boss Lion.* Mankato, MN: ABDO, 2005.

Fiction

Rohmann, Eric. *My Friend Rabbit.* Brookfield, CT: Roaring Brook Press, 2011.

Chapter 3

Second-Grade Lesson Plans

Second-grade lessons plans were created to help the busy school librarian, as he or she strives to meet the demanding needs of a school library including that of teaching literacy skills and reading appreciation. The following interactive standards-backed elementary lessons will meet the globally literate needs of today's students. The lessons are set to different standards in the desire to meet the school librarians' state or school library, Common Core State Standards (CCSS) or McREL literacy, or English language arts standards, which include the proverbial American Association of School Librarians (AASL) standards.

The quality-researched standards of AASL, CCSS, and The McREL Compendium of Standards and Benchmarks are applied with each school library lesson for purposeful school library instruction and student achieved skills. The parts of the standards chosen for this book were those that were the most essential for library instruction and could be met in the lesson time allotment of twenty minutes. The standards may be used together as given, individually, or lessons may be set to other quality standards.

Based on standards, student learning objectives are given for each lesson. Lessons include students working individually or with others for more efficient student learning. Team teaching is seen, as more can be accomplished when working together. Quality-researched resources are suggested. The streamlined, standards-based lessons for the busy school librarian will provide interactive and successful student learning. The AASL standards are stated in the first chapter as they are universally seen with all lessons in some way. The following McREL and CCSS standards are used specifically with this grade level.

Second-Grade Library Standards with Language Arts Benchmarks from McREL Language Arts Writing Standards and Benchmarks and CCSS

Second-grade students:

*Second-Grade Common Core (Literacy), Reading Literature

1. Ask and answer such questions as who, what, where, when, why, and how to demonstrate understanding of key details in a text. (CCSS.ELA-Literacy.RL.2.1)
2. Recount stories, including fables and folktales from diverse cultures, and determine their central message, lesson, or moral. (CCSS.ELA-Literacy.RL.2.2)
3. Describe how words and phrases (e.g., regular beats, alliteration, rhymes, repeated lines) supply rhythm and meaning in a story, poem, or song. (CCSS.ELA-Literacy.RL.2.4)
4. Describe the overall structure of a story, including describing how the beginning introduces the story and the ending concludes the action. (CCSS.ELA-Literacy.RL.2.5)
5. Compare and contrast two or more versions of the same story (e.g., Cinderella stories) by different authors or from different cultures. (CCSS.ELA-Literacy.RL.2.9)

*Second-Grade Common Core (Literacy), Reading Informational Texts

6. Ask and answer such questions as who, what, where, when, why, and how to demonstrate understanding of the key details in a text. (CCSS.ELA-Literacy.RI.2.1)
7. Identify the main purpose of a text, including what the author wants to answer, explain, or describe. (CCSS.ELA-Literacy.RI.2.6)

Governors Association Center for Best Practices and Council of Chief State School Officers. *Common Core State Standards (Literacy).* Washington, DC: National Governors Association Center for Best Practices and Council of Chief State School Officers, 2010. Retrieved from http://www.corestandards.org/

McREL Compendium of Standards and Benchmarks Language Arts Writing Standards and Benchmarks (Grade K–2)

*Gathers and uses information for research purposes. Standard 4

1. Uses a variety of sources to gather information (e.g., informational books, pictures, charts, indexes, video, television programs, guest speakers, internet, own observation). (McREL)

McREL Compendium of Standards and Benchmarks Language Arts Reading Standards and Benchmarks (Grade K–2)

*Uses the general skills and strategies of the reading process. Standard 5

2. Uses meaning clues (e.g., pictures, captions, illustrations, title, cover, headings, story structure, story topic) to aid comprehension and make predictions about content (e.g., action, events, character's behavior). (McREL)
3. Reads [Hear] a variety of familiar literary passages and texts (e.g., fairy tales, folktales, fiction, nonfiction, legends, fables, myths, poems, nursery rhymes, picture books, predictable books). (McREL)

*Uses skills and strategies to read a variety of literary texts.

4. Knows setting, main characters, main events, sequence, narrator, and problems in stories. (McREL)

*Uses skills and strategies to read a variety of informational texts.

5. Summarizes information found in texts (e.g., retell in own words). (McREL)
6. Relates new information to prior knowledge and experience. (McREL)

McREL. *Language Arts Standards*, 2015. Retrieved from http://www2.mcrel.org/compendium/standard

Pirates Go to the Library

Pirates go to the library! In the shape below and before pirates leave on their ship, show the pirates three ways to take care of books in the library.

Pirates Go the Library

Standards

Student(s)

- Inquire, think critically, and gain knowledge. (AASL 1)
- Draw conclusions, make informed decisions, apply knowledge to new situations, and create new knowledge. (AASL 2)
- Pursue personal and aesthetic growth. (AASL 4)
- Describe how words and phrases (e.g., regular beats, alliteration, rhymes, repeated lines) supply the rhythm and meaning in a story, poem, or song. (CCSS 3)
- Identify the main purpose of a text, including what the author wants to answer, explain, or describe. (CCSS 7).
- Uses meaning clues (e.g., pictures, captions, illustrations, title, cover, headings, story structure, story topic) to aid comprehension and make predictions about content (e.g., action, events, character's behavior). (McREL 2)
- [Reads]] Hear a variety of familiar literary passages and texts (e.g., fairy tales, folktales, fiction, nonfiction, legends, fables, myths, poems, nursery rhymes, picture books, predictable books). (McREL 3)

Objectives

Students

- Recognize the rhymes and author's purpose of a rhyming book.
- Illustrate good book care.

Directions

1. The reading teacher shows and reads an easy reading rhyming pirate book that could be related to the library or school.
2. Led by the reading teacher, students discuss the author's purpose for writing the book, and discuss illustrations and the rhymes found in the book.
3. The school librarian guides discussion on what rules should be followed in a school library.
4. Teachers guide student work as students illustrate how pirates should show book care in the library in three ways.
5. Students color their worksheets.

Teaching Team

Reading and school librarian teachers.

Suggested Sources

Demas, Corrine. *Pirates Go to School*. London: Orchard Books, 2011.
Greene, Rhonda Gowler. *No Pirates Allowed! Said Library Lou*. Mankato, MN: Sleeping Bear Press, 2013.
Teague, Mark. *The Pirate Jamboree*. London: Orchard Books, 2016.

Helping the Community

How do cars and trucks help in your community?

This is a _____. It helps in the community by _____
_____

This is a _____. It helps in the community by _____
_____

This is a _____. It helps in the community by _____
_____

This is a _____. It helps in the community by _____
_____

Show or tell how you could help your community, too:

Helping the Community

Standards

Student(s)

- Inquire, think critically, and gain knowledge. (AASL 1)
- Draw conclusions, make informed decisions, apply knowledge to new situations, and create new knowledge. (AASL 2)
- Share knowledge and participate ethically and productively as members of our democratic society. (AASL 3)
- Pursue personal and aesthetic growth. (AASL 4)
- Ask and answer such questions as who, what, where, when, why, and how to demonstrate understanding of key details in a text. (CCSS 6)
- Uses meaning clues (e.g., pictures, captions, illustrations, title, cover, headings, story structure, story topic) to aid comprehension and make predictions about content (e.g., action, events, character's behavior). (McREL 2)
- Relates new information to prior knowledge and experience. (McREL 6)

Objectives

Students

- Research for key details and briefly describe vehicles that help in a community.
- Describe how they can help a community too.

Directions

1. The school librarian reads and shows a fiction book about vehicles that help in a community.
2. The social studies teacher leads class discussion on various vehicles that help in a community and shows nonfiction books. Students discuss how they can help in a community or at school.
3. With guidance of the library and social studies teachers, students research nonfiction books through visual clues or by reading key details, and briefly describe how a garbage truck, street sweeper, police car, and fire truck help. Students illustrate or write how they can help, too.
4. The art teacher guides students as students color their papers, cut out the community vehicles, and then create a community display of vehicles at work at the top of the worksheets.

Teaching Team

Art, school librarian, and social studies teachers.

Suggested Sources

Fiction

Iwai, Melissa. *Wake Up, Engines*. New York: Clarion Books, 2007.
McMullan, Kate. *I Stink*. New York: HarperCollins, 2006.

Nonfiction

Dayton, Connor. *Street Sweepers*. New York: PowerKids Press, 2012.
Gregory, Josh. *Fire Truck*. North Mankato, MN: Cherry Lake Publishing, 2011.
Murray, Julie. *Garbage Trucks*. Mankato, MN: ABDO Kids, 2016.
Murray, Julie. *Police Cars*. Mankato, MN: ABDO Kids, 2016.
Parker, Victoria. *Helping Family and Friends*. Portsmouth, NH: Heinemann Library, 2012.

Magic Porridge Pot Fairy Tale

⭐ Answer the questions.

1. How did the girl get the porridge pot? _____

_____

2. What was the magic of the porridge pot? _____

_____

3. What can you learn from the story? _____

_____

⭐ Color the porridge pot. Add pictures to the pot to show what happened at the end of the story.

Magic Porridge Pot Fairy Tale

Standards

Student(s)

- Inquire, think critically, and gain knowledge. (AASL 1)
- Draw conclusions, make informed decisions, apply knowledge to new situations, and create new knowledge. (AASL 2)
- Ask and answer such questions as who, what, where, when, why, and how to demonstrate understanding of key details in a text. (CCSS 1)
- Recount stories, including fables and folktales from diverse cultures, and determine their central message, lesson, or moral. (CCSS 2)
- Describe the overall structure of a story, including describing how the beginning introduces the story and the ending concludes the action. (CCSS 4)
- Uses meaning clues (e.g., picture captions, illustrations, title, cover, headings, story structure, story topics) to aid comprehension and make predictions about content (e.g., action, events, character's behavior). (McREL 2)
- [Reads] Hear a variety of familiar literary passages and texts (e.g., fairy tales, folktales, fiction, nonfiction, legends, fables, myths, poems, nursery rhymes, picture books, predictable books). (McREL 3)
- Knows setting, main characters, main events, sequence, narrator, and problems in stories. (McREL 4)

Objectives

Students

- Describe a fairy tale and what makes it a fairy tale.
- Summarize beginning and ending events, setting, characters, and moral.
- Illustrate the ending event.

Directions

1. The reading and school librarian teachers introduce *The Magic Porridge Pot* fairy tale by first describing porridge and by also leading a discussion about what makes a fairy tale including the magic.
2. The reading teacher reads and shows *The Magic Porridge Pot* story.
3. Students discuss and then identify the setting, characters, the beginning and ending events, the moral or lesson learned from the story, the magic, and other key details.
4. The teachers guide the worksheet answers including the student illustrations of the story ending.

Teaching Team

Reading and school librarian teachers.

Suggested Sources

Dickins, Rosie. *The Magic Porridge Pot.* London: Usborne, 2012.
Lewis, Jan. *The Magic Porridge Pot.* New York: Penguin, 2012.
MacDonald, Alan. *The Magic Porridge Pot.* London: Penguin UK, 2012.

Simply a Machine

It Is Simply a Machine

Make a simple machine after exploring simple machines. Draw your own simple machine shapes. You can use the following shapes too.

- -

What machine did you make? _____

What can your machine do?

Simply a Machine

Standards

Student(s)

- Inquire, think critically, and gain knowledge. (AASL 1)
- Draw conclusions, make informed decisions, apply knowledge to new situations, and create new knowledge. (AASL 2)
- Share knowledge and participate ethically and productively as members of our democratic society. (AASL 3)
- Pursue personal and aesthetic growth. (AASL 4)
- Ask and answer such questions as who, what, where, when, why, and how to demonstrate understanding of key details in a text. (CCSS 6)
- Uses a variety of sources to gather information (e.g., informational books, pictures, charts, indexes, videos, television). (McREL 1)
- Uses meaning clues (e.g., pictures, captions, illustrations, title, cover, headings, story structure, story topic) to aid comprehension and make predictions about content (e.g., action, events, character's behavior). (McREL 2)
- Relates new information to prior knowledge and experience. (McREL 6)

Objectives

Students

- Research and recognize the key details of simple machines.
- Construct a simple paper machine and explain it.

Directions

1. Student sheets are copied on card stock.
2. The science teacher shows a short Internet video clip or book on simple machines.
3. The school librarian introduces simple machine nonfiction books.
4. With the guidance of the teachers, student pairs gather key details from the nonfiction sources and create simple paper machines using their worksheets and additional student paper creations.
5. Finally, students describe their simple machines in text or illustration.

Teaching Team

Science and school librarian teachers.

Suggested Sources

Adler, David. *Simple Machines; Wheels, Levers, and Pulleys*. New York: Holiday House, 2015.
Macaulay, D. *How Machines Work: Zoo Break*. New York: DK, 2015.
LaMachia, D. *Inclined Planes at Work*. Berkeley Heights, NJ: Enslow, 2016.
LaMachia, D. *Levers at Work*. Berkeley Heights, NJ: Enslow, 2016.
LaMachia, D. *Pulleys at Work*. Berkeley Heights, NJ: Enslow, 2016.
LaMachia, D. *Wheels and Axels at Work*. Berkeley Heights, NJ: Enslow, 2016.
PBS & WGBH Educational Foundation. *Simple Machines* [Video]. Updated 2015. Retrieved from http://www.pbslearningmedia.org/resource/idptv11.sci.phys.maf.d4ksim/simple-machines/

Scary Tales

by Adam Keeling

1. What is the title of the book? _____

2. Who is the author? _____

3. Draw or write the main characters:

4. Draw or write the plot:

5. Make a corner book page marker with the pumpkin shapes. Decorate.
   Cut out both shapes together with the middle strip. Fold in the middle.

Scary Tales

Standards

Student(s)

- Inquire, think critically, and gain knowledge. (AASL 1)
- Draw conclusions, make informed decisions, apply knowledge to new situations, and create new knowledge. (AASL 2)
- Explain major differences between books that tell stories and books that give information, drawing on a wide reading of a range of text types. (First Grade, CCSS 4)
- Identify the purpose of a text, including what the author wants to answer, explain, or describe. (CCSS 7)
- [Reads] Hear a variety of familiar literary passages and texts (e.g., fairy tales, folktales, fiction, nonfiction, legends, fables, myths, poems, nursery rhymes, picture books, predictable books). (McREL 3)
- Knows setting, main characters, main events, sequence, narrator, and problems in stories. (McREL 4)

Objectives

Students

- Recognize nonfiction and fiction differences and the author's purpose.
- Describe title, author, characters, and main plot.
- Create a book page marker.

Directions

1. The school librarian leads discussion on nonfiction and fiction differences and shows parts of a nonfiction pumpkin book. The author's purpose is discussed.
2. The reading teacher writes the fiction's title and author on the class board, and then reads a slightly scary fiction story. Discussion includes character and plot.
3. The art teacher guides students as students color and decorate a book corner page marker, which could look scary. Students cut out the pumpkin shapes together and fold in the middle.

Teaching Team

Art, reading, and school librarian teachers.

Suggested Sources

Fiction

Birney, Betty. *Humphrey's Creep-Crawly Camping Adventure*. New York: Puffin Books, 2015.
Brown, Margaret Wise. *Fierce Yellow Pumpkin*. New York: HarperCollins, 2006.
Reynolds, Aaron. *Creepy Carrots*. New York: Simon & Schuster, 2012.
Scotton, Rob. *Scaredy-Cat, Splat!* New York: Harper, 2010.
Van Leeuwen, Jean. *Amanda Pig and the Awful Scary Monster*. New York: Penguin, 2013.

Nonfiction

Schuh, Mari C. *Pumpkins in Fall*. Minneapolis, MN: Jump, 2014.
Shores, Erika L. *Pumpkins*. Mankato, MN: Capstone, 2016.

Turnips

Turnips are vegetables that grow in the dirt. Read a turnip story. Discuss the story. Then color the turnip and put it back in the dirt box.

Turnips

Standards

Student(s)

- Inquire, think critically, and gain knowledge. (AASL 1)
- Draw conclusions, make informed decisions, apply knowledge to new situations, and create new knowledge. (AASL 2)
- Share knowledge and participate ethically and productively as members of our democratic society. (AASL 3)
- Recount stories, including fables and folktales from diverse cultures, and determine their central message, lesson, or moral. (CCSS 2)
- Describe the overall structure of a story, including describing how the beginning introduces the story and the ending concludes the action. (CCSS 4)
- [Reads] Hear a variety of familiar literary passages and texts (e.g., fairy tales, folktales, fiction, nonfiction, legends, fables, myths, poems, nursery rhymes, picture books, predictable books). (McREL 3)
- Knows setting, main characters, main events, sequence, narrator, and problems in stories. (McREL 4)

Objectives

Students

- Recognize fiction, fairy tale, or folklore and the central message.
- Describe characters and the beginning and ending major events.

Directions

1. The reading or school librarian teacher reads a turnip fiction, fairy tale, or folklore book.
2. With teacher's help, the class discusses the characters, central message of the story, and the beginning, ending, and other major events of the story.
3. With teacher's assistance, students answer worksheet questions by drawing or writing.
4. With the art teacher's help, students color the turnip, lightly color the question/answer box brown for dirt, cut out the turnip, and vertically place the turnip back into the dirt.

Teaching Team

Art, reading, and school librarian teachers.

Suggested Sources

Brett, Jan. *The Turnip*. New York: G. P. Putnam's Sons Books for Young Readers, 2015.
Hester, Denia. *Grandma Lena's Big Ol' Turnip*. New York: Albert Whitman, 2015.
Tolstoy, Aleksei. *Gigantic Turnip*. Cambridge, MA: Barefoot Books, 2005.
Yates, Irene. *The Enormous Turnip*. New York: Penguin, 2012.

Thanksgiving Play

Read a Thanksgiving play. Act it out. Color the hat and headband for your play.

What would you say in the play? _____

_____

Thanksgiving Play

Standards

Student(s)

- Inquire, think critically, and gain knowledge. (AASL 1)
- Draw conclusions, make informed decisions, apply knowledge to new situations, and create new knowledge. (AASL 2)
- Share knowledge and participate ethically and productively as members of our democratic society. (AASL 3)
- Ask and answer such questions as who, what, where, when, why, and how to demonstrate understanding of key details in a text. (CCSS 1)
- [Reads] Hear a variety of familiar literary passages and texts (e.g., fairy tales, folktales, fiction, nonfiction, legends, fables, myths, poems, nursery rhymes, picture books, predictable books). (McREL 3)
- Knows setting, main characters, main events, sequence, narrator, and problems in stories. (McREL 4)
- Summarizes information found in texts (e.g., retells in own words). (McREL 6)

Objectives

Students

- Gather ideas for a Thanksgiving play by summarizing setting, characters, and events.
- Create a Native American headband and pilgrim's hat.
- Act out a Thanksgiving play.

Directions

1. Worksheets are copied on card stock.
2. To gather ideas for a play, the school librarian reads a fiction book showing a Thanksgiving play or a book involving pilgrims and Native Americans. A discussion includes characters, setting, and main events, as related to who, what, where, when, and why.
3. The reading teacher discusses how the class will act out the story and guides students in the creation of a colored pilgrim hat and Native American headband. Students affix the bottom strip to the pilgrim hat in back and position the patterned Native American headband in front of the same headband strip. When acting out, students turn the hat to show the correct head gear.
4. The library and reading teachers discuss and guide the writing of a simple phrase or sentence that a student actor could say, and then student pairs act out their story.

Teaching Team

Reading and school librarian teachers.

Suggested Sources

Brown, Marc. *Arthur's Thanksgiving.* New York: Little, Brown, 2011.
Dean, Kim. *The First Thanksgiving.* New York: HarperFestival, 2013.
Minden, Cecilia. *The Thanksgiving Play.* North Mankato, MN: Child's World, 2010.
Roberts, Bethany. *Thanksgiving Mice!* New York: Clarion Books, 2005.

Frog's Adventures

Read a frog book. Make a frog pencil holder, so you can write about frog's adventures. Write the book title on the front. On the back, draw what happened. Color. Cut. Tape the front to the back, but leave the top open.

Front

Back

My Froggy Pencil Holder

Title

Frog's Adventures

Standards

Student(s)

- Inquire, think critically, and gain knowledge. (AASL 1)
- Draw conclusions, make informed decisions, apply knowledge to new situations, and create new knowledge. (AASL 2)
- Ask and answer such questions as who, what, where, when, why, and how to demonstrate understanding of the key details in a text. (CCSS 1)
- Identify the main purpose of a text, including what the author wants to answer, explain, or describe. (CCSS 7)
- Uses meaning clues (e.g., pictures, captions, illustrations, title, cover, headings, story structure, story topic) to aid comprehension and make predictions about content (e.g., action, events, character's behavior). (McREL 2)
- Knows setting, main characters, main events, sequence, narrator, and problems in stories. (McREL 4)

Objectives

Students

- Compare the purpose, setting, characters, and events of two books by the same author.
- Illustrate one story event.

Directions

1. The reading and school librarian teachers each read and show a frog book by the same author and compare stories through the author's purpose, setting, main character, and events.
2. With the teacher's guidance, students select one frog story to illustrate. They first write that book title on the front frog panel.
3. The art teacher helps students create a pencil holder. Students design their selected book story on the larger space of the back frog panel, color the frogs, cut out the two frog holder panels, and tape the front panel to the back by taping the sides and bottom, but leave the top open for a pencil holder. The dotted lines can be folded over to hold the pencils inside.

Teaching Team

Art, reading, and school librarian teachers.

Suggested Sources

Bunting, Eve. *Frog's Flying Adventure*. Mankato, MN: Sleeping Bear Press, 2012.
Bunting, Eve. *Frog's Lucky Day*. Mankato, MN: Sleeping Bear Press, 2012.
London, Jonathan. *Froggy Builds a Tree House*. New York: Puffin Books, 2013.
London, Jonathan. *Froggy Is the Best*. New York: Penguin, 2015.
London, Jonathan. *Froggy Goes the Library*. New York: Viking Books, 2016.

Gifts

1. Look at the title page to answer these questions:

What is the title? _____

Who is the author? _____

Who is the illustrator? _____

2. Illustrate what happened first, in the middle, and at last in the story:

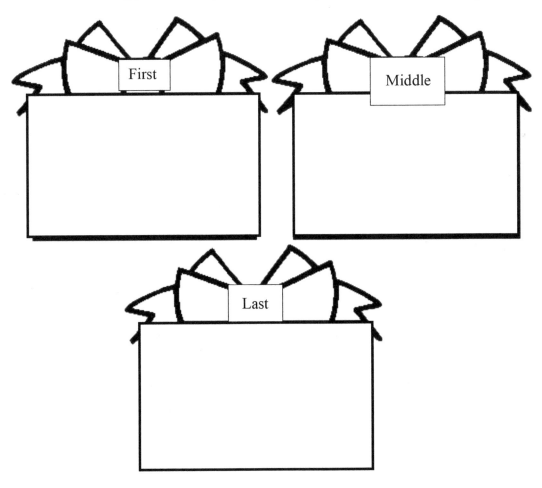

Gifts

Standards

Student(s)

- Inquire, think critically, and gain knowledge. (AASL 1)
- Draw conclusions, make informed decisions, apply knowledge to new situations, and create new knowledge. (AASL 2)
- Share knowledge and participate ethically and productively as members of our democratic society. (AASL 3)
- Pursue personal and aesthetic growth. (AASL 4)
- Describe the overall structure of a story, including describing how the beginning introduces the story and the ending concludes the action. (CCSS 4)
- Identify the main purpose of a text, including what the author wants to answer, explain, or describe. (CCSS 7)
- Uses meaning clues (e.g., picture captions, illustrations, title, cover, headings, story) to aid comprehension and make predictions about content (e.g., action, events, character's behavior). (McREL 2)
- Summarizes information found in texts (e.g., retells in own words). (McREL 5)

Objectives

Students

- Recognize ways of caring as the author's purpose.
- Recognize and list title page parts.
- Illustrate what happened first, in the middle, and at last.

Directions

1. The school librarian or reading teacher reads and shows a book about caring or caring at Christmas, which was the author's purpose.
2. The school library teacher leads discussion on title, author, and illustrator from the title page, which are written on the class board.
3. The reading teacher discusses the book's first, middle, and ending events and how caring was shown.
4. With teachers' guidance, students answer worksheet questions on title, author, illustrator, and then colorfully illustrate what happened first, in the middle, and at last on the worksheet gifts.

Teaching Team

Reading and school librarian teachers.

Suggested Sources

Bourgeois, Paulette. *Franklin's Christmas Gift*. Tonawanda, NY: Kids Can Press, 2013.
Dewney, Anna. *Llama Llama Holiday Drama*. New York: Viking, 2010.
Hale, Bruce. *Clark the Shark Dares to Share*. New York: HarperCollins, 2013.
Ruppert, Larry. *Dick and Jane: A Christmas Story*. New York: Grosset & Dunlap, 2004.

Card Catalog

E   Keeling, Blake
636.1   Horses
Kee

The library has an online catalog. It lists all library books. It tells about the books. It is on a computer. The online catalog helps you find books. Use the library online catalog.

Search for an animal. Find an animal book on the online catalog.

1. What is the title of the book? _____

_____

2. What is the call number?

3. Can you find the book in the library?

4. Draw something from your book:

Card Catalog

Standards

Student(s)

- Inquire, think critically, and gain knowledge. (AASL 1)
- Draw conclusions, make informed decisions, apply knowledge to new situations, and create new knowledge. (AASL 2)
- Share knowledge and participate ethically and productively as members of our democratic society. (AASL 3)
- Pursue personal and aesthetic growth. (AASL 4)
- Identify the main purpose of a text, including what the author wants to answer, explain, or describe. (CCSS 7)
- Uses a variety of sources to gather information (e.g., informational books, pictures, charts, indexes, video, television programs, guest speakers, internet, own observation). (McREL 1)
- Relates new information to prior knowledge and experience. (McREL 6)

Objectives

Students

- Recognize nonfiction.
- Show how to very basically use the online catalog.
- Search for any animal book on the online catalog and write the title and call number.

Directions

1. The reading teacher shows and discusses the purpose of a nonfiction book by showing and discussing a horse nonfiction book.
2. Teachers mention that students can find books by using the online catalog. The school librarian defines the online catalog and explains very basically how to use.
3. The library and reading teachers guide small groups as students answer their worksheet questions when searching for an animal book on the online catalog, and then as students select the first or second animal title.
4. Students are guided when writing the title and call number of the animal book from the online catalog.
5. Students find their book in the library. Upon finding the book, student groups examine and illustrate a key detail of their book. This lesson is best done midway through the school year, as most all second graders are ready for the online catalog by then.

Teaching Team

Reading and school librarian teachers.

Suggested Sources

Doyle, Sheri. *Horses.* Mankato, MN: Capstone, 2013.
Simon, Seymour. *Horses.* New York: HarperCollins, 2006.

Thumbs Up for Tom Thumb

Tom Thumb

Tom Thumb's parents wished for a child, who was no bigger than a thumb. They got the wish.

1. Tom was as small as a thumb. Did that help to make the story a fairy tale?
   Yes   No

2. Tell or draw about Tom Thumb and the horse:

3. Tell or draw about the end.

4. Color and cut out Tom Thumb. He will be a thumb puppet for you. Act out the story.

From *Standards-Based Lesson Plans for the Busy Elementary School Librarian* by Joyce Keeling. Santa Barbara, CA: Libraries Unlimited. Copyright © 2017.

Thumbs Up for Tom Thumb

Standards

Student(s)

- Inquire, think critically, and gain knowledge. (AASL 1)
- Draw conclusions, make informed decisions, apply knowledge to new situations, and create new knowledge. (AASL 2)
- Share knowledge and participate ethically and productively as members of our democratic society. (AASL 3)
- Recount stories, including fables and folktales from diverse cultures, and determine their central message, lesson, or moral. (CCSS 2)
- Describe the overall structure of a story, including describing how the beginning introduces the story and the ending concludes the action. (CCSS 4)
- [Reads] Hear a variety of familiar literary passages and texts (e.g., fairy tales, folktales, fiction, nonfiction, legends, fables, myths, poems, nursery rhymes, picture books, predictable books). (McREL 3)
- Knows setting, main characters, main events, sequence, narrator, and problems in stories. (McREL 4)
- Summarizes information found in texts (e.g., retells in own words). (McREL 5)

Objectives

Students

- Recognize a fairy tale and what makes it a fairy tale.
- Describe characters, and beginning, middle, and end of the story.
- Create a Tom Thumb puppet and retell the story.

Directions

1. The reading or school librarian teacher reads a Tom Thumb fairy tale.
2. Teachers lead a discussion on characters, beginning, middle, and end, and what made the story a fairy tale.
3. Under teachers' guidance, students answer their worksheet questions by illustrating or writing.
4. Students color and cut out Tom Thumb. For the thumb holder, students cut out the box strip that states the words "Tom Thumb." The thumb strip is attached to Tom Thumb for a thumb puppet, so the story can be acted out. Students act out the story in small groups.

Teaching Team

Reading and school librarian teachers.

Suggested Sources

Blair, Eric. *Tom Thumb.* Mankato, MN: Picture Window Books, 2011.
Carle, Eric. *Tom Thumb.* New York: Scholastic, 2011.
Grimm's Brothers. *Tom Thumb.* Updated 2015. Retrieved from http://www.grimmstories.com/en/grimm_fairy-tales/tom_thumb

Find an Award Book

Give an illustrator book trophy to the best illustrated easy book. Write the title of the book on the first line. Write the illustator on the second line. Illustrate the book in the box.

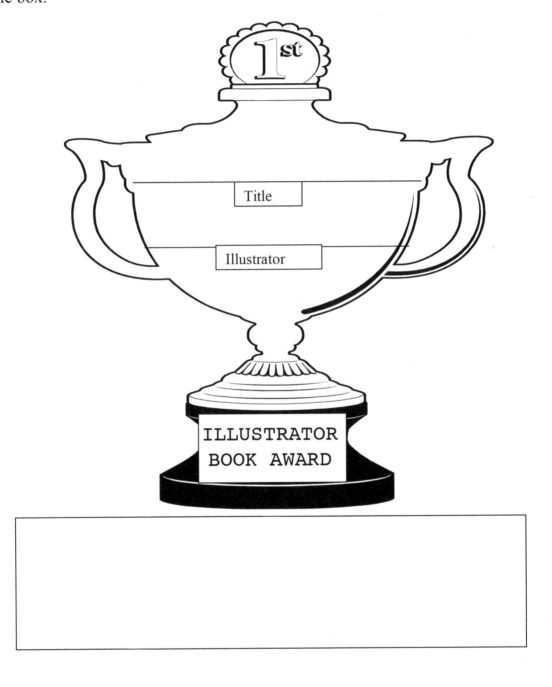

Title

Illustrator

ILLUSTRATOR BOOK AWARD

Find an Award Book

Standards

Student(s)

- Inquire, think critically, and gain knowledge. (AASL 1)
- Draw conclusions, make informed decisions, apply knowledge to new situations, and create new knowledge. (AASL 2)
- Share knowledge and participate ethically and productively as members of our democratic society. (AASL 3)
- Pursue personal and aesthetic growth. (AASL 4)
- Ask and answer such questions as who, what, where, when, why, and how to demonstrate understanding of key details in a text. (CCSS 1)
- Uses meaning clues (e.g., pictures, captions, illustrations, title, cover, headings, story structure, story topic) to aid comprehension and make predictions about content (e.g., action, events, character's behavior). (McREL 2)
- Reads a variety of familiar literary passages and texts (e.g., fairy tales, folktales, fiction, nonfiction, legends, fables, myths, poems, nursery rhymes, picture books, predictable books). (McREL 3)

Objectives

Students

- Recognize and illustrate a Caldecott award book.
- Identify and write the title and illustrator.

Directions

1. Worksheets are copied on card stock if the work will be displayed.
2. The school librarian discusses and defines the Caldecott award books and illustrators.
3. The reading teacher reads and shows two Caldecott award books. A discussion is led, asking, who, what, where about the book, and why the book is an award book.
4. The school librarian shows how to find Caldecott award books and displays some books.
5. With both teachers' assistance, student pairs select and examine a Caldecott book, and write the title and illustrator on the worksheet trophy. Students illustrate the book in the box under the trophy and lightly color the trophy.
6. If the worksheets were printed on card stock, the trophy and illustrated box are cut out as connected together, with the illustrated box folded so that the trophy can be free standing for a library display.

Teaching Team

Reading and school librarian teachers.

Suggested Source

American Librarian Association. *Caldecott Medal Winners, 1938–Present.* Updated 2016. Retrieved from http://www.ala.org/alsc/awardsgrants/bookmedia/caldecottmedal/caldecottwinners/caldecottmedal

Valentine Party

Get ready for a Valentine's Day school party. Read a book to get ideas.
Decorate and color this page. Add other Valentine party illustrations.
Put your illustrations together for a Valentine's Day card.
Finish the Valentine poem, and add the poem to your card.

Valentine's Day party at school,

Is cool.

Happy Valentine's Day

Valentine Party

Standards

Student(s)

- Inquire, think critically, and gain knowledge. (AASL 1)
- Draw conclusions, make informed decisions, apply knowledge to new situations, and create new knowledge. (AASL 2)
- Ask and answer such questions as who, what, where, when, why, and how to demonstrate understanding of the key details in a text. (CCSS 1)
- Identify the main purpose of a text, including what the author wants to answer, explain, or describe. (CCSS 7)
- Uses meaning clues (e.g., pictures, captions, illustrations, title, cover, headings, story structure, story topic) to aid comprehension and make predictions about content (e.g., action, events, character's behavior). (McREL 2)
- Knows setting, main characters, main events, sequence, narrator, and problems in stories. (McREL 4)
- Relates new information to prior knowledge and experience. (McREL 6)

Objectives

Students

- Summarize Valentine's Day party ideas.
- Illustrate different things needed for a Valentine's Day party.
- Complete the poem.

Directions

1. The reading and school librarian teachers read and show one or two Valentine's books that mention a Valentine's Day party. Teachers lead discussions on setting, events, author, and the author's purpose.
2. Under teacher's guidance, the class lists things to have for a classroom Valentine's Day party, as seen in the books and as related to what they know.
3. The teacher guides the class in completing the Valentine's Day worksheet poem.
4. Students create a Valentine's card from the worksheet colored illustrations, additional student illustrations, and the poem, as glued on construction paper. The card could be a party invitation.

Teaching Team

Reading and school librarian teachers.

Suggested Sources

Berenstain, Jan. *The Berenstain Bears' Valentine Party.* New York: HarperFestvial, 2008.
Friedman, Laurie B. *Ruby Valentine Saves the Day.* Minneapolis, MN: Carolrhoda Books, 2010.
Jennings, Sharon. *Franklin's Valentines.* Tonawanda, NY: Kids Can Press, 2013.
Schulman, Janet. *10 Valentine Friends: A Holiday Counting Book.* New York: Alfred A. Knopf, 2011.
Scotton, Rob. *Love, Splat.* New York: HarperCollins, 2008.

Fox and Crow Fable

The crow had cheese. The fox wanted it. Show or tell what happened to the fox.

What was the lesson (moral) from the story? _____

_____

_____

Fox and Crow Fable

Standards

Student(s)

- Inquire, think critically, and gain knowledge. (AASL 1)
- Draw conclusions, make informed decisions, apply knowledge to new situations, and create new knowledge. (AASL 2)
- Pursue personal and aesthetic growth. (AASL 4)
- Ask and answer such questions as who, what, where, when, why, and how to demonstrate understanding of key details in a text. (CCSS 1)
- Recount stories, including fables and folktales from diverse cultures, and determine their central message, lesson, or moral. (CCSS 2)
- [Reads] Hear a variety of familiar literary passages and texts (e.g., fairy tales, folktales, fiction, nonfiction, legends, fables, myths, poems, nursery rhymes, picture books, predictable books). (McREL 3)
- Knows setting, main characters, main events, sequence, narrator, and problems in stories. (McREL 4)
- Relates new information to prior knowledge and experience. (McREL 6)

Objectives

Students

- Recognize a fable.
- Explain character, setting, beginning, main, and ending events, and moral.
- Illustrate an event and write the moral.

Directions

1. The school librarian explains moral and fables, using students' prior knowledge.
2. The reading teacher reads "The Fox and the Crow" fable.
3. Reading and school librarian teachers guide student discussion on character, setting, beginning, main, and ending event, and the moral.
4. Teachers guide students as they draw the main event or main plot and write the moral.
5. Students share their answers with the class.

Teaching Team

Reading and school librarian teachers.

Suggested Sources

Mackinnon, Mairi. *The Fox and the Crow*. London, England: Usborne, 2007.
Marwood, Diane. *The Fox and the Crow*. New York: Crabtree, 2012.
Pinkney, Jerry. *Aesop's Fables*. New York: SeaStar Books, 2000.
Sneed, Brad. *Aesop's Fables—Retellings of 15 Fables from Aesop for Children*. New York: Dial, 2003.
Wiley, Melissa. *Fox and Crow Are Not Friends*. New York: Random House, 2012.

Soaring with Eagles

1. Describe the bald eagle:

What color is the beak? _____.

What color is the body? _____.

What color is the head? _____

2. Where do bald eagles make their homes? _____

_____

3. What do bald eagles eat? _____

4. Color the bald eagle and the flag. The bald eagle is a symbol for the United States. Add the U.S. flag to the eagle picture to make an eagle badge.

Soaring with Eagles

Standards

Student(s)

- Inquire, think critically, and gain knowledge. (AASL 1)
- Draw conclusions, make informed decisions, apply knowledge to new situations, and create new knowledge. (AASL 2)
- Pursue personal and aesthetic growth. (AASL 4)
- Ask and answer such questions as who, what, where, when, why, and how to demonstrate understanding of the key details in a text. (CCSS 6)
- Uses a variety of sources to gather information (e.g., informational books, pictures, charts, indexes, videos, television programs, guest speakers, Internet, own observation). (McREL 1)
- Uses meaning clues (e.g., pictures, captions, illustrations, title, cover, headings, story structure, story topic) to aid comprehension and make predictions about content (e.g., action, events, character's behavior). (McREL 2)
- Relates new information to prior knowledge and experience. (McREL 6)

Objectives

Students

- Research and state key facts about the bald eagle.
- Create a bald eagle badge.

Directions

1. The school librarian and social studies teachers discuss nonfiction, and read and show one to two bald eagle facts from a nonfiction book. They also discuss the fact that the eagle is a symbol for the United States.
2. The teachers guide small group research on the bald eagle, as students answer their worksheet questions by reading the text or viewing illustrations in simple nonfiction books and sources.
3. Students color their bald eagle according to their research and color the flag. They cut out and add the flag to their bald eagle picture for a badge.

Teaching Team

School librarian and social studies teachers.

Suggested Sources

Gaspar, Joe. *The Bald Eagle.* New York: PowerKids, 2014.
Herrington, Lisa M. *The Bald Eagle.* New York: Scholastic, 2015.
McDowell, Pamela. *Bald Eagles.* Mankato, MN: AV2 by Weigl, 2013.
Monroe, Tyler. *The Bald Eagle.* Mankato, MN: Capstone, 2014.
National Geographic Society. *Bald Eagles.* Updated 2015. Retrieved from http://kids.nationalgeographic.com/animals/bald-eagle/#bald-eagle-closeup.jpg
San Diego Zoo. *Bald Eagle.* Updated 2016. Retrieved from http://kids.sandiegozoo.org/animals/birds/bald-eagle

Frog Prince

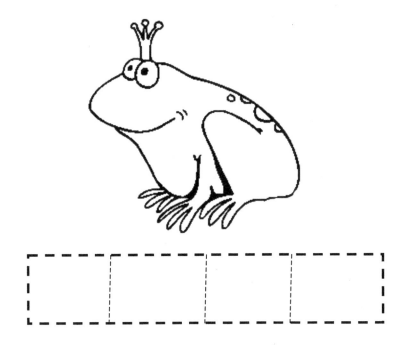

1. Who were the main characters? _____

2. What happened in the beginning of the story? _____

_____

3. In the pond, illustrate what happened in the end:

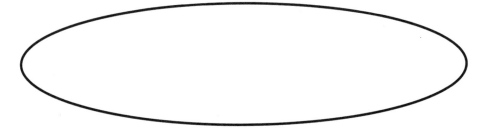

4. Color the frog, cut it out, and cut out the long strip. Fold on the dotted lines of the strip, and attach the strip to the frog so that the frog looks ready to hop.

Frog Prince

Standards

Student(s)

- Inquire, think critically, and gain knowledge. (AASL 1)
- Draw conclusions, make informed decisions, apply knowledge to new situations, and create new knowledge. (AASL 2)
- Share knowledge and participate ethically and productively as members of our democratic society. (AASL 3)
- Recount stories, including fables and folktales from diverse cultures, and determine their central message, lesson, or moral. (CCSS 2)
- Describe the overall structure of a story, including describing how the beginning introduces the story and the ending concludes the action. (CCSS 4)
- [Reads] Hear a variety of familiar literary passages and texts (e.g., fairy tales, folktales, fiction, nonfiction, legends, fables, myths, poems, nursery rhymes, picture books, predictable books). (McREL 3)
- Knows setting, main characters, main events, sequence, narrator, and problems in stories. (McREL 4)
- Summarizes information found in texts (e.g., retells in own words). (McREL 5)

Objectives

Students

- Recognize a fairy tale and understand what made it a fairy tale.
- Describe characters, and beginning, middle, and ending of the story.
- Create hopping frogs to retell the story.

Directions

1. The reading or school librarian teacher reads *The Frog Prince* tale.
2. Teachers discuss characters, setting, the beginning, ending, other major events of the stories, and what makes the story a fairy tale.
3. With guidance, students answer their worksheet questions, where students define characters and the beginning, and illustrate what happened in the end.
4. The art teacher guides students as they color and cut out the frog, and cut out the box strip. Students fold the paper strip on the dotted lines before attaching it to the end of the frog. The frog looks ready to hop. Students retell the story with their frogs.

Teaching Team

Art, reading, and school librarian teachers.

Suggested Sources

Blair, Eric. *The Frog Prince*. Mankato, MN: Picture Window Books, 2011.
Brothers, Grimm. *The Frog Prince*. Minneapolis, MN: Lerner, 2016.
Gardner, Sally. *The Frog Prince*. London: Orion Children's Books, 2011.
Urbanovic, Jackie. *Prince of a Frog*. New York: Orchard Books, 2015.

Cat's Story

It was lost at the library

Cat chewed a book

Read two fiction stories about a cat as the main character.

1. What is one cat story title? _____

2. What is the other cat story title? _____

3. Now pick one story and write about it. Write about the cat's adventure on the box lines around the larger cat. Write three to four sentences. Look at the smaller cat to see how to write the story.

Cat's Story

Standards

Student(s)

- Inquire, think critically, and gain knowledge. (AASL 1)
- Draw conclusions, make informed decisions, apply knowledge to new situations, and create new knowledge. (AASL 2)
- Ask and answer such questions as who, what, where, when, why, and how to demonstrate understanding of key details. (CCSS 1)
- Describe how words and phrases (e.g., regular beats, alliteration, rhymes, repeated lines) supply rhythm and meaning in a story, poem, or song. (CCSS 3)
- Describe the overall structure of a story, including describing how the beginning introduces the story and the ending concludes the action. (CCSS 4)
- [Reads] Hear a variety of familiar literary passages and texts (e.g., fairy tales, folktales, fiction, nonfiction, legends, fables, myths, poems, nursery rhymes, picture books, predictable books). (McREL 3)
- Knows setting, main characters, main events, sequence, narrator, and problems in stories. (McREL 4)

Objectives

Students

- Understand the similarities or differences of fiction books by the same author or illustrator.
- Define book titles.
- Paraphrase and write a cat story adventure.

Directions

1. Reading and school librarian teachers each read and show a cat fiction book by the same author or illustrator. The book titles and the author are written on the class board.
2. The teachers guide a class comparison of the books by asking what, when, and why, and by asking the story events.
3. With guidance, students list the two books' titles on their worksheets.
4. Students select one of the cat fiction books and write three to four sentences about a cat's adventure along the lines of the box around the larger cat. Students color the large cat.

Teaching Team

Reading and school librarian teachers.

Suggested Sources

Myron, Vicki. *Dewey: There's a Cat in the Library.* New York: Little Brown Books, 2009.
Myron, Vicki. *Dewey's Christmas at the Library.* New York: Little Brown Books, 2010.
Scotton, Rob. *Splat and the Cool School Trip.* New York: HarperCollins, 2013.
Scotton, Rob. *Splat the Cat: Christmas Countdown.* New York: HarperCollins, 2015.

Going Bananas Over Gorillas and Monkeys

 Gorillas and monkeys are alike and yet different

1. Do gorillas have tails? ---------

2. Where do gorillas live? --------

----

3. What do gorillas eat? ----------

----

4. Write another gorilla fact:

----

1. Do monkeys have tails? --------

2. Where do monkeys live? -------

----

3. What do monkeys eat? ---------

----

4. Write another monkey fact:

Draw or write how a gorilla and a monkey are alike:

Going Bananas Over Gorillas and Monkeys

Standards

Student(s)

- Inquire, think critically, and gain knowledge. (AASL 1)
- Draw conclusions, make informed decisions, apply knowledge to new situations, and create new knowledge. (AASL 2)
- Ask and answer such questions as who, what, where, when, why, and how to demonstrate understanding of the key details in a text. (CCSS 6)
- Identify the main purpose of a text, including what the author wants to answer, explain, or describe. (CCSS 7)
- Uses a variety of sources to gather information (e.g., informational books, pictures, charts, indexes, video, television programs, guest speakers, internet, own observation). (McREL 1)
- Uses meaning clues (e.g., pictures, captions, illustrations, title, cover, headings, story structure, story topic) to aid comprehension and make predictions about content (e.g., action, events, character's behavior). (McREL 2)
- Summarizes information found in texts (e.g., retells in own words). (McREL 5)

Objectives

Students

- Research and describe a gorilla and a monkey.
- Show the differences between gorillas and monkeys.

Directions

1. The reading teacher introduces the lesson by reading a fiction story about both a monkey and a gorilla. Students discuss the author's purpose.
2. The school librarian introduces and leads discussion on gorilla and monkey nonfiction books.
3. Teachers guide small groups as students read or examine nonfiction book illustrations to answer worksheet questions on the comparison and contrast of monkeys and gorillas.
4. Students color their worksheets. They write or draw other facts; time permitting.

Teaching Team

Reading and school librarian teachers.

Suggested Sources

Fiction

Lewis, Patrick. *Tugg and Teeny: Jungle Surprises*. Mankato, MN: Sleeping Bear Press, 2011.
Lewis, Patrick. *Tugg and Teeny: That's What Friends Are for*. Mankato, MN: Sleeping Bear Press, 2012.

Nonfiction

De La Bedoyere, Camilla. *The Wild Life of Monkeys*. Rosen, NY: Windmill Books, 2015.
Hansen, Grace. *Gorillas*. Mankato, MN: ABDO, 2014.
Riggs, Kate. *Gorillas*. New York: Creative Education, 2014.
Ryndak, Rob. *Monkeys*. Milwaukee, WI: Gareth Stevens Publishing, 2015.

Pig's Story Changed

Read and compare a different "Three Pigs" fairy tale that is not like the "Three Pigs" story you know. What would the three pigs say about their different story? Write two to three short lines that rhyme about the different story. Then illustrate the new story on the fence for the pigs.

Our Story Has Changed!

Pig's Story Changed

Standards

Student(s)

- Inquire, think critically, and gain knowledge. (AASL 1)
- Draw conclusions, make informed decisions, apply knowledge to new situations, and create new knowledge. (AASL 2)
- Share knowledge and participate ethically and productively as members of our democratic society. (AASL 3)
- Describe how words and phrases (e.g., regular beats, alliteration, rhymes, repeated lines) supply rhythm and meaning in a story, poem, or song. (CCSS 3)
- Describe the overall structure of a story, including describing how the beginning introduces the story and the ending concludes the action. (CCSS 4)
- Compare and contrast two or more versions of the same story (e.g., Cinderella stories) by different authors or from different cultures. (CCSS 5)
- [Reads] Hear a variety of familiar literary passages and texts (e.g., fairy tales, folktales, fiction, nonfiction, legends, fables, myths, poems, nursery rhymes, picture books, predictable books). (McREL 3)
- Knows setting, main characters, main events, sequence, narrator, and problems in stories. (McREL 4)

Objectives

Students

- Compare a traditional "Three Pigs" story with one or two other versions.
- Retell a "Three Pigs" version by creating a poem and illustrating.

Directions

1. The reading teacher reviews a familiar "Three Pigs" story, including discussing the beginning and ending.
2. The librarian and reading teachers read one or two other versions of the "Three Little Pigs."
3. The teachers lead discussions on the setting, main character, and plot comparisons.
4. With the teachers leading, the class creates a short two- to three-line rhyme poem of three to four words a line about a "Three Pigs" version. The poem is written on the class board.
5. Students write the class poem or create their own poem and illustrate the story.

Teaching Team

Reading and school librarian teachers.

Suggested Sources

Blackford, Andy. *The Three Little Pigs and the New Neighbor.* New York: Crabtree, 2014.
Brett, Jan. *The 3 Little Dassies.* New York: G. P. Putnam, 2010.
Cowley, Joy. *The Three Little Pigs.* Minneapolis, MN: Big & Small (Lerner), 2016.
Geist, Ken. *The Three Little Fish and the Big Bad Shark.* New York: Cartwheel Books, 2016.
Ketteman, Helen. *The Three Little Gators.* Mankato, MN: AV2 by Weigl, 2013.
Teague, Mark. *The Three Little Pigs and the Somewhat Bad Wolf.* London: Orchard Books, 2013.

April Showers

April showers in spring,

Makes the birds sing.

April showers makes things grow,

Flowers are all aglow.

Spring is here.

April Showers

Standards

Student(s)

- Inquire, think critically, and gain knowledge. (AASL 1)
- Draw conclusions, make informed decisions, apply knowledge to new situations, and create new knowledge. (AASL 2)
- Ask and answer such questions as who, what, where, when, why, and how to demonstrate understanding of key details in a text. (CCSS 6)
- Identify the main purpose of a text, including what the author wants to answer, explain, or describe. (CCSS 7)
- Uses a variety of sources to gather information (e.g., informational books, pictures, charts, indexes, videos, television programs, guest speakers, Internet, own observation). (McREL 1)
- [Reads] Hear a variety of familiar literary passages and texts (e.g., fairy tales, folktales, fiction, nonfiction, legends, fables, myths, poems, nursery rhymes, picture books, predictable books). (McREL 3)
- Relates new information to prior knowledge and experience. (McREL 6)

Objectives

Students

- Research and find facts about spring.
- Illustrate three facts about spring on the worksheet umbrella sections and create a pinwheel.

Directions

1. The science and school librarian teachers read and discuss small portions of books about spring.
2. The teachers guide small group spring research as students examine illustrations and text of simple nonfiction books. Students find four or more different things that occur in spring.
3. The art teacher guides students as they draw four colorful spring facts on the umbrella, and lightly color the umbrella. Students cut out the umbrella square, cut on the fine lines, and fold four points of the triangles to the center, and attach the points with a push pin to a pencil eraser head for a pinwheel.
4. Students recite the spring poem with their umbrella pinwheel.

Teaching Team

Art, science, and school librarian teachers.

Suggested Sources

Carole, Bonnie. *Red and Green in Spring*. Vero Beach, FL: Rourke Educational Media, 2015.

Clay, Kathryn. *Rain Showers*. Mankato, MN: Capstone, 2016.

Herrington, Lisa. *How Do You Know It's Spring?* New York: Children's Press, 2014.

Paper Source. *How to Make Pinwheels*. Updated 2015. Retrieved from http://www.paper source.com/howto/ideas/pinwheel.html

Rockwell, Anne. *My Spring Robin*. New York: Aladdin, 2015.

Chapter 4

Third-Grade Lesson Plans

The following interactive standards-backed third-grade lessons will meet the needs of today's students. The lessons are set to different standards in the desire to meet the school librarians' state or school library, Common Core State Standards (CCSS) or McREL literacy, or English language arts standards, which include the proverbial American Association of School Librarians (AASL) standards.

The quality-researched AASL standards, CCSS, and the McREL Compendium of Standards and Benchmarks are applied with each school library lesson to enhance school library instruction and aid students in achieving skills. The parts of the standards chosen for this book were those that were the most essential for library instruction and could be met in the lesson time allotment of twenty minutes. The standards may be used together as given, individually, or lessons may be set to other quality standards.

As based on standards, student learning objectives are given for each lesson. Lessons include students working individually or with others for more efficient student learning. Team teaching is recommended, as more can be accomplished when working together. Quality-researched resources are suggested. The streamlined standards-based lessons for the busy school librarian will provide interactive and successful student learning. The AASL standards are stated in the first chapter as they are universally seen with all lessons in some way. The following McREL and CCSS standards are used specifically with this grade level.

Third-Grade Library Standards with Language Arts Benchmarks from McREL Compendium of Standards and Benchmarks and Common Core Language Arts Literacy Standards (CCSS)

Third-grade students:

*Third-Grade Common Core (Literacy), Reading Literature

1. Ask and answer questions to demonstrate understanding of a text, referring explicitly to the text as the basis for the answers. (CCSS.ELA-Literacy.RL.3.1)

2. Recount stories, including fables, folktales, and myths from diverse cultures; determine the central message, lesson, or moral; and explain how it is conveyed through key details in the text. (CCSS.ELA-Literacy.RL.3.2)

3. Describe characters in a story (e.g., their traits, motivations, or feelings) and explain how their actions contribute to the sequence of events. (CCSS.ELA-Literacy.RL.3.3)

4. Refer to parts of stories, dramas, and poems, when writing or speaking about a text, using terms such as chapter, scene, and stanza, and describe how each successive part builds on earlier sections. (CCSS.ELA-Literacy.RL.3.5)

*Third-Grade Common Core (Literacy), Reading Informational Texts

5. Ask and answer questions to demonstrate understanding of a text, referring explicitly to the text for answers. (CCSS.ElA-Literacy.RI.3.1)

6. Use information gained from illustrations (e.g., maps, photographs) and the words in a text to demonstrate understanding of the text (e.g., where, when, why, and how key events occur). (CCSS.ELA-Literacy.RI.3.7)

Governors Association Center for Best Practices and Council of Chief State School Officers. *Common Core State Standards (Literacy)*. Washington, DC: National Governors Association Center for Best Practices and Council of Chief State School Officers, 2010. Retrieved from http://www.corestandards.org/

McREL Compendium of Standards and Benchmarks Language Arts Writing Standards and Benchmarks (Grades 3–5)

*Gather and use information for research purposes. Standard 4

1. Use a variety of strategies to plan research (e.g., identify possible topic by brainstorming, listing questions, and using idea webs; organize prior knowledge about a topic; develop a course of action; determine how to locate necessary information). (McREL)
2. Use encyclopedias to gather information for research topics. (McREL)
3. Use electronic media to gather information (e.g., databases, Internet, CD-ROM, television shows, videos, pull-down menus, word searches). (McREL)

McREL Compendium of Standards and Benchmarks Language Arts Reading Standards and Benchmarks (Grades 3–5)

*Use the general skills and strategies of the reading process. Standard 5

4. Use word reference materials (e.g., glossary, dictionary, thesaurus) to determine the meaning, pronunciation, and derivations of unknown words. (McREL)

*Use skills and strategies to read a variety of literary texts. Standard 6

5. Read a variety of literary passages and texts (e.g., fairy tales, folktales, fiction, nonfiction, myths, poems, fables, fantasies, historical fiction, biographies, autobiographies, chapter books). (McREL)
6. Understand the basic concept of plot (e.g., main problem, conflict, resolution, cause-and-effect). (McREL)
7. Know themes that recur across literary works. (McREL)

*Use skills and strategies to read a variety of informational texts. Standard 7

8. Use the various parts of a book (e.g., index, table of contents, glossary, appendix, preface) to locate information. (McREL)
9. Summarize and paraphrase information in texts (e.g., include the main idea and significant supporting details of a reading selection). (McREL)

McREL. *Language Arts Standards*, 2015. Retrieved from http://www2.mcrel.org/compendium/standard

Dogs Go to School

Dogs go to the library to read,

Reading is what they need.

Read a poem on dogs at school,

The poem will be cool.

After reading poems about dogs at school or elsewhere, describe a favorite dog or school poem from a book:

1. What is the poem title? _____

2. Who wrote the poem? _____

3. What is the name of the poem book? _____

4. Tell about the poem: _____

_____

_____

5. Now write your own short poem on dogs or school. Write four rhyming lines. Use a rhyming dictionary or other similar rhyming source to find more words for the poem.

_____

_____

_____

_____

_____

From *Standards-Based Lesson Plans for the Busy Elementary School Librarian* by Joyce Keeling. Santa Barbara, CA: Libraries Unlimited. Copyright © 2017.

Dogs Go to School

Standards

Student(s)

- Inquire, think critically, and gain knowledge. (AASL 1)
- Draw conclusions, make informed decisions, apply knowledge to new situations, and create new knowledge. (AASL 2)
- Share knowledge and participate ethically and productively as members of our democratic society. (AASL 3)
- Pursue personal and aesthetic growth. (AASL 4)
- Refer to parts of stories, dramas, and poems, when writing or speaking about a text, using terms such as chapter, scene, and stanza, and describe how each successive part builds on earlier sections. (CCSS 4)
- Uses word reference materials (e.g., glossary, dictionary, thesaurus) to determine the meaning, pronunciation, and derivations of unknown words. (McREL 4)
- Reads a variety of literary passages and texts (e.g., fairy tales, folktales, fiction, nonfiction, myths, poems, fables, fantasies, historical fiction, biographies, autobiographies, chapter books). (McREL 5)

Objectives

Students

- Select and describe a funny poem about dogs and/or school.
- Show how to use a rhyming dictionary.
- Compose a poem.

Directions

1. The school librarian shows how to use a rhyming dictionary in print or online.
2. The reading and school librarian teachers read funny poems about dogs in school and funny dog or school poems. Teachers recommend some poem books on those topics.
3. Student pairs find, read, and describe a funny dog, school, or other such poem and its source.
4. The teachers assist student pairs as students write their own dog or school rhyming poem using a rhyming dictionary or similar source. Students write a four-line poem.

Teaching Team

Reading and school librarian teachers.

Suggested Sources

Foster, John. *Oxford Children's Rhyming Dictionary*. Cary, NC: Oxford University Press, 2014.

Lansky, Bruce. *My Dog Ate My Homework*. Minnetonka, MN: Meadowbrook Press, 2009.

MacLachlan, Patricia. *Didn't Do It*. New York: Katherine Tegen Books (HarperCollins), 2010.

Rhyme Zone. *RhymeZone Rhyming Dictionary and Thesaurus*. Updated 2016. Retrieved from http://www.rhymezone.com

Schmidt, Amy. *Back to Dog-Gone School*. New York: Random House, 2016.

Schmidt, Amy. *Dog-Gone School*. New York: Random House, 2013.

Library Tic Tac Toe

X	O	X
X	X	O
O	X	O

Library

Library Tic Tac Toe

Standards

Student(s)

- Inquire, think critically, and gain knowledge. (AASL 1)
- Draw conclusions, make informed decisions, apply knowledge to new situations, and create new knowledge. (AASL 2)
- Share knowledge and participate ethically and productively as members of our democratic society. (AASL 3)
- Ask and answer questions to demonstrate understanding of a text, referring explicitly to the text as the basis for the answers. (CCSS 5)
- Uses the various parts of a book (e.g., index, table of contents, glossary, appendix, preface) to locate information. (McREL 8)

Objectives

Students

- Review library sections, book care, and book parts by playing library tic tac toe.

Directions

1. The school librarian and reading teachers lead a discussion on book parts (table of contents, index, title page, cover, spine, author, illustrator), book care (return books on time, do not write on or tear library books), and library areas (fiction, nonfiction, easy books).
2. The teachers divide the class into an X and O team. When a team answers a library tic tac toe question first and correctly, they place their X or O on the board drawn tic tac toe and on the student tic tac toe sheets until a team places three Xs or Os in a row to win.
3. Suggested teacher-given questions are as follows: (1) What are the pages in a book that give the chapter pages? (2) What is the name of the page of a book that tells the author, title, illustrator, publisher, and publishing place? (3) Who is the person that writes a book? (4) Who is the person that creates the pictures or illustrations? (5) What part of the book shows the spine label? (6) What is on a cover of a book? (7) Is it important to return books on time and why? (8) What is one important library book care tip? (9) Define fiction, and explain why there is an "F" for fiction on book spines. (10) What is nonfiction? (11) What are Easy books? (12) How are fiction books put on library shelves? (13) How are nonfiction books found?

Teaching Team

Reading and school librarian teachers.

Suggested Sources

None needed.

Stone Soup

On the outside of the soup pot, list scattered words to describe the story. In the steamy, wavy lines, list the story characters. Under the soup, write a two-line rhyme to describe the moral.

Stone Soup

Standards

Student(s)

- Draw conclusions, make informed decisions, apply knowledge to new situations, and create new knowledge. (AASL 2)
- Recount stories, including fables, folktales, and myths, from diverse cultures; determine the central message, lesson, or moral; and explain how it is conveyed through key details in the text. (CCSS 2)
- Describe characters in a story (e.g., their traits, motivations, or feelings) and explain how their actions contribute to the sequence of events. (CCSS 3)
- Refer to parts of stories, dramas, and poems, when writing or speaking about a text, using terms such as chapter, scene, and stanza, and describe how each successive part builds on earlier sections. (CCSS 4)
- Reads a variety of literary passages and texts (e.g., fairy tales, folktales, fiction, nonfiction, myths, poems, fables, fantasies, historical fiction, biographies, autobiographies, chapter books). (McREL 5)
- Understands the basic concept of plot (e.g., main problem, conflict, resolution, cause-and-effect). (McREL 6)

Objectives

Students

- Define characters, moral, and story events.
- Compose a two-line rhyming poem about the moral of the story.

Directions

1. The school librarian reads *Stone Soup*.
2. The reading teacher guides discussion on story events, character, and moral.
3. The teachers guide the class listing of descriptive words about the story and the characters.
4. The class generates ideas for a two-line poem on the moral, from the list of descriptive words. Students write a two-line poem on the moral or use the class-generated poem.
5. The reading teacher reads and compares another *Stone Soup* version.

Teaching Team

Reading and school librarian teachers.

Suggested Sources

Brown, Marcia. *Stone Soup* [CD]. Danbury, CT: Weston Woods, 2003.
Glaser, Linda. *Stone Soup with Matzoh Balls*: *A Passover Tale in Chelm*. Park Ridge, IL: Albert Whitman & Company, 2014.
Jorisch, Stephane. *The Real Story of Stone Soup*. New York: Dutton, 2007.
Kimmel, Eric. *Cactus Soup*. New York: Two Lions, 2004.
Muth, Jon. *Stone Soup*. New York: Scholastic, 2003.

Subject, Author, Title

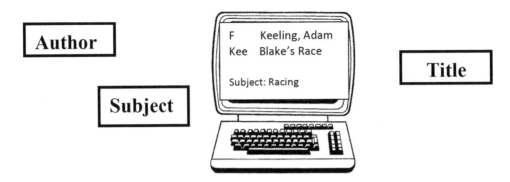

Author

Subject

F   Keeling, Adam
Kee Blake's Race

Subject: Racing

Title

Search for library books, using the online card catalog. The three major ways to search for a library book are by title, subject, and author searching.

Click on **title** (search)

1. Type in *Diary of a Wimpy Kid*. How many books have the title of *Diary of a Wimpy Kid* in the library? _____

Click on **author** (search)

2. Type in the author's last name of Roald Dahl. What is the title of one book by Dahl in the library? _____

Click on **subject** (search), and type in dogs to find fiction and nonfiction books on dogs

3. What is the title of a <u>fiction</u> book on dogs? _____
_____ Call number:

4. What is the title of a <u>nonfiction</u> book on dogs? _____
_____ Call number:

5. In your own thoughts, explain the purpose of the card catalog: _____
_____
_____

6. Find a book that you would like to read in the card catalog. What is the title? _____
_____ Call number:

Subject, Author, Title

Standards

Student(s)

- Inquire, think critically, and gain knowledge. (AASL 1)
- Draw conclusions, make informed decisions, apply knowledge to new situations, and create new knowledge. (AASL 2)
- Share knowledge and participate ethically and productively as members of our democratic society. (AASL 3)
- Pursue personal and aesthetic growth. (AASL 4)
- Use information gained from illustrations (e.g., maps, photographs) and the words in a text to demonstrate understanding of the text (e.g., where, when, why, and how key events occur). (CCSS 6)
- Use electronic media to gather information (e.g., databases, Internet, CD-ROM, television shows, videos, pull-down menus, word searches). (McREL 3)

Objectives

Students

- Recognize subject, author, and title library online catalog searching.
- Search the online catalog to answer worksheet questions.

Directions

1. The school librarian teacher shows students how to search by subject, author, and title using the library's online catalog.
2. The school librarian and reading teachers assist student pairs or small groups, as students use the online catalog to answer the worksheets.

Teaching Team

Reading and school librarian teachers.

Suggested Sources

OCLC. *Online World Libraries*. Updated 2016. Retrieved from http://www.worldcat.org

Those Bones

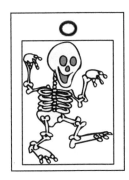

Research the human skeleton and answer the following questions in full sentences. After the questions are answered, the top skeleton square can be cut out for a key chain.

1. How many bones are in the human body?

2. What are two purposes for the skeleton?

3. What are at least two ways to build strong bones?

4. Draw lines and label _____ major bones of the following X-ray of the skeleton.

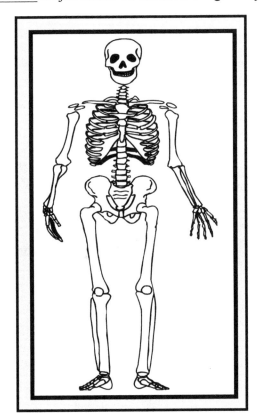

Those Bones

Standards

Student(s)

- Inquire, think critically, and gain knowledge. (AASL 1)
- Draw conclusions, make informed decisions, apply knowledge to new situations, and create new knowledge. (AASL 2)
- Share knowledge and participate ethically and productively as members of our democratic society. (AASL 3)
- Ask and answer questions to demonstrate understanding of a text, referring explicitly to the text for answers. (CCSS 5)
- Use information gained from illustrations (e.g., maps, photographs) and the words in a text to demonstrate understanding of the text (e.g., where, when, why, and how key events occur. (CCSS 6)
- Uses electronic media to gather information (e.g., databases, Internet, CD-ROM, television shows, videos, pull-down menus, word searches). (McREL 3)
- Summarizes and paraphrases information in texts (e.g., includes the main idea and significant supporting details of a reading selection). (McREL 9)

Objectives

Students

- Research the human skeletal system from nonfiction sources.
- Label some bones of the human skeleton.

Directions

1. The worksheet is copied on card stock.
2. The school librarian reads a humorous book on human bones like *Dem Bones* or other similar book. The school librarian also introduces nonfiction sources and Internet sites on bones.
3. The science teacher tells the class how many major bones students should find and label.
4. As guided by teachers, student pairs research and answer worksheet questions.
5. Students create a skeleton key chain by cutting out the top skeleton picture.

Teaching Team

Science and school librarian teachers.

Suggested Sources

Barner, Bob. *Dem Bones* [CD & Book]. Norwalk, CT: Weston Woods, 2002.

Dorling Kindersley. *Human Skeleton for Kids*. Updated 2015. Retrieved from http://www. dkfindout.com/us/human-body/skeleton-and-bones/

Loria, Laura. *The Bones in Your Body*. New York: Britannica Educational Publishing, 2015.

Nemours Foundation. *Your Bones*. Updated 2015. Retrieved from http://kidshealth.org/kid/htbw/ bones.html

Roza, Greg. *The Skeletal System*. Milwaukee, WI: Gareth Stevens Publishing, 2012.

Schoenberg, Jane. *My Bodywork: Songs about Your Bones, Muscles, Heart and More!* [CD & Book]. New York: Crocodile Books, 2005.

Sullivan, Jody. *The Human Skeleton*. Mankato, MN: Capstone, 2009.

Wild North America

Research a North American wild animal.

Circle the animal you will research: deer, raccoon, beaver, or squirrel.

1. Find a book on your animal. From looking at the table of contents of the book, list one or two chapters that are interesting: _____

_____

2. Now, find two subjects from the index of your animal book that look interesting. List those subjects:_____

3. The index and table of contents will lead to facts, so use them. Find some facts about your chosen animal. Neatly write an original five-sentence paragraph about your animal.

_____

_____

_____

_____

_____

_____

4. Find and print an online copyright free picture of the animal. Display your picture and paragraph.

Wild North America

Standards

Student(s)

- Inquire, think critically, and gain knowledge. (AASL 1)
- Draw conclusions, make informed decisions, apply knowledge to new situations, and create new knowledge. (AASL 2)
- Ask and answer questions to demonstrate understanding of text, referring explicitly to the text for answers. (CCSS 5)
- Uses a variety of strategies to plan research (e.g., identifies possible topic by brainstorming, listing questions, using idea webs; organizes prior knowledge about a topic; develop a course of action; determines how to locate necessary information). (McREL 1)
- Use the various parts of a book (e.g., index, table of contents, glossary, appendix, preface) to locate information. (McREL 8)

Objectives

Students

- Gather ideas about a North American animal, while using the table of contents and index.
- Summarize and write a paragraph.

Directions

1. The science teacher briefly introduces the North American deer, raccoon, squirrel, and beaver.
2. To narrow down researching, the school librarian guides research by showing the use of the table of contents and index.
3. The librarian and social studies teachers guide students in research of a student-chosen North American wild animal, as students use the table of contents and index to first gather ideas. Then when students finish researching, they write an original five-sentence paragraph.
4. The teachers guide students when locating a royalty-free online animal picture (iclipart).
5. Students display their picture and paragraphs in the library. This lesson takes two lesson times.

Teaching Team

Science and school librarian teachers.

Suggested Sources

Berne, Emma Carlson. *Raccoons*. New York: PowerKids Press, 2015.
Jacobs, Lee. *Beaver.* Farmington Hills, MN: Gale, 2003.
O'Sullivan, Elizabeth. *Beavers*. Minneapolis, MN: Lerner, 2007.
Petrie, Kristin. *Raccoons*. Mankato, MN: ABDO, 2015.
Petrie, Kristin. *Squirrels*. Mankato, MN: ABDO, 2015.
Triet, Trudi Strain. *Squirrels*. New York: Cavendish, 2012.
Webster, Christine. *Deer*. Mankato, MN: AV2 Weigl, 2013.
Wil, Mara. *Deer.* New York: Cavendish, 2014.
Vital Imagery. *iclipartforschools*. Updated 2014. Retrieved from http://schools.iclipart.com

Sacagawea

Sacagawea was a Shoshone Native American Indian woman who helped Lewis and Clark. Put yourself in her moccasins and write at least three sentences around her following home. Write about her life in her words. Her words have been started. Continue her words by writing around the picture.

I am called Sacagawea.

Sacagawea

Standards

Student(s)

- Inquire, think critically, and gain knowledge. (AASL 1)
- Draw conclusions, make informed decisions, apply knowledge to new situations, and create new knowledge. (AASL 2)
- Share knowledge and participate ethically and productively as members of our democratic society. (AASL 3)
- Ask and answer questions to demonstrate understanding of a text, referring explicitly to the text for answers. (CCSS 5)
- Use information gained from illustrations (e.g., maps, photographs) and the words in a text to demonstrate understanding of the text (e.g., where, when, why, and how key events occur). (CCSS 6)
- Uses a variety of strategies to plan research (e.g., identifies possible topic by brainstorming, listing questions, using idea webs; organizes prior knowledge about a topic; develops a course of action; determines how to locate necessary information). (McREL 1)
- Summarizes and paraphrases information in texts (e.g., includes the main idea and significant supporting details of a reading selection. (McREL 9)

Objectives

Students

- Research text and illustrations about Sacagawea.
- Summarize and paraphrase at least three facts.

Directions

1. The social studies teacher gives a brief overview of Sacagawea.
2. The school librarian introduces Sacagawea resources.
3. With teachers' guidance, student small groups research Sacagawea and then paraphrase at least three facts around the tepee home of Sacagawea as if the words would be told in her words.
4. Students color their sheets and share their research.

Teaching Team

School librarian and social studies teachers.

Suggested Sources

Labrecque, Ellen. *What's Your Story, Sacagawea?* Minneapolis, MN: Lerner Publications, 2016.
Lynette, Rachel. *Sacagawea.* New York: PowerKids Press, 2014.
Milton, Joyce. *Sacagawea: Her True Story.* New York: Penguin, 2011.
Nelson, Maria. *The Life of Sacagawea.* Milwaukee, WI: Gareth Stephens Publishing, 2012.
Norwich, Grace. *I Am Sacagawea.* New York: Scholastic, 2012.

Mosquitoes

1. Look at the title page and list title, author, illustrator, publisher, and publishing place below.

Title: _____

Author: _____

Illustrator: _____ Publisher: _____

Publishing Place: _____

2. Tell about the story by illustrating it in the box. In the box below, draw a story event with the main character and setting. Then cut on the dotted line, cut out the mosquito, glue the paper strip vertically to the mosquito, and put the mosquito in the cut line, so it flies around the main character.

Mosquitoes

Standards

Student(s)

- Inquire, think critically, and gain knowledge. (AASL 1)
- Draw conclusions, make informed decisions, apply knowledge to new situations, and create new knowledge. (AASL 2)
- Recount stories, including fables, folktales, and myths, from diverse cultures; determine the central message, lesson, or moral; and explain how it is conveyed through key details in the text. (CCSS 2)
- Describe characters in a story (e.g., their traits, motivations, or feelings) and explain how their actions contribute to the sequence of events. (CCSS 3)
- Reads a variety of literacy passages and texts (e.g., fairy tales, folktales, fiction, nonfiction, myths, poems, fables, fantasies, historical fiction, biographies). (McREL 5)
- Understands the basic concept of plot (e.g., main problem, conflict, resolution, cause-and-effect). (McREL 6)

Objectives

Students

- Analyze a folklore story.
- Discuss and illustrate the main event, setting, and character to recount the story.
- List title page facts.

Directions

1. After writing title page facts on the board, the reading teacher reads a mosquito folklore story.
2. The school librarian guides class discussion on story events, setting, and character.
3. The librarian and reading teachers guide students to title page answers.
4. The art teacher guides student illustrations of plot, character, and setting to recount the story. Students cut out the mosquito and paper strip. The paper strip is bent at the small line and then affixed vertically to the mosquito. Students cut on the dotted line around the story box and place the mosquito in the dotted line, so that the mosquito flies around the main character.
5. If time, students hear another mosquito folklore story or see the DVD.

Teaching Team

Art, reading, and school librarian teachers.

Suggested Sources

Aardema, Verna. *Why Mosquitoes Buzz in People's Ears.* Stamford, CT: Weekly Reader Books, 2004.

Carlos, Kelly. *Abuelito Swallowed a Mosquito*! New York: Create Space, 2015.

Simpson, Caroll. *The First Mosquito.* Phoenix, AZ: Heritage House Publishing, 2015.

Weston Woods. *Why Mosquitoes Buzz in People's Ears and Other Caldecott Classics* [DVD]. Norwalk, CT: Weston Woods, 2002.

Sleighing a Pioneer Christmas

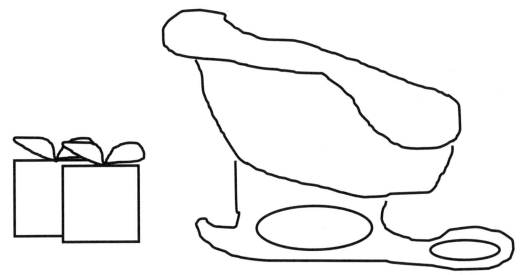

A pioneer Christmas may have a sleigh. Read a story about a pioneer Christmas.

1. What is the story title?

2. Who is the author?

3. Where did the story take place?

4. What was the main plot of the story?

5. What is the theme?

6. According to the book, what is a way that pioneers lived that is different than the way you live?

7. Either draw or write about a Christmas gift told in the story.

8. Color, cut out the sleigh and gifts, and glue the gifts on the sleigh for a sleigh gift tag.

From *Standards-Based Lesson Plans for the Busy Elementary School Librarian* by Joyce Keeling. Santa Barbara, CA: Libraries Unlimited. Copyright © 2017.

Sleighing a Pioneer Christmas

Standards

Student(s)

- Inquire, think critically, and gain knowledge. (AASL 1)
- Draw conclusions, make informed decisions, apply knowledge to new situations, and create new knowledge. (AASL 2)
- Share knowledge and participate ethically and productively as members of our democratic society. (AASL 3)
- Pursue personal and aesthetic growth. (AASL 4)
- Ask and answer questions to demonstrate understanding of a text, referring explicitly to the text as the basis for answers. (CCSS 1)
- Reads a variety of literary passages and texts (e.g., fairy tales, folktales, fiction, nonfiction, myths, poems, fables, fantasies, historical fiction, biographies, autobiographies, chapter books). (McREL 5)
- Understands the basic concept of plot (e.g., main problem, conflict, resolution, cause-and-effect). (McREL 6)
- Knows themes that recur across literary works. (McREL 7)

Objectives

Students

- Analyze a pioneer Christmas story.
- Discuss and write setting, main plot, theme, and compare pioneer life to today.

Directions

1. The reading and school librarian teachers read and show a pioneer Christmas-type story. Teachers lead discussion on setting, main plot, theme, and characters.
2. Under the teachers' guidance, students discuss and compare the pioneer way of living with the students' way of living today.
3. With teachers' assistance, students answer the worksheet questions on the book title, author, setting, main plot, theme, pioneer way of living, and the Christmas gift in the story.
4. With the art teacher's assistance, students color the sleigh and gifts and attach the gifts to the sleigh for a holiday gift tag.

Teaching Team

Art, reading, and school librarian teachers.

Suggested Sources

Greenwood, Barbara. *Pioneer Christmas, Celebrating in the Backwoods in 1841.* Tonawanda, NY: Kids Can Press, 2003.

Wilder, Laura Ingalls. *Christmas in the Big Woods (My First Little House Books).* Paradise, CA: Paw Prints, 2008.

Wilder, Laura Ingalls. *A Little House Christmas Treasury. Festive Holiday Stories.* New York: HarperCollins, 2005.

Library Dreidel

Library Dreidel

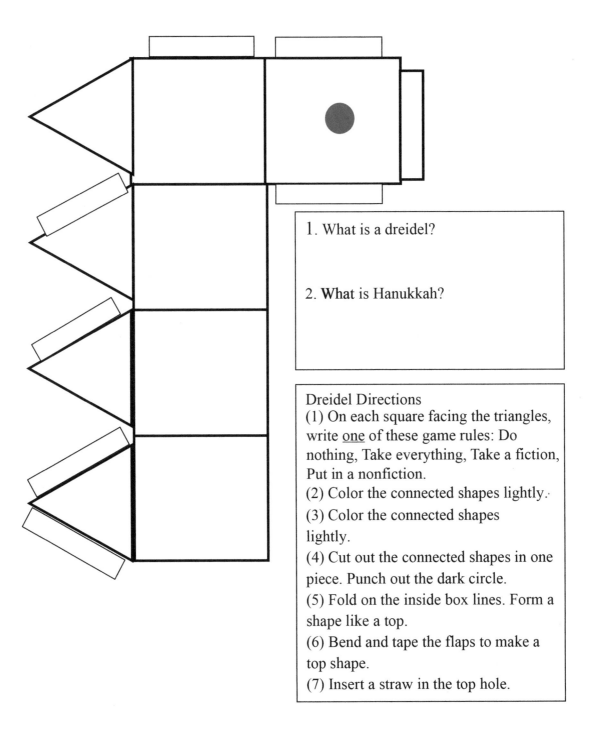

1. What is a dreidel?

2. **What** is Hanukkah?

Dreidel Directions
(1) On each square facing the triangles, write <u>one</u> of these game rules: Do nothing, Take everything, Take a fiction, Put in a nonfiction.
(2) Color the connected shapes lightly.
(3) Color the connected shapes lightly.
(4) Cut out the connected shapes in one piece. Punch out the dark circle.
(5) Fold on the inside box lines. Form a shape like a top.
(6) Bend and tape the flaps to make a top shape.
(7) Insert a straw in the top hole.

From *Standards-Based Lesson Plans for the Busy Elementary School Librarian* by Joyce Keeling. Santa Barbara, CA: Libraries Unlimited. Copyright © 2017.

Library Dreidel

Standards

Student(s)

- Inquire, think critically, and gain knowledge. (AASL 1)
- Draw conclusions, make informed decisions, apply knowledge to new situations, and create new knowledge. (AASL 2)
- Recount stories, including fables, folktales, and myths, from diverse cultures; determine the central message, lesson, or moral; and explain how it is conveyed through key details in the text. (CCSS 2)
- Ask and answer questions to demonstrate understanding of a text, referring explicitly to the text for answers. (CCSS 5)
- Reads a variety of literary passages and texts (e.g., fairy tales, folktales, fiction, nonfiction, myths, poems, fables, fantasies, historical fiction, biographies, autobiographies, chapter books). (McREL 5)

Objectives

Students

- Define Hanukkah and the dreidel.
- Make a dreidel in order to play the Library Dreidel game.

Directions

1. The worksheet should be copied on card stock.
2. The reading teacher discusses a Hanukkah source for a Hanukkah and a dreidel definition.
3. The school librarian reads and discusses a simple dreidel fiction book.
4. Students answer the worksheet questions on the definition of Hanukkah and the dreidel.
5. The art teacher helps students lightly color, cut out, fold, tape, and create a dreidel. A half straw is stuck in the dreidel middle.
6. Student groups will play Library Dreidel where a small pile of nonfiction and fiction books are set in the middle, students have books, and spin the dreidel to see what to do with the books.

Teaching Team

Art, reading, and school librarian teachers.

Suggested Sources

Fiction

Barash, Chris. *Is It Hanukkah Yet?* Park Ridge, IL: Albert Whitman & Company, 2015.
Levine, Abby. *This Is the Dreidel.* Mankato, MN: AV2 Weigl, 2013.
Simpson, Martha Seif. *The Dreidel That Wouldn't Spin: A Toyshop Tale of Hanukkah.* Bloomington, IN: Wisdom Tales Press, 2014.

Nonfiction

Dickmann, Nancy. *Hanukkah.* Portsmouth, NH: Heinemann, 2011.
Felix, Rebecca. *We Celebrate Hanukkah in Winter.* Ann Arbor, MI: Cherry Lake Pub., 2015.

Sleeping Beauty

ZZZZZ...

Review Grimm's *Sleeping Beauty* story. Then read another *Sleeping Beauty* version and discuss it.

1. What things show that the stories are fairy tales? Describe at least two or more things.

_____

_____

_____

2. How were the two story tale versions different? _____

_____

_____

3. Change the story ending to make it funny. What if the prince was tired and just slept too? Who would wake up Sleeping Beauty? _____

_____

_____

_____

4. Illustrate your story by making changes to the illustration on this page and share your story with others.

Sleeping Beauty

Standards

Student(s)

- Inquire, think critically, and gain knowledge. (AASL 1)
- Draw conclusions, make informed decisions, apply knowledge to new situations, and create new knowledge. (AASL 2)
- Share knowledge and participate ethically and productively as members of our democratic society. (AASL 3)
- Ask and answer questions to demonstrate understanding of a text, referring explicitly to the text as the basis for the answers. (CCSS 1)
- Recount stories, including fables, folktales, and myths, from diverse cultures; determine the central message, lesson, or moral; and explain how it is conveyed through key details in the text. (CCSS 2)
- Reads a variety of literary passages and texts (e.g., fairy tales, folktales, fiction, nonfiction, myths, poems, fables, fantasies, historical fiction, biographies, autobiographies, chapter books). (McREL 5)
- Understands the basic concept of plot (e.g., main problem, conflict, resolution, cause-and-effect). (McREL 6)

Objectives

Students

- Define a fairy tale.
- Compare plot, characters, and settings of two versions of the same fairy tale.
- Write a humorous ending.

Directions

1. The school librarian reviews and discusses the traditional *Sleeping Beauty* written by Grimm.
2. The reading teacher reads and discusses a different *Sleeping Beauty* version.
3. Teachers guide class discussion of the plot, character, and setting comparisons.
4. Both teachers guide the class as students compare the two story versions on their worksheets.
5. Small groups write a humorous ending.
6. Students illustrate their new story at the top of their worksheets and share their new stories.

Teaching Team

Reading and school librarian teachers.

Suggested Sources

Bardhan-Quallen, Sudipta. *Snoring Beauty.* New York: HarperCollins, 2014.
Cowley, Joy. *Sleeping Beauty.* Minneapolis, MN: Big & Small (Lerner), 2015.
Dwyer, Mindy. *Alaska's Sleeping Beauty.* Seattle, WA: Sasquatch Books, 2014.
Grimm, Jacob. *Sleeping Beauty.* New York: NorthSouth, 2012.
Hoffman, Mary. *First Book of Fairy Tales.* New York: DK Publishing, 2006.
Martin, Powell. *Sleeping Beauty: The Graphic Novel.* Mankato, MN: Stone Arch Books, 2009.
Smallman, Steve. *Get Some Rest, Sleeping Beauty!* Edina, MA: QEB, 2015.

Casey Jones

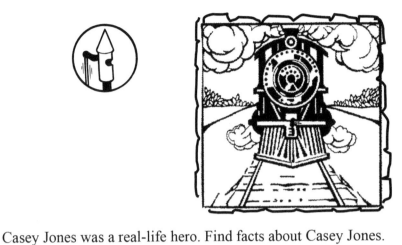

Casey Jones was a real-life hero. Find facts about Casey Jones.

1. Describe Casey Jones. _____

_____

2. Why was the time important for Casey Jones? _____

_____

_____

_____

3. What made Casey Jones a legend? _____

_____

_____

_____

4. Create a postage-type stamp of Casey Jones by using the above pictures and by adding other details.

Casey Jones

Standards

Student(s)

- Inquire, think critically, and gain knowledge. (AASL 1)
- Draw conclusions, make informed decisions, apply knowledge to new situations, and create new knowledge. (AASL 2)
- Share knowledge and participate ethically and productively as members of our democratic society. (AASL 3)
- Ask and answer questions to demonstrate understanding of a text, referring explicitly to the text as the basis for the answers. (CCSS 1)
- Recount stories, including fables, folktales, and myths, from diverse cultures; determine the central message, lesson, or moral; and explain how it is conveyed through key details in the text. (CCSS 2)
- Describes characters in a story (e.g., their traits, motivations, or feelings) and explain how their actions contribute to the sequence of events. (CCSS 3)
- Uses electronic media to get information (e.g., databases, Internet, CD-ROM, television shows, videos, pull-down menus, words searches). (McREL 3)
- Summarizes and paraphrases information in texts (e.g., includes the main idea and significant supporting details of a reading selection). (McREL 9)

Objectives

Students

- Discover what made the character a legend and other knowledge about him.
- Portray the main character's life in a postage stamp.

Directions

1. The social studies teacher introduces Casey Jones and the concept of legends.
2. The school librarian reads and discusses a Casey Jones legend story.
3. Teachers suggest online and print Casey Jones resources.
4. Under guidance of teachers, student pairs describe Casey Jones. Then students summarize the legend and answer questions on what makes a legend and why time was important.
5. The art teacher guides students in the creation of a Casey Jones postage-type stamp using the worksheet train and adding other pictures to the stamp to portray the character.

Teaching Team

Art, school librarian, and social studies teachers.

Suggested Sources

Alber, Christoper. *Casey Jones and His Railroad Legacy.* New York: Cavendish, 2014.
Casey Jones Museum. *The Legend of Casey Jones.* Updated 2008. Retrieved from http://www.caseyjones.com/caseyjones/legend.htm
Krensky, Stephen. *Casey Jones.* Minneapolis, MN: Millbrook Press, 2006.
Schlosser, S. *Railroad Folklore.* Updated 2010. Retrieved from http://americanfolklore.net/folklore/2010/07/casey_jones.html

Sending a Valentine

Give or mail a Valentine bookmark card. First write a Valentine joke or riddle on the bookmark (dotted line shape). Decorate. Cut out the following card.

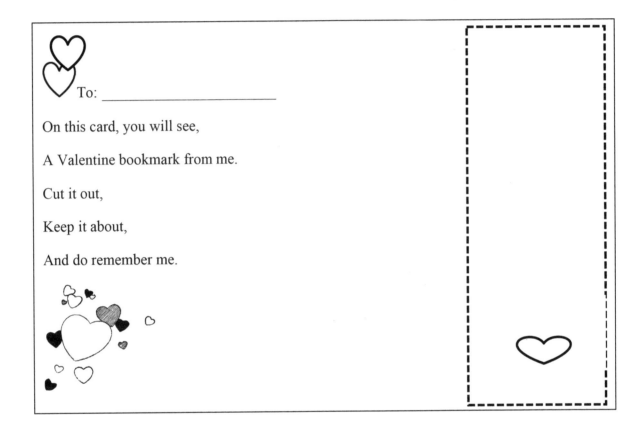

To: _____

On this card, you will see,

A Valentine bookmark from me.

Cut it out,

Keep it about,

And do remember me.

Turn the card over and on the right side, address the card to someone special. Add a short poem to the left side.

Sending a Valentine

Standards

Student(s)

- Inquire, think critically, and gain knowledge. (AASL 1)
- Draw conclusions, make informed decisions, apply knowledge to new situations, and create new knowledge. (AASL 2)
- Share knowledge and participate ethically and productively as members of our democratic society. (AASL 3)
- Refer to parts of stories, dramas, and poems, when writing or speaking about a text, using terms such as chapter, scene, and stanza, and describe how each successive part builds on earlier sections. (CCSS 4)
- Reads a variety of literary passages and texts (e.g., fairy tales, folktales, fiction, nonfiction, myths, poems, fables, fantasies, historical fiction, biographies, autobiographies, chapter books). (McREL 5)

Objectives

Students

- Discover and write two humorous riddles, jokes, or short poems.

Directions

1. The reading teacher reads part or all of a short humorous Valentine's Day story.
2. The school librarian suggests joke, humorous poem, and riddle books.
3. Students cut out the Valentine's Day card. The teachers guide student searching and copying of jokes, riddles, or short humorous poems for the Valentine's card bookmark and for the card front.
4. The art teacher guides students as they decorate their card bookmark and the card.

Teaching Team

Art, reading, and school librarian teachers.

Suggested Sources

Fiction

Berger, Samantha. *A Crankenstein Valentine.* New York: Little, Brown and Company, 2014.
Thaler, Mike. *Valentine's Day from the Black Lagoon.* New York: Scholastic, 2014.

Nonfiction

Bozzo, Linda. *Funny Valentine's Day Jokes to Tickle Your Funny Bone.* Berkeley Heights, NJ: Enslow, 2013.
Burbank, Lizzy. *Jokes for Kids: 301 Funny Holiday Jokes & Riddles.* New York: Createspace Independent Publishing Platform, 2014.
Lansky, Bruce. *Peter, Peter Pizza-Eater, and Other Silly Rhymes.* New York: Simon & Schuster, 2006.
Niven, Felicia Lowenstein. *Ha-Ha Holiday Jokes to Tickle Your Funny Bone.* Berkeley Heights, NJ: Enslow Publishers, 2014.
Silverstein, Shel. *Who Wants a Cheap Rhinoceros?* New York: Simon & Schuster, 2014.

Earth Space Adventure

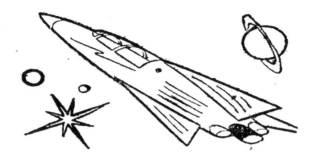

Fly into space around the earth, research, and describe your space travels. Answer the following questions.

 1. Write a fact about the sun. How far away is it from earth or how hot is it? _____

_____

 2. Write a fact about the earth's moon size or the average temperature:_____

_____

 3. What is the size (diameter) of the earth? _____

4. Why would you call earth, the blue planet? _____

_____

5. What percentage of the earth is water? _____

Create a picture of your earth space travel. Cut out the space ship, the sun, earth, and moon illustrations, and glue the space pictures on black paper.

From *Standards-Based Lesson Plans for the Busy Elementary School Librarian* by Joyce Keeling.
Santa Barbara, CA: Libraries Unlimited. Copyright © 2017.

Earth Space Adventure

Standards

Student(s)

- Inquire, think critically, and gain knowledge. (AASL 1)
- Draw conclusions, make informed decisions, apply knowledge to new situations, and create new knowledge. (AASL 2)
- Ask and answer questions to demonstrate understanding of a text, referring explicitly to the text as the basis for the answers. (CCSS 5)
- Use information gained from illustrations (e.g., maps, photographs) and the words in a text to demonstrate understanding of the text (e.g., where, when, why, and how key events occur). (CCSS 6)
- Uses encyclopedias to gather information for research topics. (McREL 2)
- Uses electronic media to gather information (e.g., databases, Internet, CD-ROM, television shows, videos, pull-down menus, word searches). (McREL 3)
- Summarizes and paraphrases information in texts (e.g., includes the main idea and significant supporting details of a reading selection). (McREL 9)

Objectives

Students

- Research simple facts about the planet earth, the moon, and the sun.
- Create an earth picture.

Directions

1. The science teacher briefly discusses one or two amazing facts about the planet earth.
2. The school librarian points out planet earth, moon, and sun books and online site resources.
3. With teachers' assistance, student groups answer worksheet questions using the resources.
4. Individual students create an earth picture using black paper and worksheet illustrations.
5. Students can find other earth facts by browsing a NASA Internet site.

Teaching Team

Science and school librarian teachers.

Suggested Sources

Cengage Learning. *Earth.* Updated 2016. Retrieved from http://encyclopedia.com

Davis, Phillips, Ed. *NASA Planetary Science Division.* Updated 2016. Retrieved from http://solarsystem.nasa.gov/planets/earth

Erickson, Kristen. *NASA.* Updated 2015. Retrieved from http://spaceplace.nasa.gov/all-about-earth/en/

Graham, Ian. *Our Sun.* Mankato, MN: Smart Apple Media, 2015.

Lawrence, Ellen. *Earth: Our Home in the Solar System.* St. Austell, Cornwall, UK: Ruby Tuesday Books, 2014.

Maloof, Torrey. *Earth and Moon.* New York: Teacher Created Materials, 2015.

Sharp, Tim. *What Is the Temperature on the Moon?* Updated 2012. Retrieved from http://www.space.com

Simon, Seymour. *Earth.* New York: Simon & Schuster, 2003.

Pot of Gold Joke

Read a leprechaun story.

1. Describe a leprechaun: _____

_____

_____

2. What does gold have to do with leprechauns? _____

_____

_____

3. In one sentence tell about the main event of the story: _____

_____

_____

4. Leprechauns played jokes. To help out with their jokes, write a St. Patrick's Day or leprechaun joke or riddle under the rainbow. Then color the illustrations.

Pot of Gold Joke

Standards

Student(s)

- Inquire, think critically, and gain knowledge. (AASL 1)
- Draw conclusions, make informed decisions, apply knowledge to new situations, and create new knowledge. (AASL 2)
- Ask and answer questions to demonstrate understanding of a text, referring explicitly to the text as the basis for the answers. (CCSS 1)
- Recount stories, including fables, folktales, and myths, from diverse cultures; determine the central message, lesson, or moral; and explain how it is conveyed through key details in the text. (CCSS 2)
- Reads a variety of literary passages and texts (e.g., fairy tales, folktales, fiction, nonfiction, myths, poems, fables, fantasies, historical fiction, biographies, autobiographies, chapter books). (McREL 5)

Objectives

Students

- Interpret the main plot and character in order to recall the story.
- Find and write a leprechaun or St. Patrick's Day joke.

Directions

1. The school librarian shows, reads, and discusses a leprechaun story and his gold.
2. The reading teacher leads a discussion on the main plot and the leprechaun from the story, as students recall the story.
3. Both teachers guide students as students answer worksheet questions.
4. Students find and write a leprechaun or St. Patrick's Day joke or riddle under the rainbow and color their sheet illustrations.

Teaching Team

Reading and school librarian teachers.

Suggested Sources

Bunting, Eve. *That's What Leprechauns Do*. New York: Clarion Books, 2005.

Edwards, Pamela Duncan. *The Leprechaun's Gold*. New York: Katherine Tegan, 2004.

Krensky, Stephen. *Too Many Leprechauns*. New York: Simon & Schuster Books for Young Readers, 2007.

Krull, Kathleen. *A Pot O'Gold: A Treasury of Irish Stories, Poetry, Folklore, and (Of Course) Blarney*. New York: Hyperion Books, 2004.

Niven, Felicia Lowenstein. *Ha-Ha Holiday Jokes to Tickle Your Funny Bone*. Berkeley Heights, NJ: Enslow, 2011.

Roop, Peter. *Let's Celebrate St. Patrick's Day*. Minneapolis, MN: Millbrook, 2003.

Rosenberg, Pam. *Holiday Jokes*. North Mankato, MN: Child's World, 2004.

Slater, Teddy. *The Luckiest St. Patrick's Day Ever*. New York: Cartwheel (Scholastic), 2008.

Celebrating Freedom

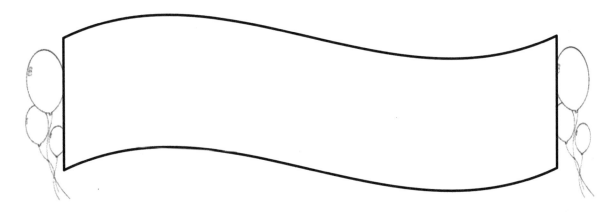

1. Use a dictionary and briefly define emancipation: _____

_____

_____

2. Use a nonfiction book or a good Internet site and describe Juneteenth: _____

_____

_____

_____

_____

3. When is Juneteenth celebrated? _____

4. What are your thoughts on the celebration of Juneteenth? _____

_____

_____

_____

5. At the top, design a banner to celebrate Juneteenth.

Celebrating Freedom

Standards

Student(s)

- Inquire, think critically, and gain knowledge. (AASL 1)
- Draw conclusions, make informed decisions, apply knowledge to new situations, and create new knowledge. (AASL 2)
- Share knowledge and participate ethically and productively as members of our democratic society. (AASL 3)
- Ask and answer questions to demonstrate understanding of a text, referring explicitly to the text as the basis for the answers. (CCSS 5)
- Use information gained from illustrations (e.g., maps, photographs) and the words in a text to demonstrate understanding of the text (e.g., where, when, why, and how key events occur). (CCSS 6)
- Uses electronic media to get information (e.g., databases, Internet, CD-ROM, television shows, videos, pull-down menus, words searches). (McREL 3)
- Uses word reference materials (e.g., glossary, dictionary, thesaurus) to determine the meaning, pronunciation, and derivations of unknown words. (McREL 4)
- Summarizes and paraphrases information in texts (e.g., includes the main idea and significant supporting details of a reading selection). (McREL 9)

Objectives

Students

- Define emancipation.
- Research and describe Juneteenth.
- Design a freedom or Juneteenth banner.

Directions

1. The social studies teacher briefly guides the student to use a dictionary to search the word, emancipation.
2. The school librarian reads and discusses a book on Juneteenth or a fiction source on the topic.
3. Teachers guide students to research online and print Juneteenth resources for small group work. Students give personal thoughts also.
4. The class will discuss their worksheet answers.
5. The art teacher will guide students in the design of a Juneteenth or freedom banner.

Teaching Team

Art, school librarian, and social studies teachers.

Suggested Sources

Acosta, Teresa Palomo. *Juneteenth. Handbook of Texas Online.* Updated 2015. Retrieved from https://tshaonline.org/handbook/online/articles/lkj01

Coleman, Wim. *Follow the Drinking Gourd: Come Along the Underground Railroad.* Concord, MA: Red Chair Press, 2015.

Cooper, F. *Juneteenth for Mazie.* Mankato, MN: Capstone, 2015.

Johnson, Angela. *All Different Now: Juneteenth, the First day of Freedom.* New York: Simon & Schuster, 2014.

Merriam-Webster Incorporated. *Learners Dictionary.* Updated 2006. Retrieved from http://learnersdictionary.com

Thumbelina

Read the fairy tale of *Thumbelina.* Answer the questions. Color the characters. In the bird's box, colorfully illustrate the setting and add the characters. The bird and box is a door hanger.

1. List the main characters. 2. In three short sentences, tell the beginning, middle, and end of the story.	

Thumbelina

Standards

Student(s)

- Inquire, think critically, and gain knowledge. (AASL 1)
- Draw conclusions, make informed decisions, apply knowledge to new situations, and create new knowledge. (AASL 2)
- Share knowledge and participate ethically and productively as members of our democratic society. (AASL 3)
- Recount stories, including fables, folktales, and myths, from diverse cultures; determine the central message, lesson, or moral; and explain how it is conveyed through key details in the text. (CCSS 2)
- Describe characters in a story (e.g., their traits, motivations, or feelings) and explain how their actions contribute to the sequence of events. (CCSS 3)
- Reads a variety of literary passages and texts (e.g., fairy tales, folktales, fiction, nonfiction, myths, poems, fables, fantasies, historical fiction, biographies, autobiographies, chapter books). (McREL 5)
- Understands the basic concept of plot (e.g., main problem, conflict, resolution, cause-and-effect). (McREL 6)

Objectives

Students

- Explain why the story is a fairy tale.
- Deduce and write the beginning, middle, and end of the story and characters.
- Illustrate the setting and create a door hanger of the story.

Directions

1. The reading and school librarian teachers read a *Thumbelina* fairy tale and lead discussion on setting, moral, beginning, middle, and ending, characters, and why *Thumbelina* is a fairy tale.
2. With teachers' support, students write the beginning, middle, and ending and characters.
3. With the art teacher's assistance, students create a *Thumbelina* door hanger of the bird and its box, after coloring and then adding the pictures from the worksheet to the bird's box.

Teaching Team

Art, reading, and school librarian teachers.

Suggested Sources

Alderson, Brian. *Thumbelina*. New York: Candlewick Press, 2009.

Americanliterature. *Thumbelina*. (n.d.). Retrieved from http://americanliterature.com/childrens-stories/thumbelina

Anderson, Hans Christian. "Thumbelina." *Hans Christian Andersen: The Complete Fairy Tales.* San Diego, CA: Canterbury Classics, 2014.

Long, Sylvia. *Sylvia Long's Thumbelina*. San Francisco, CA: Chronicle Books, 2010.

Wizard of Oz

(1) Inside the first tornado swirl, list main characters.

(2) Inside the second tornado swirl, describe the problem of the story in a few words.

(3) Inside the third tornado swirl, describe the solution in a few words.

Create a twirling tornado hanger for your locker. Color the tornado front and back and cut around the solid circular lines of the tornado without cutting apart the tornado box frame. Attach the wizard to the top to hang the tornado.

From *Standards-Based Lesson Plans for the Busy Elementary School Librarian* by Joyce Keeling. Santa Barbara, CA: Libraries Unlimited. Copyright © 2017.

Wizard of Oz

Standards

Student(s)

- Inquire, think critically, and gain knowledge. (AASL 1)
- Draw conclusions, make informed decisions, apply knowledge to new situations, and create new knowledge. (AASL 2)
- Share knowledge and participate ethically and productively as members of our democratic society. (AASL 3)
- Recount stories, including fables, folktales, and myths, from diverse cultures; determine the central message, lesson, or moral; and explain how it is conveyed through key details in the text. (CCSS 2)
- Describe characters in a story (e.g., their traits, motivations, or feelings) and explain how their actions contribute to the sequence of events. (CCSS 3)
- Reads a variety of literacy passages and texts (e.g., fairy tales, folktales, fiction, nonfiction, myths, poems, fables, fantasies, historical fiction, biographies). (McREL 5)
- Understands the basic concept of plot (e.g., main problem, conflict, resolution, cause-and-effect). (McREL 6)

Objectives

Students

- Identify a fantasy.
- Define and write character, setting, and the problem/solution of the story.
- Create a twirling story locker hanger to recount the story.

Directions

1. The school librarian reads a shortened version or a picture book of *The Wizard of Oz*.
2. The reading teacher guides discussion about characters, setting, and the story's problem/solution, in order to recall the story.
3. The school librarian and reading teachers guide student descriptive word answers, as students briefly describe character, the story problem, and solution in the tornado swirls.
4. The art teacher guides students to lightly color the tornado on the writing side but color brightly on the reverse side. Students cut out around the solid circular lines of the tornado to maintain a tornado shape while not cutting apart the box framework and then attach the wizard at the top of the tornado. The tornado shape is a twirling locker decoration recounting the story.

Teaching Team

Art, reading, and school librarian teachers.

Suggested Sources

Baum, Frank. *The Wizard of Oz*. New York: Applesauce Press (Simon and Shuster), 2015.
Bracken, Beth. *The Wizard of Oz*. Mankato, MN: Capstone Young Readers, 2013.
Filippini, Anouk. *The Wizard of Oz*. Paris, France: Auzou Publishing, 2016.

Donkey in Lion's Skin

1. The Donkey in Lion's Skin fable is about a donkey who found a lion's skin and put it on to fool others. Draw a lion's face on the donkey.

2. When the donkey saw the fox, he forgot, and he said, "Hee-haw." Then the fox knew it was the donkey. What could the fox say to the donkey? Write the fox's words in the fox word bubble.

3. What would the donkey say back to the fox? Put the donkey's words in the donkey word bubble.

4. Colorfully draw the setting with the donkey and fox on this sheet.

5. The moral of the fable suggests a lesson. What was the moral or lesson in the fable?_____

_____

_____

_____

_____

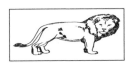

From *Standards-Based Lesson Plans for the Busy Elementary School Librarian* by Joyce Keeling. Santa Barbara, CA: Libraries Unlimited. Copyright © 2017.

Donkey in Lion's Skin

Standards

Student(s)

- Inquire, think critically, and gain knowledge. (AASL 1)
- Draw conclusions, make informed decisions, apply knowledge to new situations, and create new knowledge. (AASL 2)
- Share knowledge and participate ethically and productively as members of our democratic society. (AASL 3)
- Ask and answer questions to demonstrate understanding of a text, referring explicitly to the text as the basis for the answers. (CCSS 1)
- Recount stories, including fables, folktales, and myths, from diverse cultures; determine the central message, lesson, or moral; and explain how it is conveyed through key details in the text. (CCSS 2)
- Describe characters in a story (e.g., their traits, motivations, or feelings) and explain how their actions contribute to the sequence of events. (CCSS 3)
- Reads a variety of literacy passages and texts (e.g., fairy tales, folktales, fiction, nonfiction, myths, poems, fables, fantasies, historical fiction, biographies). (McREL 5)
- Understands the basic concept of plot (e.g., main problem, conflict, resolution, cause and effect). (McREL 6)

Objectives

Students

- Analyze a fable.
- Identify character, moral, and plot.
- Illustrate the setting.

Directions

1. The reading teacher reads and shows the fable of the "Donkey in Lion's Skin."
2. Students discuss characters, plot, setting, and moral under teacher guidance.
3. The librarian and reading teachers guide students to work on worksheet work, adding the characters' conversation and giving their opinion on the moral.
4. The art teacher helps students create the setting and the lion face for the donkey.

Teaching Team

Art, school librarian, and social studies teachers.

Suggested Sources

Blair, Eric. *The Donkey in the Lion's Skin: A Retelling of Aesop's Fable.* Mankato, MN: Picture Window Books, 2011.

McGovern, Ann. *Aesop's Fables.* New York: Scholastic, 2013.

Parker, Victoria. *The Lion and the Bull and Other Fables.* Milwaukee, WI: Gareth Stevens, 2014.

Celebrate Cinco de Mayo

1. What is Cinco de Mayo? _____

_____

2. Write two to three facts about the history of Cinco de Mayo:

_____

_____

_____

_____

3. How would you suggest celebrating Cinco de Mayo? Using bright festive colors, list some ways to celebrate around the dancer holding the maracas.

4. Brightly color the following maracas.

From *Standards-Based Lesson Plans for the Busy Elementary School Librarian* by Joyce Keeling.
Santa Barbara, CA: Libraries Unlimited. Copyright © 2017.

Celebrate Cinco de Mayo

Standards

Student(s)

- Inquire, think critically, and gain knowledge. (AASL 1)
- Draw conclusions, make informed decisions, apply knowledge to new situations, and create new knowledge. (AASL 2)
- Pursue personal and aesthetic growth. (AASL 4)
- Ask and answer questions to demonstrate understanding of a text, referring explicitly to the text for answers. (CCSS 5)
- Use information gained from illustrations (e.g., maps, photographs) and the words in a text to demonstrate understanding of the text (e.g., where, when, why, and how key events occur). (CCSS 6)
- Reads a variety of literary passages and texts (e.g., fairy tales, folktales, fiction, nonfiction, myths, poems, fables, fantasies, historical fiction, biographies, autobiographies, chapter books). (McREL 5)
- Summarizes and paraphrase information in texts (e.g., includes the main idea and significant supporting details of a reading selection). (McREL 9)

Objectives

Students

- Determine events.
- Discover and summarize basic facts about Cinco de Mayo.

Directions

1. The school librarian reads and shows a Cinco de Mayo fiction book.
2. The social studies teacher guides a book discussion on events of the book.
3. Upon receiving teacher guidance and references for basic Cinco de Mayo research, students define Cinco de Mayo, briefly write about the history, and then write about the celebration.
4. With the art teacher's assistance, students celebrate Cinco de Mayo with maracas by coloring and then sealing the maracas with rice or sand.

Teaching Team

Art, school librarian, and social studies teachers.

Suggested Sources

Fiction

Bullard, Lisa. *Marco's Cinco de Mayo*. Minneapolis, MN: Cloverleaf Books, 2012.

Nonfiction

Carr, Aaron. *Cinco de Mayo*. Mankato, MN: AV2 by Weigl, 2012.
Doering, Amanda. *Cinco de Mayo: Day of Mexican Pride*. Mankato, MN: Capstone Press, 2006.
Otto, Carolyn. *Holidays around the World: Celebrate Cinco de Mayo: With Fiestas, Music, and Dance*. Washington, DC: National Geographic Children's Books, 2008.
Rissman, Rebecca. *Cinco de Mayo*. Portsmouth, NH: Heinemann, 2010.

Chapter 5

Fourth-Grade Lesson Plans

The following interactive standards-based elementary lessons for fourth-grade students meet the needs of today's students. The lessons are set to different standards in the desire to meet the needs of school librarians' state or school library, Common Core State Standards (CCSS) or McREL literacy, or English language arts standards, which include the proverbial American Association of School Librarians (AASL) standards.

The quality-researched standards of AASL, the CCSS, and The McREL Compendium of Standards and Benchmarks are applied with each school library lesson for purposeful school library instruction and student achieved skills. The parts of the standards chosen for this book were those that were the most essential for library instruction and could be met in the lesson time allotment of twenty minutes. The standards may be used together as given, individually, or lessons may be set to other quality standards.

Student learning objectives are given for each lesson. Lessons include students working individually or with others for more efficient student learning. Team teaching is seen, as more can be accomplished when working together. Quality-researched resources are suggested. The streamlined, standards-based lessons for the busy school librarian will provide interactive and successful student literacy learning. The AASL standards are stated in the first chapter as they are universally seen with all lessons in some way. The following McREL and CCSS standards are used specifically with the fourth-grade level.

Fourth-Grade Library Standards with Language Arts Benchmarks from McREL Language Arts Writing Standards and Benchmarks, and CCSS

Fourth-grade students:

*Fourth-Grade Common Core (Literacy), Reading Literature

1. Refer to details and examples in a text when explaining what the text says explicitly and when drawing inferences from the text. (CCSS.ELA-Literacy.RL.4.1)
2. Determine a theme of a story, drama, or poem from details in the text; summarize the text. (CCSS.ELA-Literacy.RL.4.2)
3. Describe in depth a character, setting, or event in a story or drama, drawing on specific details in the text (e.g., a character's thoughts, words, or actions). (CCSS.ELA-Literacy.RL.4.9)
4. Compare and contrast the treatment of similar themes and topics (e.g., opposition of good and evil) and patterns of events (e.g., the quest) in stories, myths, and traditional literature from different cultures. (CCSS.ELA-Literacy.RL.4.9)

*Fourth-Grade Common Core (Literacy), Reading Informational Texts

5. Refer to details and examples in a text, when explaining what the text says explicitly and when drawing inferences from the text. (CCSS.ElA-Literacy.RI.4.1)
6. Interpret information presented visually, orally, or quantitatively (e.g., in charts, graphs, diagrams, timelines, animations, or interactive elements on Web pages) and explain how the information contributes to an understanding of the text in which it appears. (CCSS.ELA-Literacy.RI.4.7)

Governors Association Center for Best Practices and Council of Chief State School Officers. *Common Core State Standards (Literacy).* Washington, DC: National Governors Association Center for Best Practices and Council of Chief State School Officers, 2010. Retrieved from http://www.corestandards.org/

McREL Compendium of Standards and Benchmarks Language Arts Writing Standards and Benchmarks (Grade 3–5)

*Gathers and uses information for research purposes. Standard 4

1. Uses a variety of strategies to plan research (e.g., identifies possible topic by brainstorming, listing questions, using idea webs; organizes prior knowledge about a topic; develops a course of action; determines how to locate necessary information). (McREL)
2. Uses encyclopedias to gather information for research topics. (McREL)
3. Uses electronic media to gather information (e.g., databases, Internet, CD-ROM, television shows, videos, pull-down menus, word searches). (McREL)

McREL Compendium of Standards and Benchmarks Language Arts Reading Standards and Benchmarks (Grade 3–5)

*Uses the general skills and strategies of the reading process. Standard 5

4. Uses word reference materials (e.g., glossary, dictionary, thesaurus) to determine the meaning, pronunciation, and derivations of unknown words. (McREL)

*Uses skills and strategies to read a variety of literary texts. Standard 6

5. Reads a variety of literary passages and texts (e.g., fairy tales, folktales, fiction, nonfiction, myths, poems, fables, fantasies, historical fiction, biographies, autobiographies, chapter books). (McREL)
6. Knows the defining characteristics (e.g., rhyme and rhythm in poetry; settings and dialogue in drama, make believe in folktales and fantasies, life stories in biography; illustrations in children's stories) and structural elements (e.g., chapter, scene, stanza, verse, meter) of a variety of genres. (McREL)
7. Understands the basic concept of plot (e.g., main problem, conflict, resolution, cause-and-effect). (McREL)
8. Knows themes that recur across literary works. (McREL)

*Uses skills and strategies to read a variety of informational texts. Standard 7

9. Uses the various parts of a book (e.g., index, table of contents, glossary, appendix, preface) to locate information. (McREL)
10. Understands similarities and differences within and among literary works from various genre and cultures (e.g., in terms of settings, character types, events, point of view, role of natural phenomena). (McREL)
11. Summarizes and paraphrases information in texts (e.g., include the main idea and significant supporting details of a reading selection). (McREL)

McREL. Language Arts Standards, 2015. Retrieved from http://www2.mcrel.org/compendium/standard

Searching the Library

To find library books, use the online catalog. Three major ways to find books are by author, title, and subject searches. Use the online catalog to go on a scavenger hunt.

1. Author search. Search for author, Dr. Seuss. How many Seuss books are found in the easy or picture book section? _____

2. Title search. Find the title of the book called *Harry Potter and the Goblet of Fire*. What is the call number? _____

3. Subject search. Search for nonfiction horse books. What is the call number for a nonfiction book on horses? _____

4. Author search. Search for the author, Rick Riordan. What is the title of one of his books?

_____

5. Subject search. Search for either volleyball or football fiction. What is the title of a volleyball or football fiction book? _____

6. Subject search. Find a biography on Abraham Lincoln. What is the call number? _____

7. Subject search. Find a joke or riddle book. What is the call number? _____

8. Title search. Find the *Guinness Book of World Records*. Go the shelf to use the book. Write any short fact from the first two pages: _____

_____

Bonus. In your opinion, what are two or more popular authors for fourth graders: _____

_____

From *Standards-Based Lesson Plans for the Busy Elementary School Librarian* by Joyce Keeling. Santa Barbara, CA: Libraries Unlimited. Copyright © 2017.

Searching the Library

Standards

Student(s)

- Inquire, think critically, and gain knowledge. (AASL 1)
- Draw conclusions, make informed decisions, apply knowledge to new situations, and create new knowledge. (AASL 2)
- Share knowledge and participate ethically and productively as members of our democratic society. (AASL 3)
- Pursue personal and aesthetic growth. (AASL 4)
- Interpret information presented visually, orally, or quantitatively (e.g., in charts, graphs, diagrams, timelines, animations, or interactive elements on Web pages) and explain how the information contributes to an understanding of the text in which it appears. (CCSS 6)
- Uses electronic media to get information (e.g., databases, Internet, CD-ROM, television shows, videos, pull-down menus, words-searches). (McREL 3)

Objectives

Students

- Research the online catalog using author, title, and subject searches.

Directions

1. The school librarian demonstrates how to search the online catalog using author, title, and subject search. If the library catalog is not online, use the OCLC online World Libraries.
2. With the reading and school librarian teachers' guidance, student pairs research the online catalog using author, title, and subject searches. Students write the answers on their worksheets.
3. Students share their last answer with the class.
4. If time, students will find a short fact from another nonfiction book as well.

Teaching Team

Reading and school librarian teachers.

Suggested Sources

OCLC. *Online World Libraries*. Updated 2015. Retrieved from http://www.worldcat.org

Acting Out in the Library

Act out a scene from your library. You will use pantomime or acting without sound. Select a library scene for your group and have the class guess your scene.

Look at these ways to create a successful scene:

1. Brainstorm some plans with your group first.

2. Select one major plan for the scene and decide who will be the actors.

3. Think of some ways to present the scene, using precise body expressions.

4. Brainstorm some ways to use exaggerated facial expressions in the scene.

5. Show confidence and excitement.

6. Do not use any sounds, as this is pantomime

7. Select someone to help keep track of time.

Now, on with your successful show!

From *Standards-Based Lesson Plans for the Busy Elementary School Librarian* by Joyce Keeling. Santa Barbara, CA: Libraries Unlimited. Copyright © 2017.

Acting Out in the Library

Standards

Student(s)

- Inquire, think critically, and gain knowledge. (AASL 1)
- Draw conclusions, make informed decisions, apply knowledge to new situations, and create new knowledge. (AASL 2)
- Share knowledge and participate ethically and productively as members of our democratic society. (AASL 3)
- Pursue personal and aesthetic growth. (AASL 4)
- Refer to details and examples in a text when explaining what the text says explicitly and when drawing inferences from the text. (CCSS 1)
- Knows the defining characteristics (e.g., rhyme and rhythm in poetry; settings and dialogue in drama, make believe in folktales and fantasies, life stories in biography; illustrations in children's stories) and structural elements (e.g., chapter, scene, stanza, verse, meter) of a variety of genres. (McREL 6)
- Uses the various parts of a book in texts (e.g., includes the main ideas and significant supporting details of a reading selection). (McREL 9)

Objectives

Students

- Review book care, book parts, and the Dewey Decimal system.
- Act out a library scene using pantomime.

Directions

1. The language arts teacher describes and gives tips on pantomime by using the worksheets.
2. The school librarian leads discussion on general library knowledge, including book care, book parts, the Dewey Decimal System, and fiction. This activity is a good review to start out the year.
3. The librarian and language arts teachers divide the class into smaller groups. Group acts out a topic without sound, with pantomime. The class guesses the topic.
4. Groups discretely select a topic and decide how to act out the following topics that are written, cut out, and folded into paper strips:

Not showing book care	Mystery	Baseball (700)
A librarian	Table of Contents	Spine
Humorous Fiction	Statue of Liberty (900)	Illustrator
Author	Pet Dog (600)	Adventure Fiction
Jokes (800)	Returning a book on time	Call Number
Snakes (500)	Book Covers	Lincoln Biography

Teaching Team

Language arts and school librarian teachers.

Suggested Sources

Mediwiki. *How to Pantomime*(n.d.). Retrieved from http://www.wikihow.com/Pantomime

In Danger

| Polar Bear | Gray Wolf | Grizzly |

There are many animals in danger of being extinct or that are endangered. You are on a mission to help. Create a caution sign for your chosen animal after explaining why it is in danger. Which animal you will research on? Polar Bear   Gray Wolf   Grizzly

1. Write at least two reasons why the animal is in danger: _____

_____

_____

2. On the colored caution sign, place your chosen animal. Then boldly write groups of two- or three-word phrases inside the sign to explain how to save the animal.

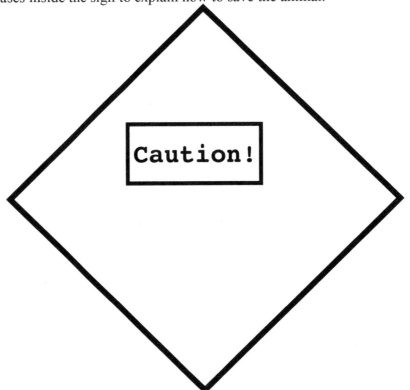

Caution!

In Danger

Standards

Student(s)

- Inquire, think critically, and gain knowledge. (AASL 1).
- Draw conclusions, make informed decisions, apply knowledge to new situations, and create new knowledge. (AASL 2)
- Share knowledge and participate ethically and productively as members of our democratic society. (AASL 3)
- Refer to details and examples in a text when explaining what the text says explicitly and when drawing inferences from the text. (CCSS 5)
- Interpret information presented visually, orally, or quantitatively (e.g., in charts, graphs, diagrams, timelines, animations, or interactive elements on Web pages) and explain how the information contributes to an understanding of the text in which it appears. (CCSS 6)
- Uses a variety of strategies to plan research (e.g., identifies possible topic by brainstorming, listing questions, using idea webs; organizes prior knowledge about a topic; develops a course of action; determines how to locate necessary information). (McREL 1)
- Uses electronic media to get information. (McREL 3)

Objectives

Students

- Analyze the key factual details to discover why their selected endangered animal is in danger.
- Design a caution sign describing ways to save the animal after researching for key facts.

Directions

1. The science teacher briefly discusses endangered animals and gives examples.
2. The school librarian teacher guides research for key factual details and suggests resources.
3. Both teachers guide students with animal research and worksheets. Students examine key details as they research and answer two or more reasons why their chosen animal is in danger.
4. Students glue their colored animal and animal name under the Caution word. Ask students to write two or three different researched descriptive phrases about how to save the animal.
5. The class discusses their findings.

Teaching Team

Science and school librarian teachers.

Suggested Sources

Close, Edward. *Endangered Animals.* New York: PowerKids Press, 2014.

Slade, Suzanne. *What Can We Do About Endangered Animals?* New York: PowerKids, 2010.

Somervill, Barbara A. *Gray Wolf.* Ann Arbor, MI: Cherry Lake Publishing, 2008.

Somervill, Barbara A. *Grizzly Bear.* Ann Arbor, MI: Cherry Lake Publishing, 2009.

Spilsbury, Louise. *Polar Bear: Killer King of the Arctic.* New York: Windmill Books, 2013.

United States Fish and Wildlife Service. *Endangered Species.* Updated 2015. Retrieved from http://www.fws.gov/endangered/

Down the Rabbit Hole

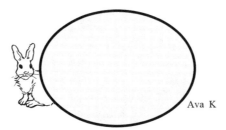

Ava K

Alice went through a rabbit hole to get to her story. In the top rabbit hole, write the title and author name. Then describe Alice's story. In complete sentences, write the beginning, middle, and ending of the story. Around the following bottom hole and Alice, illustrate two or more ways that show the fantasy parts of the story.

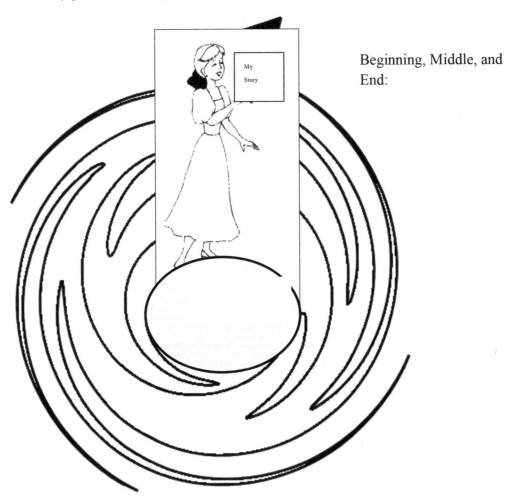

Beginning, Middle, and End:

Down the Rabbit Hole

Standards

Student(s)

- Inquire, think critically, and gain knowledge. (AASL 1)
- Draw conclusions, make informed decisions, apply knowledge to new situations, and create new knowledge. (AASL 2)
- Share knowledge and participate ethically and productively as members of our democratic society. (AASL 3)
- Describe in depth a character, setting, or event in a story or drama, drawing on specific details in the text (e.g., a character's thoughts, words, or actions). (CCSS 3)
- Compare and contrast the treatment of similar themes and topics (e.g., opposition of good and evil) and patterns of events (e.g., the quest) in stories, myths, and traditional literature from different cultures. (CCSS 4)
- Reads a variety of literary passages and texts (e.g., fairy tales, folktales, fiction, nonfiction, myths, poems, fables, fantasies, historical fiction, biographies, autobiographies, chapter books). (McREL 5)
- Understands the basic concept of plot (e.g., main problem, conflict, resolution, cause-and-effect). (McREL 7)

Objectives

Students

- Define fantasy and illustrate parts of a fantasy.
- Describe character and setting, and then describe and write the beginning, middle, and ending events.
- Identify title and author.

Directions

1. The reading and school librarian teachers read a shortened version of *Alice in Wonderland* or a section from the story. Teachers discuss fantasy.
2. With guided discussion, students discuss main character, setting, the story beginning, middle, and ending events.
3. Both teachers guide student worksheet answers on events, title, and author. Students illustrate two or more of the fantasy story parts.

Teaching Team

Reading and school librarian teachers.

Suggested Sources

Carroll, Lewis. *Alice in Wonderland: The Magical Story*. New York: Parragon, 2010.

Carroll, Lewis. *Alice in Wonderland: Down the Rabbit Hole* [DVD]. Holland, OH: Dreamscape Media, 2015.

Carroll, Lewis. *Lewis Carroll's Alice's Adventures in Wonderland: Down the Rabbit Hole*. Minneapolis, MN: Magic Wagon, 2008.

Safe Travels

Be **safe**, and also learn how to find good information when exploring the Internet.

<u>S</u>ee who wrote the Internet information, and why they wrote the information on the site.

<u>A</u>lways look for references or where the information was found.

<u>F</u>ew can you trust on the Internet, so do not give out personal information.

<u>E</u>valuate information for possible writing errors like spelling errors, and check the date. Choose a planet and write the planet name here: _____.

Find good Internet information on the planet. Have safe travels!

1. What is the Internet address of the site? _____

2. Was year of the site given?   Yes   No

3. Were references given?   Yes   No

4. Circle why the site was written?   Give Information   Sell Something   Entertain

5. Neatly write five planet facts in your own words. Then print a picture.

_____

_____

_____

_____

_____

Safe Travels

Standards

Student(s)

- Inquire, think critically, and gain knowledge. (AASL 1)
- Draw conclusions, make informed decisions, apply knowledge to new situations, and create new knowledge. (AASL 2)
- Share knowledge and participate ethically and productively as members of our democratic society. (AASL 3)
- Interpret information presented visually, orally, or quantitatively (e.g., in charts, graphs, diagrams, timelines, animations, or interactive elements on web pages) and explain how the information contributes to an understanding of the text in which it appears. (CCSS 6)
- Uses electronic media to get information (e.g., databases, Internet, CD-ROM, television shows, videos, pull-down menus, words-searches). (McREL 3)
- Summarizes and paraphrases information in texts (e.g., includes the main idea and significant supporting details of a reading selection). (McREL 11)

Objectives

Students

- Evaluate an Internet site.
- By using the Internet, research a planet and summarize the planet facts.

Directions

1. The school librarian and technology teachers briefly discuss Internet safety (do not give out personal information and so on), and then discuss how to find good online information, like check for references, look for a site with a current date and a creditable author with no obvious spelling and grammatical errors.
2. The science teacher guides brainstorming about planets.
3. The teachers provide Internet sites on planets for student research.
4. Teachers guide research, as student pairs select a planet and answer their worksheet questions with information from a given Internet site. Students evaluate the site, write five planet facts, and print a planet picture.
5. Student fact boxes and pictures are displayed.

Teaching Team

Science, school librarian, and technology teachers.

Suggested Sources

Britt, Robert Roy. *Solar System Planets: Order of the 8 (or 9) Planets*. Updated 2015. Retrieved from http://www.space.com/15216-dwarf-planets-facts-solar-system-sdcmp.html

Greller, J. *A Media Specialist Guide to Evaluating Web Sites*. Updated 2008. Retrieved from http://mediaspecialistsguide.blogspot.ie/2015/12/updated-post-do-your-students-know-how.html

NASA Planetary Science Division. "Planets." *National Aeronautics and Space Administration*. Updated 2015. Retrieved from http://solarsystem.nasa.gov/planets/solarsystem

Totem Poles

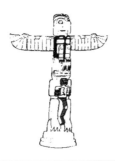

Read Native American Indian folklore and answer the questions before designing a totem pole.

1 What was the title of the folklore story? _____

_____

2. Who were the main characters? _____

_____

3. What was the main event of the story? _____

_____

4. Was there a pattern of events? Quickly describe them: _____

_____

_____

5. What was the Native American Indian tribe?

_____

6. Now finish designing the totem pole. Add two more animals. Color and cut out the totem pole and round stand. Cut the circle slit. Fold the last totem pole box after sliding the totem pole into the stand.

Totem Poles

Standards

Student(s)

- Share knowledge and participate ethically and productively as members of our democratic society. (AASL 3)
- Compare and contrast the treatment of similar themes and topics (e.g., opposition of good and evil) and patterns of events (e.g., the quest) in stories, myths, and traditional literature from different cultures. (CCSS 4)
- Refer to details and examples in a text when explaining what the text says explicitly and when drawing inferences from the text. (CCSS 5)
- Reads a variety of literary passages and texts (e.g., fairy tales, folktales, fiction, nonfiction, myths, poems, fables, fantasies, historical fiction, biographies, autobiographies, chapter books). (McREL 5)
- Understands similarities and differences within and among literary works from various genre and cultures (e.g., in terms of settings, character types, events, point of view, role of natural phenomena). (McREL 10)

Objective

Students

- Describe folklore.
- Acquire brief totem pole key details and design a totem pole.
- Describe character, main plot, theme, pattern of events.

Directions

1. The worksheet is copied on card stock.
2. The social studies teacher leads a brief class research project about totem poles.
3. The school librarian reads an American Indian folklore containing a totem pole.
4. The librarian and social studies teachers lead discussion on character, theme, main plot, pattern of events, and the American Indian tribe featured as students answer their worksheet questions.
5. The art teacher guides the student to design totem poles. The base of the totem pole will need the slit cut so that the cut out totem pole can stand when inserted in that slit.

Teaching Team

Art, school librarian, and social studies teachers.

Suggested Resources

McDermott, Gerald. *Raven: A Trickster Tale from the Pacific Northwest.* Boston, MA: Harcourt, 2001.

Tipiheaven. *Totem Poles and Their Meanings.* Updated 2009. Retrieved from https://tipiheaven .wordpress.com/page/7/

Vanasse, Deb. *Totem Tale.* Seattle, WA: Sasquatch Books, 2006.

Wolfson, Evelyn. *Mythology of the Inuit.* Berkley Heights, NJ: Enslow, 2014.

Rip Van Winkle

Rip Van Winkle is an American legend that takes place in a mountain area.

1. In the bird's speech bubble, answer Rip Van Winkle's question of what happened.

2. Describe the beginning of the story: _____

_____

_____

3. Describe the ending of the story: _____

_____

_____

_____

4. If you had slept for twenty years like Rip Van Winkle, how would your world change?

_____

_____

5. Colorfully illustrate the worksheet illustrations at the top of the paper by adding two to three trees to make it look more like a Catskill mountain scene in the story. Color the bird and Rip Van Winkle and give Van Winkle a longer beard.

Rip Van Winkle

Standards

Student(s)

- Share knowledge and participate ethically and productively as members of our democratic society. (AASL 3)
- Describe in depth a character, setting, or event in a story or drama, drawing on specific details in the text (e.g., a character's thoughts, words, or actions). (CCSS 3)
- Compare and contrast the treatment of similar themes and topics (e.g., opposition of good and evil) and patterns of events (e.g., the quest) in stories, myths, and traditional literature from different cultures. (CCSS 4)
- Reads a variety of literary passages and texts (e.g., fairy tales, folktales, fiction, nonfiction, myths, poems, fables, fantasies, historical fiction, biographies, autobiographies, chapter books). (McREL 5)
- Understands the basic concept of plot (e.g., main problem, conflict, resolution, cause-and-effect). (McREL 7)

Objective

Students

- Analyze a folktale legend.
- Distinguish the main character, theme, and beginning and ending story events.
- Illustrate the setting.

Directions

1. The reading and school librarian teachers read and discuss *Rip Van Winkle.*
2. The teachers guide discussion about what made the story a folktale legend and discuss the main character, theme, plot, and setting.
3. With guidance, students answer the worksheet questions, as well as how their world would change in twenty years.
4. Students color the worksheet illustrations, add a long beard to Rip Van Winkle, and add other things to the scene to resemble mountains since the story took place in the mountains.

Teaching Team

Reading and school librarian teachers.

Suggested Resources

Foehner, Ashley. *Washington Irving's Rip Van Winkle*. Golden, CO: Fulcrum Publishing, 2008.
Franklin, Phoebe. *Rip Van Winkle*. New Rochele, NY: Newmark Learning, 2015.
Harasymiw, Mark. *Legend of Rip Van Winkle*. Milwaukee, WI: Gareth Stevens Publishing, 2016.
HowStuffWorks. *Rip Van Winkle*. Updated 2015. Retrieved from http://www.howstuffworks.com/
    rip-van-winkle-story

Nutcracker Magic

1. Write the following information from the title page and copyright page of *The Nutcracker*
Story:
Title:
Author:
Illustrator:
Publishing Place: Publisher: Copyright:

2. What were the major problem and the effect?

3. What were the least three events that made the story a fairy tale?

4. Were there bad and good characters in the story? If so, who were they?

5. In the box below, have the Nutcracker write an invitation to the girl:

You are invited

Nutcracker Magic

Standards

Student(s)

- Inquire, think critically, and gain knowledge. (AASL 1)
- Draw conclusions, make informed decisions, apply knowledge to new situations, and create new knowledge. (AASL 2)
- Share knowledge and participate ethically and productively as members of our democratic society. (AASL 3)
- Pursue personal and aesthetic growth. (AASL 4)
- Describe in depth a character, setting, or event in a story or drama, drawing on specific details in the text (e.g., a character's thoughts, words, or actions). (CCS 3)
- Compare and contrast the treatment of similar themes and topics (e.g., opposition of good and evil) and patterns of events (e.g., the quest) in stories, myths, and traditional literature from different cultures. (CCSS 4)
- Reads a variety of literary passages and texts (e.g., fairy tales, folktales, fiction, nonfiction, myths, poems, fables, fantasies, historical fiction, biographies, autobiographies, chapter books). (McREL 5)
- Understands the basic concept of plot (e.g., main problem, conflict, resolution, cause-and-effect). (McREL 7)

Objectives

Students

- Interpret a fairy tale and the events that made it a fairy tale.
- Define setting, theme, major problem and effect, characters, and title page.
- Create an invitation from the Nutcracker for the girl.

Directions

1. The music and school librarian teachers briefly introduce *The Nutcracker* story. Title page information is discussed and listed on the board.
2. The class sees and hears *The Nutcracker* easy or shortened book version. Students discuss the main character, theme, setting, and main plot.
3. Both teachers guide student answers as students cite the source from the title page and as students answer the good and bad characters, event or plot happenings that made the story a fairy tale, and the major problem and effect.
4. Students write an invitation from the Nutcracker to the girl.
5. A follow-up option is viewing a Nutcracker movie.

Teaching Team

Music and school librarian teachers.

Suggested Sources

Engelbreit, Mary. *Mary Engelbriet's Nutcracker.* New York: HarperCollins, 2014.
Jeffers, Susan. *The Nutcracker.* New York: HarperCollins, 2007.
VisionFilms. *Nutcracker Sweet* [DVD]. Sherman Oaks, CA: VisionFilms, 2016.

Magical Christmas

Read a Christmas miracle story. List the characters, main plot, setting, or theme in the stars. In the middle shape, draw the story. Connect the story into a mobile.

Theme   Characters

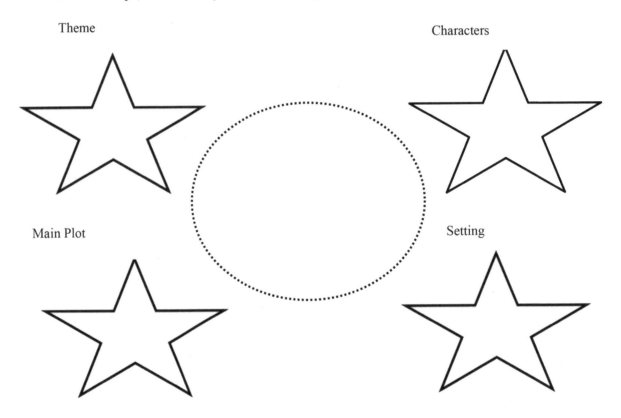

Main Plot   Setting

Magical Christmas

Standards

Student(s)

- Inquire, think critically, and gain knowledge. (AASL 1)
- Draw conclusions, make informed decisions, apply knowledge to new situations, and create new knowledge. (AASL 2)
- Determine a theme of a story, drama, or poem from details in the text; summarize the text. (CCSS 2)
- Describe in depth a character, setting, or event in a story or drama, drawing on specific details in the text (e.g., a character's thoughts, words, or actions). (CCSS 3).
- Reads a variety of literary passages and texts (e.g., fairy tales, folktales, fiction, nonfiction, myths, poems, fables, fantasies, historical fiction, biographies, autobiographies, chapter books). (McREL 5)
- Understands the basic concept of plot (e.g., main problem, conflict, resolution, cause-and-effect). (McREL 7)
- Knows themes that recur across literary works. (McREL 8)

Objectives

Students

- Describe theme, main plot, setting, and characters.
- Illustrate an event.
- Create a winter or Christmas mobile connecting the story elements.

Directions

1. The reading and school librarian teachers read and discuss a short Christmas story or an easy book that is an age-appropriate book about a type of miracle or Christmas wonder.
2. With guided discussion, students discuss and write the theme, middle event, setting, and characters on the stars. Students also draw the story in the middle shape.
3. The art teacher helps students connect the story parts into a mobile. Students color the top star design. Students connect the smaller stars to the circle, and finally connect the circle to the top star with ribbons or yarn for a Christmas or winter holiday mobile.

Teaching Team

Art, reading, and school librarian teachers.

Suggested Sources

Barnes, Laura. *Ernest's Special Christmas.* Stockton, NJ: Barnesyard Books, 2003.
Devlin, Wende. *Cranberry Christmas.* Cynthiana, KY: Purple House, 2004.
Wojciechowski, Susan. *The Christmas Miracle of Jonathan Toomey.* Somerville, MA: Candlewick Press, 2015.

Reading Is Sweet

Sweet Key to Reading

<u>Across:</u> (1) Someone who illustrates, (2) A not-true story, (3) A story location, (4) Someone who publishes books.

<u>Down:</u> (1) Writer, (2) A true story or facts, (3) A person's life, (4) A book name, (5) The purpose of the book, (6) The problem/solution.

1. What is a good holiday fiction book title? _____

   What is that fiction book call number? _____

2. What is a holiday nonfiction book title? _____

   What is that nonfiction book call number? _____

Reading Is Sweet

Standards

Student(s)

- Inquire, think critically, and gain knowledge. (AASL 1)
- Draw conclusions, make informed decisions, apply knowledge to new situations, and create new knowledge. (AASL 2)
- Share knowledge and participate ethically and productively as members of our democratic society. (AASL 3)
- Pursue personal and aesthetic growth. (AASL 4)
- Describe in depth a character, setting, or event in a story or drama, drawing on specific details in the text (e.g., a character's thoughts, words, or actions). (CCSS 3)
- Use[s] electronic media to gather information (e.g., databases, Internet, CD-ROM, television shows, videos, pull-down menus, word searches). (McREL 3)
- Use[s] the various parts of a book (e.g., index, table of contents, glossary, appendix, preface) to locate information. (McREL 9)

Objectives

Students

- Review and define book parts, fiction/nonfiction, biography, and story elements.
- List holiday fiction and then nonfiction book titles with call numbers.

Directions

1. The reading and school librarian teachers lead discussion on the following ten words: illustrator, author, fiction, nonfiction, setting, publisher, biography, title, theme (purpose), and plot (problem/solution). Those words are listed on the class board for the students' word puzzle key.
2. Students answer the candy cane worksheet puzzles using the listed words.
3. Then students use the card catalog to find a holiday fiction and nonfiction book and write the titles and call numbers on worksheets.
4. Students share fiction and nonfiction holiday titles.

Teaching Team

Reading and school librarian teachers.

Suggested Sources

None needed.

The Donkey's Turn

The Miller, His Son, and the Donkey

The Miller, His Son, and the Donkey fable is about a miller and his son who wanted to get their donkey to the market. Many people had ideas on how to get the donkey there; someone even recommended that the son and father carry the donkey. In the end, the miller and his son did not get the donkey to the market, as the donkey fell into the river and probably swam away.

1. What is a fable? _____

_____

2. What was the moral of this donkey fable? _____

_____

3. What was one guess or inference that you made during the story: _____

_____

4. Now, it is the donkey's turn. Write a funny different ending of the fable, from the donkey's

view: _____

_____

_____

_____

_____

_____

From *Standards-Based Lesson Plans for the Busy Elementary School Librarian* by Joyce Keeling.
Santa Barbara, CA: Libraries Unlimited. Copyright © 2017.

The Donkey's Turn

Standards

Student(s)

- Draw conclusions, make informed decisions, apply knowledge to new situations, and create new knowledge. (AASL 1)
- Pursue personal and aesthetic growth. (AASL 4)
- Refer to details and examples in a text when explaining what the text says explicitly and when drawing inferences from the text. (CCSS 1)
- Describe in depth a character, setting, or event in a story or drama, drawing on specific details in the text. (CCSS 3)
- Compare and contrast the treatment of similar themes and topics (e.g., opposition of good and evil) and patterns of events (e.g., the quest) in stories, myths, and traditional literature from different cultures. (CCSS 4)
- Reads a variety of literary passages and texts (e.g., fairy tales, folktales, fiction, nonfiction, myths, poems, fables, fantasies, historical fiction, biographies, autobiographies, chapter books). (McREL 5)
- Understands the basic concept of plot (e.g., main problem, conflict, resolution, cause-and-effect). (McREL 7)

Objective

Students

- Analyze a fable.
- Retell character, story inferences, moral, and plot.
- Write another ending for the fable.

Directions

1. The school librarian discusses and reads the fable of *The Miller, His Son, and the Donkey.*
2. The reading teacher leads a discussion of what is a fable, and then leads discussion on the moral, theme, character, inferences, and main plot.
3. Under the direction of the teachers, students rewrite the fable ending, but with a humorous look from the donkey's view.
4. Revised fables will be shared.

Teaching Team

Reading and school librarian teachers.

Suggested Resources

Pinkney, Jerry. *Aesop's Fables*. New York: SeaStar Books, 2000.
Salem, Lynn. *The Miller, His Son, and the Donkey*. Elizabethtown, PA: Continental Press, 2005.
Sommer, Carl. *The Miller, His Son and Their Donkey*. Houston, TX: Advance Publishing, 2014.

Rosa and Ruby

Rosa Parks and Ruby Bridges showed courage. Write a newspaper article on either Rosa Parks or Ruby Bridges. First share your thoughts and then find some unfamiliar facts on both.

1. <u>Ruby Bridges</u>. In your opinion, what were Ruby's feelings about going to a school where she did not feel welcome? _____

_____

List two or more facts about Ruby Bridges: _____

_____

2. <u>Rosa Parks.</u> In your opinion, what were Rosa Parks' feelings about her bus ride?

_____

_____

List two or more facts about Rosa Parks: _____

_____

3. Write a short news article on either Rosa Parks or Ruby Bridges.

Read All About It: A Courageous Person!

_____

_____

_____

_____

_____

From *Standards-Based Lesson Plans for the Busy Elementary School Librarian* by Joyce Keeling.
Santa Barbara, CA: Libraries Unlimited. Copyright © 2017.

Rosa and Ruby

Standards

Student(s)

- Inquire, think critically, and gain knowledge. (AASL 1)
- Draw conclusions, make informed decisions, apply knowledge to new situations, and create new knowledge. (AASL 2)
- Share knowledge and participate ethically and productively as members of our democratic society. (AASL 3)
- Refer to details and examples in a text when explaining what the text says explicitly and when drawing inferences from the text. (CCSS 5)
- Uses electronic media to get information (e.g., databases, Internet, CD-ROM, television shows, videos, pull-down menus, words-searches). (McREL 3)
- Knows the defining characteristics (e.g., rhyme and in poetry, settings and dialog in drama, make believe in folktales and fantasies, life stories in biography; illustrations in children's stories) and structural elements (e.g., chapter, scene, stanza, verse, meter) of a variety of genres. (McREL 6)
- Summarizes and paraphrases information in texts (e.g., includes the main idea and significant supporting details of a reading selection). (McREL 11)

Objectives

Students

- Research and summarize two or more facts about Rosa Parks and Ruby Bridges.
- Write a brief newspaper article.

Directions

1. The social studies teacher briefly discusses segregation and introduces Rosa Parks and Ruby Bridges and for what Parks and Bridges are best known.
2. The school librarian teacher suggests resources about Parks and Bridges.
3. Teachers guide research using online sites and print sources, as student groups discuss and list two or more unfamiliar facts about Parks and Bridges. Students write their opinion.
4. Teachers guide students to create a brief newspaper article on either Parks or Bridges.

Teaching Team

School librarian and social studies teachers.

Suggested Sources

Biography.com. *Rosa Parks*. Updated 2015. Retrieved from http://www.biography.com/people/rosa-parks-9433715/videos/rosa-parks-civil-rights-pioneer-17181763791

Biography.com. *Ruby Bridges*. Updated 2015. Retrieved from http://www.biography.com/people/ruby-bridges-475426#synopsis

Bridges, Ruby. *Ruby Bridges Goes to School*. New York: Scholastic, 2009.

Hansen, Grace. *Rosa Parks Activist for Equality*. Mankato, MN: ABDO, 2016.

Kemp, Kristin. *Rosa Parks*. New York: Teacher Created Materials, 2015.

Rubke, Simone. *Ruby Bridges*. New York: Scholastic, 2015.

Valentine's Day Poems Take the Cake

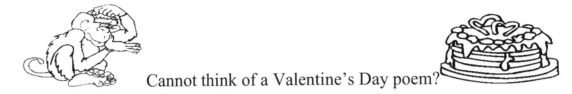

Cannot think of a Valentine's Day poem?

Use a thesaurus and make a list of descriptive words for Valentine's Day in the box. Then inside the Valentine shape, write a form poem.

Way to go!

Valentine's Day Poems Take the Cake

Standards

Student(s)

- Share knowledge and participate ethically and productively as members of our democratic society. (AASL 3)
- Determine a theme of a story, drama, or poem from details in the text; summarize the text. (CCSS 2)
- Uses word reference materials (e.g., glossary, dictionary, thesaurus) to determine the meaning, pronunciation, and derivations of unknown words. (McREL 4)
- Knows the defining characteristics (e.g., rhyme and rhythm in poetry; settings and dialogue in drama, make believe in folktales and fantasies, life stories in biography; illustrations in children's stories) and structural elements (e.g., chapter, scene, stanza, verse, meter) of a variety of genres. (McREL 6)

Objective

Students

- Show how to use a thesaurus and list descriptive words.
- Compose a heart-shaped form poem.

Directions

1. The school librarian reads a Valentine's Day picture book.
2. The reading teacher reads a funny poem or Valentine's Day poem.
3. The teachers discuss how to use a thesaurus and why it is used for writing.
4. Teachers guide students to use a thesaurus and list descriptive words about Valentine's Day.
5. From the word list, students write a two- to three-line Valentine form poem in a heart shape.
6. Students lightly color the Valentine and give their heart poems to someone of their choice.

Teaching Team

Reading and school librarian teachers.

Suggested Sources

Fiction

De Groat, Diane. *Roses Are Pink, Your Feet Really Stink.* Pine Plains, NY: Live Oak Media, 2009.
Jackson, Alison. *The Ballad of Valentine.* New York: Puffin, 2006.

Nonfiction

Chatterton, Martin. *Kingfisher First Thesaurus.* Boston, MA: Houghton Mifflin Harcourt, 2011.
Hellweg, Paul. *The American Heritage Children's Thesaurus.* Boston, MA: Houghton Mifflin Harcourt, 2016.
Prelutsky, Jack. *It's Valentine's Day.* New York: HarperCollins, 2013.
Prelutsky, Jack. *I've Lost My Hippopotamus: More Than 100 Poems.* New York: Greenwillow, 2014.

Horses

Read a short fiction book about a horse. Then answer the following questions.

1. In a complete sentence, explain the main event: _____

_____

2. In a complete sentence, describe the main character: _____

_____

_____

3. In a complete sentence, tell about the setting of the story: _____

_____

3. Inside the horseshoe, neatly write the theme.

4. Lightly color the horseshoe. On the horseshoe, neatly write the name of the horse or give the horse a name. Cut out the horseshoe for a locker decoration.

Horses

Standards

Student(s)

- Draw conclusions, make informed decisions, apply knowledge to new situations, and create new knowledge. (AASL 2)
- Share knowledge and participate ethically and productively as members of our democratic society. (AASL 3)
- Determine a theme of a story, drama, or poem from details in the text; summarize the text. (CCSS 2)
- Describe in depth a character, setting, or event in a story or drama, drawing on specific details in the text (e.g., a character's thoughts words, or actions). (CCSS 3)
- Understands the basic concept of plot (e.g., main problem, conflict, resolution, cause-and-effect). (McREL 7)
- Knows themes that recur across literary works. (McREL 8)

Objective

Students

- Determine theme.
- Describe main character, major events, and setting.

Directions

1. After discussing the title and author, the school librarian reads and shows a grade-appropriate horse picture book.
2. The reading teacher leads a discussion on theme, character, setting, and the major events.
3. Both librarian and social studies teachers assist students as students answer their worksheet questions in complete sentences. Students write the name of the horse inside the horseshoe, and neatly and boldly write the theme on the horseshoe.
4. The horse can be colored. The horseshoe with the horse can be cut out for a locker decoration.

Teaching Team

Reading and school librarian teachers.

Suggested Sources

Brett, Jan. *Fritz and the Beautiful Horses*. New York: G. P. Putnam's Sons Books for Young Readers, 2016.

Dubowski, Cathy East. *Anna Sewell's Black Beauty*. New York: Penguin Young Readers, 2011.

Friedrich, Elizabeth. *Leah's Pony*. Honesdale, PA: Boyd's Mill Press, 1999.

McCully, Emily Arnold. *Wonder Horse*: *The True Story of the World's Smartest Horse*. New York: Henry Holt and Company, 2010.

Morton, Sasha. *Black Beauty*. London: Ticktock, 2014.

Look in the Mirror, Snow White

Look in the Mirror

Read a traditional *Snow White* story and another *Snow White* story version. Compare the two versions in the mirrors.

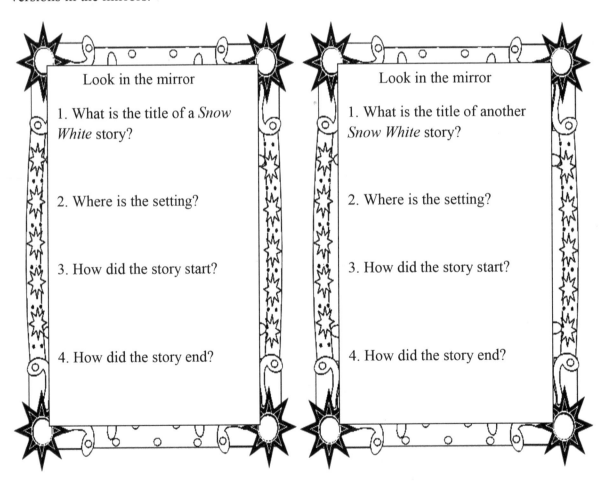

Look in the mirror

1. What is the title of a *Snow White* story?

2. Where is the setting?

3. How did the story start?

4. How did the story end?

Look in the mirror

1. What is the title of another *Snow White* story?

2. Where is the setting?

3. How did the story start?

4. How did the story end?

Look in the Mirror, Snow White

Standards

Student(s)

- Share knowledge and participate ethically and productively as members of our democratic society. (AASL 3)
- Refer to details and examples in a text when explaining what the text says explicitly and when drawing inferences from the text. (CCSS 1)
- Compare and contrast the treatment of similar themes and topics (e.g., opposition of good and evil) and patterns of events (e.g., the quest) in stories, myths, and traditional literature from different cultures. (CCSS 4)
- Reads a variety of literary passages and texts (e.g., fairy tales, folktales, fiction, nonfiction, myths, poems, fables, fantasies, historical fiction, biographies, autobiographies, chapter books). (McREL 5)
- Understands similarities and differences within and among literary works from various genre and cultures (e.g., in terms of settings, character types, events, point of view, role of natural phenomena). (McREL 10)

Objective

Students

- Describe a traditional fairy tale and a nontraditional version.
- Compare characters, theme, setting, and plot of different fairy tale versions.

Directions

1. The teachers read, show, and discuss a traditional and nontraditional Snow White story.
2. The teachers lead a comparison of the two stories, including setting, characters, theme, beginning and ending events, possible inferences, and what makes the story a fairy tale.
3. Teachers guide student work, as students compare the two versions through setting, and the starting and ending of the versions.

Teaching Team

Reading and school librarian teachers.

Suggested Sources

Cali, Davide. *Snow White and the 77 Dwarfs*. Toronto, Canada: Tundra Books, 2015.

Dwyer, Mindy. *Alaska's Snow White and Her Seven Sled Dogs*. Seattle, WA: Sasquatch, 2015.

Gag, Wanda. *Snow White and the Seven Dwarfs*. Minneapolis, MN: University of Minnesota Press, 2004.

Grimm, Jacob. *Snow White and the Seven Dwarfs: A Fairy Tale*. New York: Abbeville Kids, 2001.

Stop

 No Plagiarism

Stop plagiarism! <u>Internet plagiarism</u> could mean not giving credit to authors or creators of Internet work. It is taking something written or created without permission. Some take movies or music off the Internet without permission, which can be seen as <u>Internet piracy</u>.

1. List four or more ways describing how plagiarism could happen with the Internet:

   1.

   2.

   3.

   4.

2. Why is it important not to plagiarize?

3. What is one thing that you want to remember in order to prevent plagiarism?

4. Be a plagiarism official who stops plagiarism! Wear the badge.

From *Standards-Based Lesson Plans for the Busy Elementary School Librarian* by Joyce Keeling. Santa Barbara, CA: Libraries Unlimited. Copyright © 2017.

Stop

Standards

Student(s)

- Inquire, think critically, and gain knowledge. (AASL 1)
- Draw conclusions, make informed decisions, apply knowledge to new situations, and create new knowledge. (AASL 2)
- Share knowledge and participate ethically and productively as members of our democratic society. (AASL 3)
- Pursue personal and aesthetic growth. (AASL 4)
- Interpret information presented visually, orally, or quantitatively (e.g., in charts, graphs, diagrams, timelines, animations, or interactive elements on web pages) and explain how the information contributes to an understanding of the text in which it appears. (CCSS 6)
- Uses electronic media to get information (e.g., databases, Internet, CD-ROM, television shows, videos, pull-down menus, words-searches). (McREL 3)
- Summarizes and paraphrases information in texts (e.g., includes the main idea and significant supporting details of a reading selection). (McREL 11)

Objectives

Students

- Explain Internet plagiarism.

Directions

1. The school librarian and technology teachers briefly discuss Internet plagiarism. The class views an online video on plagiarism or on a similar topic to stimulate discussion. The school librarian also briefly mentions that plagiarism should be carefully watched with books and other such sources as well.
2. After suggesting resources, teachers guide small group discussion and consequent worksheet answers on listing how plagiarism is done, and the importance of plagiarism prevention.
3. Students share their group results with the class.
4. Students cut out and wear the No Plagiarism badge.

Teaching Team

School librarian and technology teachers.

Suggested Sources

Copyright Society of U.S.A. *Copyright Facts*. Updated 2007. Retrieved from http://www.copyrightkids.org/cbasicsframes.htm

Cyberbee. *Cyberbee Copyright* [Game]. Updated 2015. Retrieved from http://www.cyberbee.com/cb_copyright.swf

Nemours. *What Is Plagiarism?* Updated 2016. Retrieved from http://kidshealth.org/kid/feeling/school/plagiarism.html

Youtube.com. *You Tube Copyright School* [Video]. Updated 2012. Retrieved from https://www.youtube.com/watch?v=InzDjH1-9Ns

Wright Flight

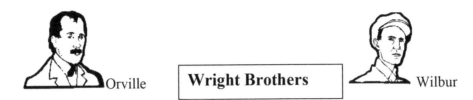

Orville   **Wright Brothers**   Wilbur

Find four facts and then write a final thought on Orville and Wilbur Wright's plane and flight. Write each fact in a complete sentence and write the year. Paraphrase.

Two facts with dates:

Two more facts with dates:

Final thought:

Wright Flight

Standards

Student(s)

- Inquire, think critically, and gain knowledge. (AASL 1)
- Draw conclusions, make informed decisions, apply knowledge to new situations, and create new knowledge. (AASL 2)
- Share knowledge and participate ethically and productively as members of our democratic society. (AASL 3)
- Interpret information presented visually, orally, or quantitatively (e.g., in charts, graphs, diagrams, timelines, animations, or interactive elements on Web pages) and explain how the information contributes to an understanding of the text in which it appears. (CCSS 6)
- Uses encyclopedia to gather information for research topics. (McREL 2)
- Uses electronic media to get information (e.g., databases, Internet, CD-ROM, television shows, videos, pull-down menus, words-searches). (McREL 3)
- Summarizes and paraphrases information in texts (e.g., includes the main idea and significant supporting details of a reading selection). (McREL 11)

Objectives

Students

- Research and summarize the information found about the Wright brothers and state four dates and facts.
- Relate personal thoughts.

Directions

1. The social studies teacher briefly shows an actual Wright brother's plane picture.
2. The school librarian discusses books and Internet sites to use in doing research about the Wright brothers.
3. Both teachers guide student research, as student pairs find four facts with dates on the Wright brothers' plane and flight. Students also give their opinion on the Wright brothers. Students answer in complete original sentences.
4. If the worksheets are copied on card stock, students create a plane. They cut out the two fact strips connected together. They cut out the final thought, bend that final thought strip at the dotted lines, and attach it vertically to the two fact strips for a free-standing biplane.

Teaching Team

School librarian and social studies teachers.

Suggested Sources

Crouch, Tom. "Wright Brothers." *Encyclopedia Britannica*. Updated 2016. Retrieved from http://www.britannica.com/biography/Wright-brothers

Dunn, Joeming W. *The Wright Brothers* [Graphic Novel]. Edina, MN: Magic Wagon, 2008.

MacLeod, Elizabeth. *The Wright Brothers*. Tonawanda, NY: Kids Can Press, 2008.

National Air and Space Museum. *Wright Brothers*. Washington, DC: National Air and Space Museum. Updated 2016. Retrieved from http://airandspace.si.edu/explore-and-learn/topics/wright-brothers.cfm

Old, Wendie, C. *To Fly: The Story of the Wright Brothers*. New York: Clarion Books, 2002.

O'Sullivan, Robyn. *The Wright Brothers Fly*. Washington, DC: National Geographic, 2007.

Weather Forecaster

Forecast:

Be a weather forcaster. Forcast the weather.

1. Use a dictionary to define forecast: _____

_____

2. What will be your forecast? A tornado, hurricane, or a thunderstorm? Write your weather storm choice on the bottom of the weather map.

3. Find three or four facts, like what your storm looks like and how it forms. Use your own words:

_____

_____

_____

_____

Now forecast your storm! **"This is Library TV,** _____

(Your name)

forecasting. The weather is looking like a _____.

(Your storm)

This is what the storm may look like_____

_____

_____

From *Standards-Based Lesson Plans for the Busy Elementary School Librarian* by Joyce Keeling. Santa Barbara, CA: Libraries Unlimited. Copyright © 2017.

Weather Forecaster

Standards

Student(s)

- Inquire, think critically, and gain knowledge. (AASL 1)
- Draw conclusions, make informed decisions, apply knowledge to new situations, and create new knowledge. (AASL 2)
- Interpret information presented visually, orally, or quantitatively (e.g., in charts, graphs, diagrams, timelines, animations, or interactive elements on Web pages) and explain how the information contributes to an understanding of the text in which it appears. (CCSS 6)
- Uses a variety of strategies to plan research (e.g., identifies possible topic by brainstorming, listing questions, using idea webs; organizes prior knowledge about a topic; develops a course of action; determines how to locate necessary information). (McREL 1)
- Uses electronic media to gather information (e.g., databases, Internet, CD-ROM, television shows, videos, pull-down menus, word searches). (McREL 3)
- Uses word reference materials (e.g., glossary, dictionary, thesaurus) to determine the meaning, pronunciation, and derivations of unknown words. (McREL 4)

Objectives

Students

- Define forecast from a dictionary source.
- Research and summarize three or four facts about a storm to forecast the weather.

Directions

1. The science teacher guides student research of the word forecast from a dictionary.
2. The school librarian provides tornado, hurricane, and thunderstorm resources.
3. With guidance from teachers, student pairs select a tornado, hurricane, or thunderstorm, and collect three to four facts on their worksheets for their weather forecast.
4. Student pairs write about and then forecast the weather to small student groups.

Teaching Team

Science and school librarian teachers.

Suggested Sources

Hansen, Grace. *Tornadoes*. Mankato, MN: ABDO, 2016.
Merriam-Webster Editors. *Webster's Dictionary for Students*. Darien, CT: Federal Street Press, 2015.
Miller, Petra. *Hurricanes*. New York: Cavendish Square, 2015.
Otfinoski, Steven. *Tornadoes*. Danbury, CT: Children's Press, 2016.
Robin, Johnson. *What Is a Hurricane?* New York: Crabtree Publishing, 2016.
Robin, Johnson. *What Is a Thunderstorm?* New York: Crabtree Publishing, 2016.
Sandbox Networks. *Infoplease Encyclopedia*. Updated 2016. Retrieved from http://www .infoplease.com
Stiefel, Chana. *Thunderstorms*. Danbury, CT: Children's Press, 2009.
Wicker, Crystal. *WeatherWhizKids*. Updated 2016. Retrieved from http://www.weatherwizkids .com/

Mike Fink

Mike Fink was a legend. He liked keelboats. Keelboats moved by pushing long poles in the river.

1. Describe the character of Mike Fink in a sentence:

_____

_____

2. Why do you think that Mike Fink was called the King of Keelboatman? _____

_____

3. Write two events from the story of Mike Fink that did <u>not</u> sound true: _____

_____

_____

4. Write one or two events that sounded true:

_____

_____

_____

5. Write a three-line rhyming poem about Mike Fink. The title is Mike Fink, the keelboat captain.

Mike Fink, the Keelboat Captain

_____

_____

_____

From *Standards-Based Lesson Plans for the Busy Elementary School Librarian* by Joyce Keeling.
Santa Barbara, CA: Libraries Unlimited. Copyright © 2017.

Mike Fink

Standards

Student(s)

- Draw conclusion, make informed decisions, apply knowledge to new situations, and create new knowledge. (AASL 2)
- Determine a theme of a story, drama, or poem from details in the text; summarize the text. (CCSS 2)
- Compare and contrast the treatment of similar themes and topics (e.g., opposition of good and evil) and patterns of events (e.g., the quest) in stories, myths, and traditional literature from different cultures. (CCSS 4)
- Reads a variety of literary passages and texts (e.g., fairy tales, folktales, fiction, nonfiction, myths, poems, fables, fantasies, historical fiction, biographies, autobiographies, chapter books). (McREL 5)
- Knows the defining characteristics (e.g., rhyme and in poetry, settings and dialog in drama, make believe in folktales and fantasies, life stories in biography; illustrations in children's stories) and structural elements (e.g., chapter, scene, stanza, verse, meter) of a variety of genres. (McREL 6)

Objectives

Students

- Describe a tall tale and the events that make it a tall tale.
- Distinguish character and story events.
- Compose a poem.

Directions

1. The social studies teacher states some true facts about Mike Fink from an online encyclopedia.
2. The school librarian reads a Mike Fink tall tale and discusses what made the story a tall tale.
3. Under teacher's guidance, students discuss and answer character and story event questions.
4. In small groups, students create a three-line rhyming poem about Mike Fink.

Teaching Team

School librarian and social studies teachers.

Suggested Sources

Encyclopedia Britannica Editors. *Mike Fink: American Frontiersman.* Updated 2016. Retrieved from http://www.britannica.com/biography/Mike-Fink

Hoberman, Mary Ann. *You Read to Me, I'll Read to You: Very Short Tall Tales to Read Together.* New York: Little, Brown Books for Young Readers, 2014.

Kellogg, Steven. *Mike Fink: A Tall Tale.* New York: HarperCollins, 1998.

Krensky, Stephen. *Mike Fink.* Minneapolis, MN: Millbrook Press, 2007.

Sandbox Networks. "Mike Fink." *Infoplease Columbia Encyclopedia.* Updated 2016. Retrieved from http://www.infoplease.com/encyclopedia/people/fink-mike.html

Hitting a Home Run

Choose an unfamiliar sport and find facts about it. Hit a home run with good facts. Find three to five facts in a print nonfiction book or print encyclopedia and put those facts on one ball, and then find three to five other facts from an online encyclopedia for the other ball. Around the top baseball player, write one or more similar facts that are found in both places. Be careful not to plagiarize.

First what is your sports topic: _____

How would you summarize your facts from both sources? What did you find out? Write a paragraph: _____

_____

_____

_____

_____

Hitting a Home Run

Standards

Student(s)

- Inquire, think critically, and gain knowledge. (AASL 1)
- Draw conclusions, make informed decisions, apply knowledge to new situations, and create new knowledge. (AASL 2)
- Refer to details and examples in a text, when explaining what the text says explicitly and when drawing inferences from the text. (CCSS 5)
- Interpret information presented visually, orally, or quantitatively (e.g., in charts, graphs, diagrams, timelines, animations, or interactive elements on Web pages) and explain how the information contributes to an understanding of the text in which it appears. (CCSS 6)
- Uses a variety of strategies to plan research (e.g., identifies possible topic by brainstorming, listing questions, using idea webs; organizes prior knowledge about a topic; develops a course of action; determines how to locate necessary information). (McREL 1)
- Uses encyclopedias to gather information for research topics. (McREL 2)
- Summarizes and paraphrase information in texts (e.g., includes the main idea and significant supporting details of a reading selection). (McREL 11)

Objectives

Students

- Compare key detailed facts about an unfamiliar sport's rules from two different sources.
- Summarize and paraphrase findings in a paragraph.

Directions

1. The physical education teacher guides student brainstorming of different and unfamiliar sports. They discuss narrowing a sports research topic to rules of the sport.
2. The school librarian provides print and Internet sport resources.
3. With teacher's guidance, students pick an unfamiliar sport, find three to five sport's rule facts from a print nonfiction source, and summarize on the worksheet on one of the baseballs. On the other baseball, they find and write three to five sport rule facts from an online encyclopedia.
4. Around the top page baseball player, students compare one or more similar facts from the two sources.
5. Students write and paraphrase a paragraph summarizing their findings.

Teaching Team

Physical education and school librarian teachers.

Suggested Sources

Academic Kids Encyclopedia. *Academic Kids Encyclopedia*. Updated 2016. Retrieved from http://academickids.com/encyclopedia/index.php/List_of_sports

Factmonster. "Information Please." *Columbia Encyclopedia*. Updated 2012. Retrieved from http://www.factmonster.com

Fortin, Francois, Ed. *Sports: The Complete Visual Reference*. Richmond, ON: Firefly Books, 2003.

Hammond, Tim. *DK Eyewitness Books: Sports.* New York: DK, 2005.

World Book. *World Book Encyclopedia.* Chicago, IL: World Book, 2016.

Zweig, Eric. *National Geographic Kids Everything Sports: All Photos, Facts, and Fun to Make You Jump!* Washington, DC: National Geographic Kids, 2016.

Chapter 6

Fifth-Grade Lesson Plans

The fifth-grade lesson plans are created to help the busy school librarian, as he or she works to meet the demanding needs of a school library including that of teaching needed skills. The following interactive standards-backed elementary lessons will meet the globally literate needs of today's students. The lessons are set to different standards in the desire to meet the school librarians' state or school library, Common Core State Standards (CCSS) or McREL literacy, or English language arts standards, which include the American Association of School Librarians (AASL) standards.

The quality-researched standards of AASL, CCSS, and the McREL Compendium of Standards and Benchmarks are applied with each school library lesson for purposeful school library instruction and to enable students to achieve skills. The parts of the standards chosen for this book were those that were the most essential for library instruction and could be met in the lesson time allotment of twenty minutes. The standards may be used together as given, individually, or lessons may be set to other quality standards.

Student learning objectives are given for each lesson. Lessons include students working individually or with others for more efficient student learning. Team teaching is seen, as more can be accomplished when working together. Quality-researched resources are suggested. The streamlined, standards-based lessons for the busy school librarian provide interactive and successful student literacy learning. The AASL standards are stated in the first chapter as they are universally seen with all lessons. The following McREL and CCSS standards are used specifically with this grade level.

Fifth-Grade Library Standards with Language Arts Benchmarks from McREL Language Arts Writing Standards and Benchmarks and Common Core Language Arts Literacy Standards (CCSS)

Fifth-grade students:

*Fifth-Grade Common Core (Literacy), Reading Literature

1. Determine a theme of a story, drama, or poem from details in the text, including how characters in a story or drama respond to challenges or how the speaker in a poem reflects upon a topic; summarize the text. (CCSS.ELA-Literacy.RL.5.2)

2. Compare and contrast two or more characters, setting, or events in a story or drama, drawing on specific details in a text (e.g., how characters interact). (CCSS.ELA-Literacy.RL.5.3)

3. Analyze how visual and multimedia elements contribute to the meaning, tone, or beauty of a text (e.g., graphic novel, multimedia presentation of fiction, folktale, myth, poem). (CCSS.ELA-Literacy.RL.5.7)

4. Compare and contrast stories in the same genre (e.g., mysteries and adventure stories) on their approaches to similar themes and topics. (CCSS.ELA-Literacy.RL.5.9)

*Fifth-Grade Common Core (Literacy), Reading Informational Texts

5. Explain the relationships or interactions between two or more individuals, events, ideas, or concepts in a historical, scientific, or technical text based on specific information in the text. (CCSS.ElA-Literacy.RI.5.3)

6. Draw on information from multiple print or digital sources, demonstrating the ability to locate an answer to a question quickly or to solve a problem efficiently. (CCSS.ELA-Literacy.RI.5.7)

7. Integrate information from several texts on the same topic in order to write or speak about the subject knowledgeably. (CCSS.ELA-Literacy.R.I.5.9)

McREL Compendium of Standards and Benchmarks Language Arts Writing Standards and Benchmarks (Grades 3–5)

*Gather and use information for research purposes. Standard 4

1. Use a variety of strategies to plan research (e.g., identifies possible topic by brainstorming, listing questions, using idea webs; organizes prior knowledge about a topic; develosp a course of action; determines how to locate necessary information). (McREL)
2. Use encyclopedias to gather information for research topics. (McREL)
3. Use electronic media to gather information (e.g., databases, Internet, CD-ROM, television shows, videos, pull-down menus, word searches). (McREL)

McREL Compendium of Standards and Benchmarks Language Arts Reading Standards and Benchmarks (Grades 3–5)

*Use the general skills and strategies of the reading process. Standard 5

4. Use word reference materials (e.g., glossary, dictionary, thesaurus) to determine the meaning, pronunciation, and derivations of unknown words. (McREL)
   *Use skills and strategies to read a variety of literary texts. Standard 6
5. Read a variety of literary passages and texts (e.g., fairy tales, folktales, fiction, nonfiction, myths, poems, fables, fantasies, historical fiction, biographies, autobiographies, chapter books). (McREL)
6. Know the defining characteristics (e.g., rhyme and rhythm in poetry; settings and dialogue in drama, make believe in folktales and fantasies, life stories in biography; illustrations in children's stories) and structural elements (e.g., chapter, scene, stanza, verse, meter) of a variety of genres. (McREL)
7. Understand the basic concept of plot (e.g., main problem, conflict, resolution, cause-and-effect). (McREL)
8. Understand similarities and differences within and among literacy works from various genres and cultures (e.g., in terms of settings, character types, events, point of view, role of natural phenomena). (McREL)
9. Know themes that recur across literary works. (McREL)

*Use skills and strategies to read a variety of informational texts. Standard 7

10. Use the various parts of a book (e.g., index, table of contents, glossary, appendix, preface) to locate information. (McREL)
11. Summarize and paraphrase information in texts (e.g., include the main idea and significant supporting details of a reading selection). (McREL)

Permission received from McREL. *Language Arts Standards*, 2015. Retrieved from http://www2.mcrel.org/compendium/standard

DO YOU KNOW THE LIBRARY?

Review what your team knows about the following subjects: (1) Book parts (like the glossary and other book parts), (2) Online catalog (three main ways to search the online catalog and other facts), and (3) Fiction and nonfiction. Then challenge teams for 100–400 points on the subjects.

BOOK PARTS

100.200.300.400

ONLINE CATALOG

100.200.300.400

FICTION NONFICTION

100.200.300.400

Know Your Library

Standards

Students

- Inquire, think critically, and gain knowledge (AASL 1)
- Draw conclusions, make informed decisions, apply knowledge to new situations, and create new knowledge (AASL 2)
- Share knowledge and participate ethically and productively as members of our democratic society (AASL 3)
- Draw on information from multiple print or digital sources, demonstrating the ability to locate an answer to a question quickly or to solve a problem efficiently (CCSS 6)
- Use[s] the various parts of a book (e.g. index, table of contents, glossary, appendix, preface) to locate information (McREL 10)

Objectives

Students

- Review card catalog, book parts, and fiction and nonfiction
- Challenge teams when recalling the card catalog, book parts, fiction and nonfiction

Directions

1. The school librarian divides the class into two-three teams, and introduces the subjects of the card catalog, book parts, fiction and nonfiction. Teams briefly review the subjects.
2. In large font, the reading teacher posts the worksheets subjects and numbers, so that teams can select a subject and 100, 200, 300, or 400 point category for their library jeopardy type questions.
3. Teachers read the questions and cross off point categories and questions as answered.
4. Teams keep track of points, as subject and point categories are team selected, quietly and quickly team discussed, and then answered in lightning fast paces. This is a fun library review.

Teaching Team

Reading and school librarian teachers.

Questions with 100 to 400 Points:

Book Parts. For100 points—what is the page called that shows the title, author, illustrator, publisher, and publishing place? 200—What is the book part called that gives the page numbers for chapters? 300—What book part give pages numbers for many subjects in the book? 400—What is the book part that gives word meanings for the book, like a dictionary?

Card Catalog. For 100 points—how do you search the card catalog for a certain author? 200—How do you find a specific book title on the card catalog? 300—If you were looking for any book on a certain subject, how will you search on the card catalog? 400—When you use the card catalog to find a book, how do you find the book in the library?

Fiction or Nonfiction. For 100 points—what is a biography? 200—Where would you find a true book on football facts; in the nonfiction or fiction? 300—What is fiction, and where is it located? 400—In a short sentence explain the difference between nonfiction and fiction?

Suggested Sources

None needed

King Arthur and the Sword in the Stone

King Arthur had real and legendary stories told about him. A popular story was *The Sword in the Stone*. Read a brief version of it. Then create a short graphic novel showing beginning, middle, and ending events of the tale.

King Arthur & the Sword in the Stone		

King Arthur and the Sword in the Stone

Standards

Student(s)

- Inquire, think critically, and gain knowledge. (AASL 1)
- Draw conclusions, make informed decisions, apply knowledge to new situations, and create new knowledge. (AASL 2)
- Determine a theme of a story, drama, or poem from details in the text, including how characters in a story or drama respond to challenges or how the speaker in a poem reflects upon a topic; summarize the text. (CCSS 1)
- Analyze how visual and multimedia elements contribute to the meaning, tone, or beauty of a text (e.g., graphic novel, multimedia presentation of fiction, folktale, myth, poem). (CCSS 3)
- Reads a variety of literary passages and texts (e.g., fairy tales, folktales, fiction, nonfiction, myths, poems, fables, fantasies, historical fiction, biographies, autobiographies, chapter books). (McREL 5)
- Understands similarities and differences within and among literacy works from various genres and cultures (e.g., in terms of settings, character types, events, point of view, role of natural phenomena). (McREL 8)

Objectives

Students

- Define a legend, point of view, setting, theme, plot, and character.
- Create a graphic novelette.

Directions

1. The reading and school librarian teachers introduce and read King Arthur and his sword or *The Sword in the Stone* story.
2. Teachers lead the class in discussing plot, point of view, setting, theme, and character.
3. The library teacher provides an example of a graphic novel.
4. Students create a graphic novelette of the story.

Teaching Team

Reading and school librarian teachers.

Suggested Sources

Brooks, Felicity. "King Arthur and the Sword in the Stone." *Tales of King Arthur.* London, England: Usborne Publishing, 2007.

Courta, Sarah. *Illustrated Tales of King Arthur.* London, England: Usborne, 2014.

Ganeri, Anita. *King Arthur's Tale.* New York: Crabtree Publishing, 2012.

Limke, Jeff. *King Arthur: Excalibur Unsheathed: An English Legend.* Minneapolis, MN: Graphic Universe Publishing, 2006.

Miester, Carl. *King Arthur and the Sword in the Stone.* Mankato, MN: Picture Window Books, 2009.

Internet Diving

When diving into the Internet, it can be fun. However, can you believe everything you see on the Internet? Use the Internet life preserver AABC check list for quality searching. Quality searching will give you an Internet site with a credible author, the right audience (for you), a big purpose (to help you), and current information. Cut out the preserver sign and keep it near!

Try out the Internet life preserver checklist for good searches. Find five facts about an ocean.
(1) First circle your chosen ocean: Pacific, Atlantic, Artic, or Indian Ocean.

(2) Find a good Internet site on your chosen ocean that meets the Internet life preserver checklist. Write down the Internet site address: _____

(3) Now, use the site. Paraphrase and write five short facts on your ocean in a paragraph.

_____

_____

_____

_____

_____

Internet Diving

Standards

Student(s)

- Inquire, think critically, and gain knowledge. (AASL 1)
- Draw conclusions, make informed decisions, apply knowledge to new situations, and create new knowledge. (AASL 2)
- Share knowledge and participate ethically and productively as members of our democratic society. (AASL 3)
- Pursue personal and aesthetic growth. (AASL 4)
- Draw on information from multiple print or digital sources, demonstrating the ability to locate an answer to a question quickly or to solve a problem efficiently. (CCSS 6)
- Uses encyclopedias to gather information for research topics. (McREL 2)
- Uses electronic media to gather information (e.g., databases, Internet, CD-ROM, television shows, videos, pull-down menus, word searches). (McREL 3)
- Summarizes and paraphrases information found in texts (e.g., retells the main ideas and significant supporting details of a reading selection). (McREL 11)

Objectives

Students

- Discuss quality ways to search the Internet.
- Search for facts about the Pacific, Atlantic, Artic, or Indian Ocean.
- Summarize facts in a five-sentence paragraph.

Directions

1. The science teacher introduces the lesson by briefly mentioning the major oceans.
2. The school librarian and technology teachers discuss ways to find quality sources on the Internet and discuss the life preserver checklist.
3. Teachers give Internet sites for general facts on Pacific, Atlantic, Artic, and Indian Oceans.
4. Teachers guide student pairs to search for general ocean facts for a five-sentence paragraph.
5. Students write and share their information. They cut out the preserver sign to keep in their billfolds.

Teaching Team

Social studies, school librarian, and technology teachers.

Suggested Sources

Briney, Amanda. *Geography of the World's Oceans*. Updated 2016. Retrieved from http://geography.about.com/od/locateplacesworldwide/tp/fiveoceans.htm

Encyclopedia Britannica. *Oceans*. Updated 2016. Retrieved from http://www.britannica.com/search?query=oceans

Graeff, Regina. *Ocean Facts for Kids*. Updated 2015. Retrieved from http://www.kids-world-travel-guide.com/ocean-facts-for-kids.html

Greller, J. *A Media Specialist Guide to Evaluating Web Sites*. Updated 2008. Retrieved from http://mediaspecialistsguide.blogspot.ie/2015/12/updated-post-do-your-students-know-how.html

Piracy

1. In your own words, define plagiarism in one sentence.

2. In your own words, define Internet piracy in one sentence.

3. What are some things on the Internet that you cannot copy without permission?

   1.

   2.

   3.

   4.

   5.

4. What are a few things that can be done to avoid piracy and plagiarism on the Internet? Write those facts around the pirate chest.

Piracy

Standards

Student(s)

- Inquire, think critically, and gain knowledge. (AASL 1)
- Draw conclusions, make informed decisions, apply knowledge to new situations, and create new knowledge. (AASL 2)
- Share knowledge and participate ethically and productively as members of our democratic society (AASL 3)
- Pursue personal and aesthetic growth. (AASL 4)
- Draw on information from multiple print or digital sources, demonstrating the ability to locate an answer to a question quickly or to solve a problem efficiently. (CCSS 6)
- Uses electronic media to gather information (e.g., databases, Internet, CD-ROM, television shows, videos, pull-down menus, word searches). (McREL 3)
- Summarizes and paraphrases information found in texts (e.g., retells the main ideas and significant supporting details of a reading selection). (McREL 11)

Objectives

Students

- Describe plagiarism and list ways to avoid plagiarism.
- Define Internet piracy and list ways to avoid piracy.

Directions

1. While using online resources, the school librarian and technology teachers define and tell about Internet piracy and Internet plagiarism through an online video or similar source.
2. The librarian and technology teachers lead a class discussion on Internet plagiarism and piracy.
3. Small student groups or pairs discuss and answer the worksheet questions on plagiarism and piracy. Around the pirate's chest, students write facts on Internet piracy prevention.
4. Students discuss their answers with the class.

Teaching Team

School librarian and technology teachers.

Suggested Sources

Common Sense Media. *Teaching Kids about Copyright & Piracy* [Video]. Updated 2016. Retrieved from https://www.commonsensemedia.org/videos/teaching-kids-about-copyright-piracy

Harris, Jennifer. *Plagiarism.* Updated 2012. Retrieved from http://edtech2.boisestate.edu/jenniferharris2/502/scavenger.html

Hartman, Molly. *Plagiarism.* Updated 2015. Retrieved from http://www.factmonster.com/spot/plagiarism.html

Nemours. *What Is Plagiarism?* Updated 2016. Retrieved from http://kidshealth.org/kid/feeling/school/plagiarism.html

St. Andrews College Library. *Plagiarism – Don't Do It!!!* (n.d.). Retrieved from https://librarysac.wordpress.com/research/dont-do-it/

Race for the Win

Your group will race to find the following answers about books. You must use the library online catalog half the time and an Internet site the other half. First, circle the source that you are using to find the answers (Internet site or online catalog). Then research to answer each question.

(1) Used Internet site or online catalog? Who is the author of *Where the Red Fern Grows*?

_____

(2) Used Internet site or online catalog? List the main character from *Hatchet* by Paulsen.

_____

(3) Used Internet site or online catalog? Who is the publisher and where is the publishing place for *Harry Potter and the Sorcerer's Stone* by Rowling? _____

_____

(4) Used Internet site or online catalog? List five books written by Matt Christopher.

_____

_____

(5) Used Internet site or online catalog? List two book awards for the book called *Charlotte's Web* by White. _____

(6) Used Internet site or online catalog? Where is a location (setting) for *Lighting Thief* by Riodoran? _____

(7) Used Internet site or online catalog? How many pages long is *Charlie and Chocolate Factory* by Dahl? _____

(8) Used Internet site or online catalog? Write a short sentence describing *Island of the Blue Dolphins* by O'Dell: _____

_____

_____

Race for the Win

Standards

Student(s)

- Inquire, think critically, and gain knowledge. (AASL 1)
- Draw conclusions, make informed decisions, apply knowledge to new situations, and create new knowledge. (AASL 2)
- Share knowledge and participate ethically and productively as members of our democratic society. (AASL 3)
- Pursue personal and aesthetic growth. (AASL 4)
- Draw on information from multiple print or digital sources, demonstrating the ability to locate an answer to a question quickly or to solve a problem efficiently. (CCSS 6)
- Uses electronic media to gather information (e.g., databases, Internet, CD-ROM, television shows, videos, pull-down menus, word searches). (McREL 3)

Objectives

Students

- Review using the online catalog and review how to locate sources online.
- Locate information regarding books with both the online catalog and the Internet.

Directions

1. The school librarian reviews how to search subject, author, and title with the online catalog. If there is not an available online catalog, students use an online world library catalog (OCLC).
2. The technology teacher briefly reminds students how to find quick, accurate information with the Internet.
3. Student teams are established to see how quickly and accurately worksheet questions can be answered.
4. In order to find popular book answers from the worksheet questions, student teams must use the online catalog for half of the questions and then an Internet web site for the other half of the questions.
5. Students first circle their source of either online catalog or Internet for the questions and then they research to answer the questions.
6. Answers are shared. In a class chart, the results of using the Internet versus the online catalog are tallied to see which resource gave the best, fastest, or easier answers.

Teaching Team

School librarian and technology teachers.

Suggested Sources

Automated Card Catalog and Internet

OCLC. *Online World Libraries* (World Cat). Updated 2015. Retrieved from http://www.worldcat .org

Native American Indian Horse

1. Read two Native American Indian fiction books that have a horse character and was written by the same author. Note: the Native American Indian rider may have a leather bag as seen below.

2. What is the title of one book? _____

3. What is the title of the other book? _____

4. Who is the author? _____

5. How were the books similar? _____

_____

6. Now, how were the books different from each other? _____

_____

7. In descriptive words, tell the theme of one book around the American Indian bag.

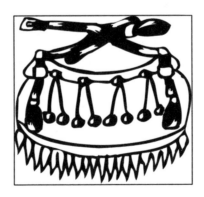

Native American Indian Horse

Standards

Student(s)

- Inquire, think critically, and gain knowledge. (AASL 1)
- Draw conclusions, make informed decisions, apply knowledge to new situations, and create new knowledge. (AASL 2)
- Share knowledge and participate ethically and productively as members of our democratic society. (AASL 3)
- Pursue personal and aesthetic growth. (AASL 4)
- Compare and contrast two or more characters, setting, or events in a story or drama, drawing on specific details in a text (e.g., how characters interact). (CCSS 2)
- Compare and contrast stories in the same genre (e.g., mysteries and adventure stories) on their approaches to similar themes and topics. (CCSS 4)
- Understands similarities and differences within and among literacy works from various genres and cultures (e.g., in terms of settings, character types, events, point of view, role of natural phenomena). (McREL 8)
- Knows themes that recur across literary works. (McREL 9)

Objectives

Students

- Compare two books by the same author.
- Describe title, author, plot, characters, and theme.

Directions

1. The school librarian and social studies teacher each reads a Native American Indian horse story written by the same author. Theme, characters, and setting are compared and discussed.
2. Teachers guide student discussion and then worksheet answers on the comparison of the story's plot similarities and differences and titles. The author is also listed.
3. Students will tell the theme of one story around the Native American Indian bag on the worksheet.

Teaching Team

School librarian and social studies teachers.

Suggested Sources

Fiction

> Bruchac, Joseph. *The Hunter's Promise: An Abenaki Tale.* Bloomington, IN: Wisdom Tales, 2015.
> Bruchac, Joseph and Nelson, S. D. *Crazy Horse's Vision.* New York: Lee & Low Books, 2000.
> Nelson, S. D. *Gift Horse.* New York: Henry N. Abrams Books for Young Readers, 2012.

Nonfiction

> Nelson, S. D. *Greet the Dawn the Lakota Way.* Pierre, SD: South Dakota State Historical Society, 2002.

Squanto

Squanto was a Native American Indian from the Patuxet (Pawtuxet) tribe. Research Squanto and also find out how Squanto helped the Pilgrims in two or more ways. Research using (1) an Internet site source and (2) a book source.

A. Describe two or more facts in Squanto's life that helped the Pilgrims. Paraphrase.

1.

2.

3.

B. Describe two or more other facts about Squanto. Paraphrase.

1.

2.

3.

C. Record where you found your information.

1. From a book

Author: Title:

Publisher: Publishing Place:

Copyright:

2. From an online source

Author: Title:

Copyright: Internet Address:

From *Standards-Based Lesson Plans for the Busy Elementary School Librarian* by Joyce Keeling. Santa Barbara, CA: Libraries Unlimited. Copyright © 2017.

Squanto

Standards

Student(s)

- Inquire, think critically, and gain knowledge. (AASL 1)
- Draw conclusions, make informed decisions, apply knowledge to new situations, and create new knowledge. (AASL 2)
- Explain the relationships or interactions between two or more individuals, events, ideas, or concepts in a historical, scientific, or technical text based on specific information in the text. (CCSS 5)
- Draw on information from multiple print or digital sources, demonstrating the ability to locate and answer to a question quickly or to solve a problem efficiently. (CCSS 6)
- Integrate information from several texts on the same topic in order to write or speak about the subject knowledgeably. (CCSS 7)
- Uses encyclopedias to gather information for research topics. (McREL 2)
- Uses electronic media to gather information (e.g., databases, Internet, CD-ROM, television shows, videos, pull down menus, word searches). (McREL 3)

Objectives

Students

- Research and describe Squanto along with his impact on Thanksgiving.
- Cite sources.

Directions

1. The school librarian and the social studies teachers introduce Squanto and his importance in American history. Students are asked to research Squanto.
2. Students are given Squanto Internet links and print sources by the school librarian.
3. Teachers guide small student groups research as students answer the worksheet questions on how Squanto helped the Pilgrims and two or more other facts about him.
4. With teachers' guidance, students cite both online and print sources.

Teaching Team

School librarian and social studies teachers.

Suggested Sources

Biography.Com. *Squanto*. Updated 2015. Retrieved from http://www.biography.com/people/squanto-9491327

Bruchac, Joseph. *Squanto's Journey: The Story of the First Thanksgiving*. Boston, MA: Harcourt, 2007.

Encyclopedia Britannica. *Squanto*. Updated 2014. Retrieved from http://www.britannica.com/biography/Squanto

Ghiglieri, Carol. *Early Reader Biographies: Squanto: A Friend to the Pilgrims*. New York: Scholastic, 2007.

Metaxas, Eric. *Squanto and the Miracle of Thanksgiving*. Nashville, TN: Thomas Nelson, 2012.

Molly Pitcher

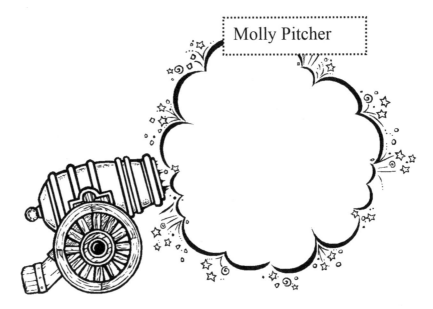

Molly Pitcher

1. Describe the story of Molly Pitcher in a list of words:

2. Use the list of descriptive words to create a four-line ballad poem. A ballad poem can tell about a historical event in a story. Write about the historical story of Molly Pitcher. Rhyme the first and third lines of the four-line poem.

From *Standards-Based Lesson Plans for the Busy Elementary School Librarian* by Joyce Keeling. Santa Barbara, CA: Libraries Unlimited. Copyright © 2017.

Molly Pitcher

Standards

Student(s)

- Inquire, think critically, and gain knowledge. (AASL 1)
- Draw conclusions, make informed decisions, apply knowledge to new situations, and create new knowledge. (AASL 2)
- Determine a theme of a story, drama, or poem from details in the text, including how characters in a story or drama respond to challenges or how the speaker in a poem reflects upon a topic; summarize the text. (CCSS 1)
- Analyze how visual and multimedia elements contribute to the meaning, tone, or beauty of a text (e.g., graphic novel, multimedia presentation of fiction, folktale, myth, poem). (CCSS 3)
- Reads a variety of literary passages and texts (e.g., fairy tales, folktales, fiction, nonfiction, myths, poems, fables, fantasies, historical fiction, biographies, autobiographies, chapter books). (McREL 5)
- Knows the defining characteristics (e.g., rhyme and rhythm in poetry; settings and dialogue in drama, make believe in folktales and fantasies, life stories in biography; illustrations in children's stories) and structural elements (e.g., chapter, scene, stanza, verse, meter) of a variety of genres. (McREL 6)

Objectives

Students

- Research and tell about Molly Pitcher through a listing of words.
- Identify a ballad poem and write a ballad poem.

Directions

1. The reading teacher introduces a ballad poem and gives a short example.
2. The social studies and librarian teachers present Molly Pitcher resources.
3. As guided by teachers, small student groups research Molly Pitcher and jot down words describing Pitcher.
4. Under the guidance of teachers, small groups create a short Molly Pitcher ballad or poem.

Teaching Team

Reading, school librarian, and social studies teachers.

Suggested Sources

A & E Television Networks. *Molly Pitcher*. Biography.com. Updated 2016. Retrieved from http://www.biography.com

Bright, J. E. *Famous American Folktales*. Paris, France: Auzuou Publisher, 2015.

Glaser, Jason. *Molly Pitcher: Young American Patriot* (Graphic Biographies). Mankato, MN: Capstone Press, 2006.

Mitchel, Kathi. "Ballads." *Poetry for Kids*. Updated 2015. Retrieved from http://www.kathi mitchell.com/poemtypes.html

Rockwell, Anne F. *They Called Her Molly Pitcher*. New York: Dragonfly Books, 2006.

Reaching for the Olympic Facts

Reaching for the Facts with the Olympics

<u>In the top three circles discuss the Olympics</u>: (1) Describe the five Olympic rings in the first circle. (2) List two to three winter Olympic events in the second circle. (3) List two to three summer Olympic events in the third circle.

<u>In the bottom two circles discuss one event</u>: (1) Choose and describe one Olympic event in one circle. (2) List two to three countries that have won medals at your chosen Olympic event in the final circle.

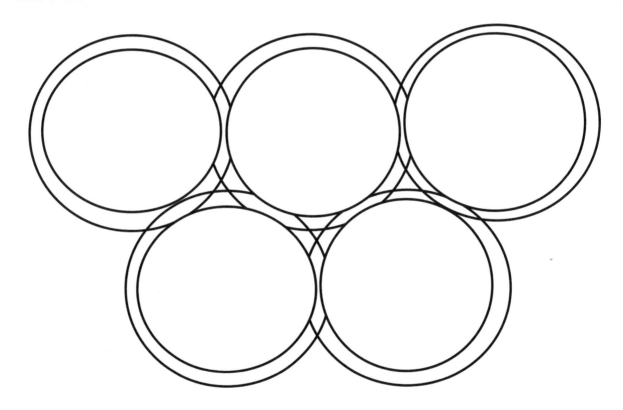

From *Standards-Based Lesson Plans for the Busy Elementary School Librarian* by Joyce Keeling.
Santa Barbara, CA: Libraries Unlimited. Copyright © 2017.

Reaching for the Olympic Facts

Standards

Student(s)

- Inquire, think critically, and gain knowledge. (AASL 1)
- Draw conclusions, make informed decisions, apply knowledge to new situations, and create new knowledge. (AASL 2)
- Share knowledge and participate ethically and productively as members of our democratic society. (AASL 3)
- Pursue personal and aesthetic growth. (AASL 4)
- Draw on information from multiple print or digital sources, demonstrating the ability to locate an answer to a question quickly or to solve a problem efficiently. (CCSS 6)
- Uses electronic media to gather information (e.g., databases, Internet, CD-ROM, television shows, videos, pull-down menus, word searches). (McREL 3)
- Summarizes and paraphrases information found in texts (e.g., retells the main ideas and significant supporting details of a reading selection). (McREL 11)

Objectives

Students

- Research and briefly paraphrase basic facts about the Olympic.
- Research and briefly describe an Olympic event by paraphrasing.

Directions

1. The social studies teacher introduces the lesson by showing a short Olympic video clip.
2. The school librarian suggests Olympic resources and describes the worksheet.
3. The teachers guide student research.
4. Small student groups answer the worksheet questions about the Olympic rings, winter and summer Olympic events, and then describe one event in the bottom worksheet circles.

Teaching Team

School librarian and social studies teachers.

Suggested Sources

Butterfield, Moira. *Events*. North Mankato, MN: Sea-to-Sea Publications, 2012.

Enchantedlearning.com. *The Olympic Games*. Updated 2015. Retrieved from http://www.enchantedlearning.com/olympics/

Factmonster. *Olympic Fun Facts*. Updated 2016. Retrieved from http://www.factmonster.com/ipka/A0771580.html

Hurley, Michael. *Great Olympic Moments*. Portsmouth, NH: Heinemann Library, 2012.

Kidskonnect. *Olympic Facts*. Updated 2016. Retrieved from https://kidskonnect.com/sports/olympics/

Kortemeier, Todd. *Inside the Olympics*. North Mankato, MN: The Child's World, Inc., 2016.

Olympic.org. *Video Galleries*. Updated 2015. Retrieved from http://www.olympic.org/videos

Rosenberg, Jennifer. *Interesting Olympic Facts*. Updated 2016. Retrieved from http://history1900s.about.com/od/greateventsofthecentury/a/olympicfacts.htm

Team USA. Updated 2016. Retrieved from http://www.teamusa.org/usa

Framing a Medal

Framing a Medal

Read a Newbery award winner, a Coretta Scott King award winner, or a state award book winner for your age level. Then frame the book: (1) Colorfully illustrate the plot in the large picture area, (2) Neatly state the award in the bottom of the frame, and (3) In the top of the frame, neatly state the title and author. Vertically attach the box that says "Framing a Medal" to the back of the following framed work so that your framed work stands independently.

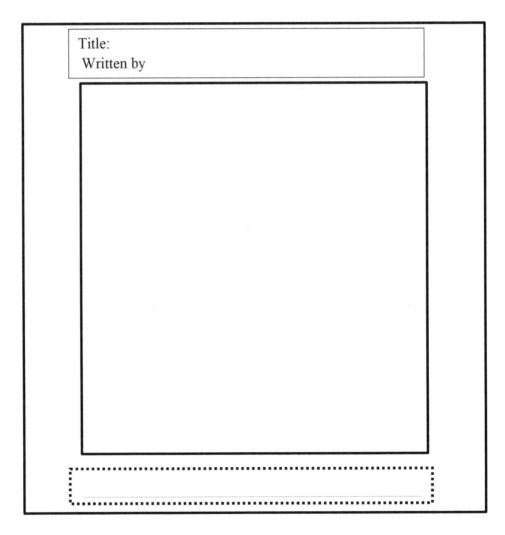

Framing a Medal

Standards

Student(s)

- Inquire, think critically, and gain knowledge. (AASL 1)
- Draw conclusions, make informed decisions, apply knowledge to new situations, and create new knowledge. (AASL 2)
- Compare and contrast stories in the same genre (e.g., mysteries and adventure stories) on their approaches to similar themes and topics. (CCSS 4)
- Reads a variety of literary passages and texts (e.g., fairy tales, folktales, fiction, nonfiction, myths, poems, fables, fantasies, historical fiction, biographies, autobiographies, chapter books). (McREL 5)
- Understands similarities and differences within and among literacy works from various genres and cultures (e.g., in terms of settings, character types, events, point of view, role of natural phenomena). (McREL 8)

Objectives

Students

- Read and describe a Newbery book or other book award book.
- Illustrate plot, and state the award, title, and author.
- Give an oral book report on plot, genre, award, title, and author.

Directions

1. Student sheets are copied on card stock.
2. The reading and school librarian teachers discuss genres and give examples of Newbery book awards, Coretta Scott King author book awards, and state book awards or other book awards.
3. After reading books, students colorfully illustrate the book's main plot in the worksheet frame, and neatly write the award, title, and author on the picture frame. They cut out the framed picture and "Framing a Medal" strip. The strip is attached vertically to the picture back as an easel stand.
4. Students present their picture and give a brief oral report of the major event, genre, title, and author of the book and explain why the book should or should not get the award.
5. This activity requires time for students to read their book, before completing the lesson.

Teaching Team

Reading and school librarian teachers.

Suggested Sources

American Library Association. *Coretta Scott King Book Awards-All Recipients-1970-Present.* Updated 2016. Retrieved from http://www.ala.org/emiert/coretta-scott-king-book-awards-
American Library Association. *Newbery Medal Winners, 1922-Present.* Updated 2016. Retrieved from http://www.ala.org/alsc/awardsgrants/bookmedia/newberymedal/newbery/winners/
Iowa Association of School Librarians. *Iowa Children's Choice Award.* Updated 2016. Retrieved from http://www.iasl-ia.org/p/iowa-teen-award.html

Christmas around the World

 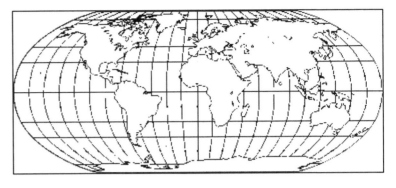

Research how Christmas is traditionally celebrated around the world. Select a country. (1) Draw a line from the Santa to the country's location on the world map. (2) Then create a colorful holiday wreath of that country's Christmas traditions: Write the country's name under the wreath ribbon. Colorfully draw or write about the country's Christmas traditions on the wreath balls. Color the wreath.

Merry Christmas from the country of:

Christmas around the World

Standards

Student(s)

- Inquire, think critically, and gain knowledge. (AASL 1)
- Draw conclusions, make informed decisions, apply knowledge to new situations, and create new knowledge. (AASL 2)
- Draw on information from multiple print or digital sources, demonstrating the ability to locate an answer to a question quickly or to solve a problem efficiently. (CCSS 6)
- Summarizes and paraphrases information in texts (e.g., includes the main idea and significant supporting details of a reading selection). (McREL 11)

Objectives

Students

- Select a country, and locate it on the world worksheet map.
- Research and summarize a country's Christmas traditions.

Directions

1. The school librarian and social studies teachers give examples of countries and their location.
2. The school librarian teacher points out resources on a country's Christmas traditions.
3. Students select a country and use a globe to locate the country on the worksheet world map.
4. As guided by teachers, students research the country's Christmas traditions.
5. Students colorfully illustrate or colorfully write four Christmas traditions for their country on the holiday worksheet wreath balls. Students write the country name under the bow. Students color the rest of the wreath and display their country wreaths.

Teaching Team

School librarian and social studies teachers.

Suggested Sources

Cooper, James. *Christmas around the World*. Updated 2016. Retrieved from http://www.why christmas.com/cultures/mexico.shtml

Enderlein, Cheryl. *Christmas in Mexico*. Mankato, MN: Capstone, 2013.

Enderlein, Cheryl. *Christmas in the Philippines*. Mankato, MN: Capstone, 2014.

Heiligman, Deborah. *Holidays around the World: Celebrate Christmas with Carols, Presents, and Peace*. Washington, DC: National Geographic Children's Books, 2016.

National Geographic. *World Globe*. Margate, FL: National Geographic Store, 2016.

Lankford, Mary D. *Christmas around the World*. New York: Morrow Junior Books, 2008.

Manning, Jack. *Christmas in France*. Mankato, MN: Capstone, 2014.

Manning, Jack. *Christmas in Germany*. Mankato, MN: Capstone, 2013.

Manning, Jack. *Christmas in Italy*. Mankato, MN: Capstone, 2013.

Ringing in Goodness

Goodness rang out in the final scene of *A Christmas Carol*. Complete a simple reader's theatre script on that final scene and then act it out:

Narrator: A relieved and happy Scrooge awoke and dressed on Christmas morning. He remembered saying that he would be a better person, after his scary night adventure of seeing his past, present, and future. He ran outside.

On the street, Scrooge asks a boy selling a turkey: What is today?

Boy: Why, it is Christmas Day.

Scrooge: I will buy the turkey. Take the turkey and deliver it to Bob's house. Hurry!

Narrator: Later, Scrooge went to Bob's house. He is welcomed into Bob's house.

Bob:

Scrooge:

Bob:
Scrooge:
Tim:

Scrooge:

Bob:

Scrooge:

Narrator:

Ringing in Goodness

Standards

Student(s)

- Inquire, think critically, and gain knowledge. (AASL 1)
- Draw conclusions, make informed decisions, apply knowledge to new situations, and create new knowledge. (AASL 2)
- Determine a theme of a story, drama, or poem from details in the text, including how characters in a story or drama respond to challenges or how the speaker in a poem reflects upon a topic; summarize the text. (CCSS 1)
- Compare and contrast two or more characters, setting, or events in a story or drama, drawing on specific details in a text (e.g., how characters interact). (CCSS 2)
- Knows the defining characteristics (e.g., rhyme and rhythm in poetry; settings and dialogue in drama, make believe in folktales and fantasies, life stories in biography; illustrations in children's stories) and structural elements (e.g., chapter, scene, stanza, verse, meter) of a variety of genres. (McREL 6)
- Understands the basic concept of plot (e.g., main problem, conflict, resolution, cause-and-effect). (McREL 7)

Objectives

Students

- Describe Dickens's *A Christmas Carol* final scene by writing it into a play script.
- Summarize characters, theme, setting, and plot.
- Act out the story.

Directions

1. The teachers give a brief overview of *A Christmas Carol*, explaining that the character was not good at sharing and had a scary life changing experience on Christmas Eve.
2. If reading just the final scene, the previous scenes are briefly explained first. Teachers read a picture book or just the final scene of Dickens's *A Christmas Carol* and discuss plot, theme, setting, and characters.
3. Guided by teachers, the class writes a reader's theatre play from the story or final story scene. The play script may continue onto the back of the page.
4. Students act out the story.

Teaching Team

Reading and school librarian teachers.

Suggested Sources

Davidson, Susanna. *A Christmas Carol* (Picture Book). London, England: Usborne, 2007.
Dickens, Charles. *A Christmas Carol*. New York: Balzer + Bray (HarperCollins), 2009.
McKeown, Adam. *A Christmas Carol*. New York: Doubleday Books, 2015.
Snagfilms. *A Christmas Carol* [1964 Animated Film]. Updated 2015. Retrieved from http://www.snagfilms.com/films/title/christmas_carol

Snow Queen

The Snow Queen Game

Snow Queen Game Questions

1) What was the title and author of the book?
2) Who were the main characters?
3) What was the first event?
4) What was the theme?
5) What was the strength of the girl?
6) What was the plot?
7) Describe the Snow Queen's palace.
8) How did the story end?

*Add two other questions and list their spinner number:

Snow Flake Spinner

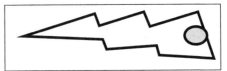

Ice Arrow for the spinner
(Add a metal fastener)

Snow Queen

Standards

Student(s)

- Draw conclusions, make informed decisions, apply knowledge to new situations, and create new knowledge. (AASL 2)
- Share knowledge and participate ethically and productively as members of our democratic society. (AASL 3)
- Determine a theme of a story, drama, or poem from details in the text, including how characters in a story or drama respond to challenges or how the speaker in a poem reflects upon a topic; summarize the text. (CCSS 1)
- Compare and contrast two or more characters, settings, or events in a story or drama, drawing on specific details in the text (e.g., how characters interact). (CCSS 2)
- Reads a variety of literary passages and texts (e.g., fairy tales, folktales, fiction, nonfiction, myths, poems, fables, fantasies, historical fiction, biographies, autobiographies, chapter books). (McREL 5)
- Understands the basic concept of plot (e.g., main problem, conflict, resolution, cause-and-effect). (McREL 7)

Objectives

Students

- Describe a fairy tale.
- Explain theme, characters, major events, setting, title, and author.
- Review the story elements by playing the Snow Queen game.

Directions

1. Copy worksheets on card stock for small student group's game board spinners.
2. The reading teacher states title and author and reads *The Snow Queen* fairy tale.
3. The school librarian guides discussion of theme, characters, major events, and setting.
4. For the game, students write two or more game questions regarding the story.
5. Students form small groups to play *The Snow Queen* game and cut out the question box, arrow box, and the game spinner. A metal fastener attaches the arrow box to the spinner.
6. The game is played by spinning the spinner and then answering numbered questions correctly in the game's time limit. After answering the questions, students then answer additional student questions. Student groups keep track of how many of their answered questions are correctly given within the time limit.
7. Game answers are discussed with the class.

Teaching Team

Reading and school librarian teachers.

Suggested Sources

Anderson, Hans Christian. *The Snow Queen*. New York: HarperCollins, 2016.
Baroni, Giorgio. *The Snow Queen*. Paris, France: Auzou Publishing, 2013.
Lowes, Sarah. *The Snow Queen*. Cambridge, MA: Barefoot Books, 2013.

Roaring Dragons

Dragons were often main characters in fairy tales, legends, and myths. Dragon stories came from China, Japan, and other cultures. Read a fairy tale, legend, or myth about a dragon.

1. What is the dragon story title? _____

2. What type of a dragon story is it? Is it a fairy tale, legend, or myth? _____

3. Describe the main plot. _____

_____

4. Make a list of words to describe the dragon. _____

_____

5. Write a Japanese lantern poem about the dragon. The poem has five lines of few words:
First Line: One syllable noun (beast). Second Line: Describe the word in two syllables (Scaly).
Third Line: Describe the word in three syllables (bright, shiny). Fourth Line: Describe the word in four syllables. Fifth Line: Rename the noun in one syllable. Write the poem below.

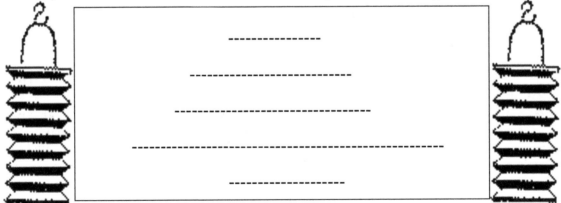

Roaring Dragons

Standards

Student(s)

- Draw conclusions, make informed decisions, apply knowledge to new situations, and create new knowledge. (AASL 2)
- Share knowledge and participate ethically and productively as members of our democratic society. (AASL 3)
- Analyze how visual and multimedia elements contribute to the meaning, tone, or beauty of a text (e.g., graphic novel, multimedia presentation of fiction, folktale myth poem). (CCSS 3)
- Uses word reference materials (e.g., glossary, dictionary, thesaurus) to determine the meaning, pronunciation, and derivations of unknown words. (McREL 4)
- Reads a variety of literary passages and texts (e.g., fairy tales, folktales, fiction, nonfiction, myths, poems, fables, fantasies, historical fiction, biographies, autobiographies, chapter books). (McREL 5)
- Understands the basic concept of plot (e.g., main problem, conflict, resolution, cause-and-effect). (McREL 7)

Objectives

Students

- Discuss and identify the story type.
- Analyze characters, plot, and setting.
- Use a thesaurus to create a word list.
- Compose a dragon poem.

Directions

1. The school librarian teacher reads and shows a short oriental dragon fairy tale, legend, or myth and discusses that story type and title. Students identify the story type.
2. The reading and librarian teachers guide discussion of characters, plot, and country setting, with emphasis on the dragon character. Students write the main plot.
3. While using a thesaurus, small student groups list words to describe the dragon.
4. While using the word lists, teachers guide student Japanese lantern poem writing about dragons.

Teaching Team

Reading and school librarian teachers.

Suggested Sources

Howard, Ann. *The Mystery of Dragon Bridge: A Peach Blossom Village Story*. Berkeley, CA: North Atlantic Books, 2014.

Jian, Li. *The Water Dragon: A Chinese Legend. English and Chinese*. Shanghai, China: Shanghai Press, 2012.

Sims, Lesley. *The Dragon and the Phoenix*. London: Usborne Publishing, 2012.

Sorin, Antonia. "How to Write a Lantern Poem." *Ehow* (n.d.). Retrieved from http://www.ehow.com/how_4928414_write-lantern-poem.html

Thesaurus.com. *Roget's 21st Century Thesaurus, Third Edition*. Wingdale, NY: Philip Lief Group. Updated 2009. Retrieved from http://www.thesaurus.com/browse/novice

Wang, Ping. *The Dragon Emperor: A Chinese Folktale*. Minneapolis, MN: Millbrook Press, 2008.

Snowy Road

When going down a snowy road, there are snowy scenes, which give us ideas for poems. Write a

short snowy poem on the car.

Fifth Reader

Snowy Road

Standards

Student(s)

- Inquire, think critically, and gain knowledge. (AASL 1)
- Share knowledge and participate ethically and productively as members of our democratic society. (AASL 3)
- Determine a theme of a story, drama, or poem from details in the text, including how characters in a story or drama respond to challenges or how the speaker in a poem reflects upon a topic; summarize the text. (CCSS 1)
- Analyze how visual and multimedia elements contribute to the meaning, tone, or beauty of a text (e.g., graphic novel, multimedia presentation of fiction, folktale myth poem). (CCSS 3)
- Uses word reference materials (e.g., glossary, dictionary, thesaurus) to determine the meaning, pronunciation, and derivations of unknown words. (McREL 4)
- Knows the defining characteristics (e.g., rhyme and rhythm in poetry; settings and dialogue in drama, make believe in folktales and fantasies, life stories in biography; illustrations in children's stories) and structural elements (e.g., chapter, scene, stanza, verse, meter) of a variety of genres. (McREL 6)

Objectives

Students

- Use a rhyming dictionary source.
- Compose a winter or Valentine's Day poem.

Directions

1. The reading teacher reads a short winter poem.
2. Teachers guide student discussions about how to create their poems, which means thinking of a snow or Valentine's Day topic and words associated with the topic.
3. Student pairs use a rhyming dictionary or similar source to create a rhyming-type poem.
4. Teachers guide students to write a short winter or Valentine's Day poem on the worksheet car.

Teaching Team

Reading and school librarian teachers.

Suggested Sources

Frost, Robert. *Stopping by Woods on a Snowy Evening*. New York: Dutton Children's Books, 2001.
Datamuse. *Rhyme Zone*. Updated 2016. Retrieved from http://www.rhymezone.com
Dictionary.com. Updated 2015. Retrieved from http://dictionary.reference.com/
Nesbitt, Kenn. "Poetry 4 Kids." *Poetry Lessons for Kids*. Updated 2008. Retrieved from http://www.poetry4kids.com/blog/lessons/poetry-writing-lessons/
Prelutsky, Jack. *It's Snowing! It's Snowing! Winter Poems*. New York: HarperCollins, 2006.
Yolen, Jane. *Snow, Snow: Winter Poems for Children*. Honesdale, PA: Boyd's Mill Press, 2005.

What Is My State?

Research this state: _____. Let the class guess your state from your facts.

Find the following facts about the state. Later read your facts, so that the class can guess the state. Start and end your reading by asking "What is my state?"

<u>What is my state?</u>

(1) The state is located in the _____ part of the United States.

(2) The statehood or when the state became part of the United States was number: _____

(3) The nickname for the state is: _____

(4) The capital of the state is: _____

(5) The state's abbreviation is: _____

<u>What is my state?</u>

For your own information, tell where you found your facts:

Internet Site Address: Internet Author:

Date of the Site:

Book Title: Book Author:

Publishing Place: Publisher: Copyright:

What Is My State?

Standards

Students

- Inquire, think critically, and gain knowledge. (AASL 1)
- Draw conclusions, make informed decisions, apply knowledge to new situations, and create new knowledge. (AASL 2)
- Share knowledge and participate ethically and productively as members of our democratic society. (AASL 3)
- Explain the relationships or interactions between two or more individuals, events, ideas, or concepts in a historical, scientific, or technical text based on specific information in the text. (CCSS 5)
- Draw on information from multiple print or digital sources, demonstrating the ability to locate and answer to a question quickly or to solve a problem efficiently. (CCSS 6)
- Uses a variety of strategies to plan research (e.g., identifies possible topic by brainstorming, listing questions, and using idea webs; organizes prior knowledge about a topic; develops a course of action; determines show to locate necessary information). (McREL 1)

Objectives

Students

- Research and relate facts about a state.
- Guess a state from student given facts.
- Discover title page facts and cite resources.

Directions

1. The school librarian teacher points out print and online sources in order for students to find quick facts on a state. Students are reminded to cite their information.
2. The social studies teacher discusses the worksheet questions.
3. Student pairs research an assigned state. To stump the class, students add another state fact to the worksheets.
4. Student pairs read their state facts to the class, until someone in the class guesses the state.
5. This will take two lessons due to the time needed for writing the citations and then guessing.

Teaching Team

School librarian and social studies teachers.

Suggested Sources

Bockenhauer, Mark. *Our Fifty States.* Washington, DC: National Geographic, 2004.

Children's Press. *America the Beautiful* [series]. New York: Children's Press, 2014.

Factmonster. "50 States." *Information Please.* Updated 2016. Retrieved from http://www.factmonster.com/states.html

USA.Gov. *Learn about the States.* Updated 2015. Retrieved from https://kids.usa.gov/learn-about-the-states/index.shtml

Stormalong

A tall tale is a story that has parts that seem to be true and then exaggerated parts. Stormalong (Alfred Bulltop Stormalong) became a tall tale. Answer the following questions to explain how Stormalong became a tall tale.

1. Stormalong's height or weight helped to make *Stormalong* a tall tale. Describe his height or weight: _____

2. Explain Stormalong's adventure with the great white whale. How did the adventure create more of a tall tale for Stormalong? _____

_____

_____

_____

3. If you were telling the story to make it even more exaggerated, what would you add to the tall tale? _____

_____

_____

_____

_____

From *Standards-Based Lesson Plans for the Busy Elementary School Librarian* by Joyce Keeling.
Santa Barbara, CA: Libraries Unlimited. Copyright © 2017.

Stormalong

Standards

Student(s)

- Inquire, think critically, and gain knowledge. (AASL 1)
- Draw conclusions, make informed decisions, apply knowledge to new situations, and create new knowledge. (AASL 2)
- Share knowledge and participate ethically and productively as members of our democratic society. (AASL 3)
- Determine a theme of a story, drama, or poem from details in the text, including how characters in a story or drama respond to challenges or how the speaker in a poem reflects upon a topic; summarize the text. (CCSS 1)
- Analyze how visual and multimedia elements contribute to the meaning, tone, or beauty of a text (e.g., graphic novel, multimedia presentation of fiction, folktale myth poem). (CCSS 3)
- Reads a variety of literary passages and texts (e.g., fairy tales, folktales, fiction, nonfiction, myths, poems, fables, fantasies, historical fiction, biographies, autobiographies, chapter books). (McREL 5)
- Understands the basic concept of plot (e.g., main problem, conflict, resolution, cause-and-effect). (McREL 7)
- Understands similarities and differences within and among literacy works from various genres and cultures (e.g., in terms of settings, character types, events, point of view, role of natural phenomena). (McREL 8)

Objectives

Students

- Describe a tall tale.
- Discuss character, major events, and setting.
- Create a different story event.

Directions

1. While showing the illustrations, the school librarian teacher reads *Stormalong* to the class.
2. The reading teacher guides discussion of characters, setting, events, and defines the term, tall tale.
3. Students answer character and plot questions and make the tall tale more exaggerated.
4. Students share their stories. If desired, students color the ship scene and add the whale.

Teaching Team

Reading and school librarian teachers.

Suggested Sources

Brimner, Larry. *Captain Stormalong*. Minneapolis, MN: Compass Point Books, 2004.

Metaxas, Eric. *Stormalong*. Mankato, MN: ABDO Publishers, 2005.

Schloser, S. "Old Stormalong and the Octopus." *American Folklore*. Updated 2010. Retrieved from http://americanfolklore.net/folklore/2010/08/old_stormalong_and_the_octopus.html

Amelia and Eleanor

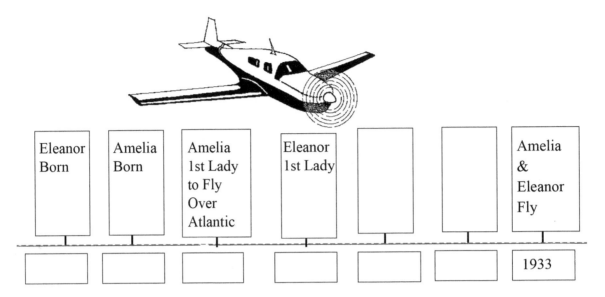

Eleanor Born	Amelia Born	Amelia 1st Lady to Fly Over Atlantic	Eleanor 1st Lady			Amelia & Eleanor Fly
						1933

The Timeline of Amelia Earhart and Eleanor Roosevelt

Amelia Earhart and Eleanor Roosevelt flew a plane together in 1933. Research Amelia Earhart and Eleanor Roosevelt. Write the year for each person's event on the timeline in the small boxes. Then plot another event and year for each person. The year of their flight together is already plotted.

On the timeline give the year for the following events:

1. Write (plot) the birthdate of Amelia.

2. Write (plot) the birthdate of Eleanor.

3. Write (plot) the date of Amelia's famous first flight as a lady pilot over the Atlantic.

4. Write (plot) the date when Eleanor became first lady of the United States of America.

5. Now, plot another important date and event for each person.

6. In your opinion, why would you describe both the characters of both Amelia Earhart and Eleanor Roosevelt as courageous?

_____

_____

Amelia and Eleanor

Standards

Student(s)

- Inquire, think critically, and gain knowledge. (AASL 1)
- Draw conclusions, make informed decisions, apply knowledge to new situations, and create new knowledge. (AASL 2)
- Share knowledge and participate ethically and productively as members of our democratic society. (AASL 3)
- Explain the relationships or interactions between two or more individuals, events, ideas, or concepts in a historical, scientific, or technical text based on specific information in the text. (CCSS 5)
- Draws on information from multiple print or digital sources, demonstrating the ability to locate an answer to a question quickly or to solve a problem efficiently. (CCSS 6)
- Uses electronic media to gather information (e.g., databases, Internet, CD-ROM, television shows, videos, pull-down menus, word searches). (McREL 3)
- Summarizes and paraphrases information in texts (e.g., includes the main idea and significant supporting details of a reading selection). (McREL 11)

Objectives

Students

- Compare Eleanor Roosevelt and Amelia Earhart.
- Research and plot timeline dates for both Amelia and Eleanor.

Directions

1. The social studies teacher leads a brief discussion about Eleanor Roosevelt and Amelia Earhart.
2. The school librarian teacher reads *Amelia and Eleanor Go for a Ride* or other similar source and discusses the fact that Earhart and Roosevelt flew together in a plane piloted by Amelia.
3. The librarian teacher guides research of Eleanor and Amelia from books and Internet sources.
4. Under guidance from teachers, student pairs complete a timeline about Roosevelt and Earhart.

Teaching Team

School librarian and social studies teachers.

Suggested Sources

Barton, Jan. *What's Your Story, Amelia Earhart?* Minneapolis, MN: Lerner Publications, 2016.

Calkhoven, Laurie. *Women Who Changed the World: 50 Amazing Americans.* New York: Scholastic, 2016.

History.Com. *Amelia Earhart.* Updated 2015. Retrieved from http://www.history.com/topics/amelia-earhart

History.Com. *Eleanor Roosevelt.* Updated 2015. Retrieved from http://www.history.com/topics/first-ladies/eleanor-roosevelt

Hollingsworth, Tamara. *Eleanor Roosevelt: A Friend to All.* New York: Teacher Created Materials, 2011.

Ryan, Pam Munoz. *Amelia and Eleanor Go for a Ride.* New York: Scholastic, 2000.

Horse of Troy

After hearing the story of the Trojan horse, discuss the story by using complete sentences to answer the following questions.

1. Who were the two groups at war in the story?

2. Compare two major characters of the story, by stating who they were and how they were different.

3. What was the main problem (main conflict) in the story?

4. Discuss the wooden horse and how it changed things.

5. What is the moral of the story?

Bonus: Write a new story title in the box under the horse.

Horse of Troy

Standards

Student(s)

- Inquire, think critically, and gain knowledge. (AASL 1)
- Draw conclusions, make informed decisions, apply knowledge to new situations, and create new knowledge. (AASL 2)
- Compare and contrast two or more characters, setting, or events in a story or drama, drawing on specific details in a text (e.g., how characters interact). (CCSS 2)
- Explain the relationships or interactions between two or more individuals, events, ideas, or concepts in a historical, scientific, or technical text based on specific information in the text. (CCSS 5)
- Reads a variety of literary passages and texts (e.g., fairy tales, folktales, fiction, nonfiction, myths, poems, fables, fantasies, historical fiction, biographies, autobiographies, chapter books). (McREL 5)
- Understands the basic concept of plot (e.g., main problem, conflict, resolution, cause-and-effect). (McREL 7)
- Knows themes that recur across literary works. (McREL 9)

Objectives

Students

- Analyze a myth.
- Summarize character, plot or problem/conflict, theme, and moral.
- State the story title and create a new title.

Directions

1. The school librarian teacher reads and shows an illustrated Trojan Horse myth story.
2. The social studies teacher leads discussion on comparing characters, theme, problem/conflict, setting, and moral.
3. As guided by teachers, students answer worksheet questions on characters, plots, and moral. If desired, students create a new title.
4. Students color the Trojan horse as copied on card stock, which is cut out with the base attached for a display.

Teaching Team

School librarian and social studies teachers.

Suggested Sources

Holub, Joan. *Surprise, Trojans! The Story of the Trojan Horse.* New York: Simon Spotlight, 2014.
Little, Emily. *The Trojan Horse: How the Greeks Won the War.* New York: Random House, 2003.
Meister, Cari. *The Wooden Horse of Troy: A Retelling.* Mankato, MN: PictureWindow Books (Capstone), 2012.

Save the Earth

Research and then list ways to help save the earth:

1.   5.

2.   6.

3.   7.

4.   8.

List at least five ways that you would personally help save the earth:

Tell where you found your information.

Book

Author:

Title:

Publishing Place:

Publisher: Copyright:

Internet

Author:

Internet Address:

Year of the Internet Site:

Then make a mini notebook out of recycled paper. Here is the cover:

Save the Earth

Standards

Student(s)

- Inquire, think critically, and gain knowledge. (AASL 1)
- Share knowledge and participate ethically and productively as members of our democratic society. (AASL 3)
- Draw on information from multiple print or digital sources, demonstrating the ability to locate an answer to a question quickly or to solve a problem efficiently. (CCSS 6)
- Integrate information from several texts on the same topic in order to write or speak about the subject knowledgeably. (CCSS 7)
- Uses a variety of strategies to plan research (e.g., identifies possible topic by brainstorming, listing questions, using idea webs; organizes prior knowledge about a topic; develops a course of action; determines how to locate necessary information). (McREL 1)
- Summarizes and paraphrases information in texts (e.g., includes the main idea and significant supporting details of a reading selection). (McREL 11)

Objectives

Students

- Research and list ways of saving the earth.
- Cite sources.

Directions

1. The school librarian teacher reads and discusses a picture book about ways to save the earth.
2. The science teacher briefly explains a couple of ways to save the earth.
3. Teachers suggest book and Internet resources on saving the earth.
4. Guided by teachers, small student groups research and write eight ways to save the earth and cite resources. Students personally write how they could individually help save the earth, too.
5. The worksheet tree makes a notebook cover, and pages should come from classroom recycled paper.

Teaching Team

School librarian and science teachers.

Suggested Sources

Fiction

Shore, Diane Z. and Alexander, Jessica. *This Is the Earth.* New York: HarperCollins, 2016.
Silverstein, Shel. *The Giving Tree.* New York: HarperCollins, 2004.

Nonfiction

Antill, Sara. *10 Ways I Can Save the Earth.* Vero Beach, FL: Rourke Publishing, 2012.
Gagne, Tammy. *Take Care of the Earth Every Day.* Mankato, MN: Amicus, 2014.
Project A. *50 Simple Things Kids Can Do to Save the Earth.* Updated 2009. Retrieved from http://50simplekids.scarabmedia.com/Default.asp
Webb, Barbara L. *What Does Green Mean?* New York: Crabtree, 2014.

Bibliography

American Association of School Librarians. *Standards for the 21st-Century Learner.* Chicago, Ill: American Library Association, 2007.

Governors Association Center for Best Practices and Council of Chief State School Officers. *Common Core State Standards.* "Literacy." Washington, D.C: National Governors Association Center for Best Practices and Council of Chief State School Officers, 2010.

McREL. *The McREL Compendium Standards and Benchmarks.* "Standards and Curriculum." "Language Arts." Aurora, CO: McREL International, 2015. Accessed January 2016. http://www.mcrel.org/standards-curriculum/

Nova. *Art Explosion 500,000.* Riverside, CA: Avanquest, 2004

Index

About the Author

JOYCE KEELING is the author of two similar popular books to help the busy school librarian. In 2006, she was recognized by the Iowa State Senate for her second book. She is and has been a school librarian and teacher for elementary and middle school library students at Clarion-Goldfield-Dows Schools, Clarion, IA for over twenty years. This involves directing libraries, teaching information literacy and library skills, guided student reading enjoyment, and more as busy school librarians can expound. She has taught communication skills and information technology to college students for many years for Buena Vista University, Mason City, IA, and the University of Phoenix, Phoenix, AZ. She has her BA in elementary teaching, MA in K-12 Library, and finally her EdS in Curriculum and Teaching.